IN PURSUIT OF
THE ENGLISH

ALSO BY DORIS LESSING

NOVELS

The Grass Is Singing
The Golden Notebook
Briefing for a Descent into Hell
The Summer Before the Dark
The Memoirs of a Survivor
The Diaries of Jane Somers:
 The Diary of a Good Neighbor
 If the Old Could . . .
The Good Terrorist
The Fifth Child
Love, Again

"CANOPUS IN ARGOS: ARCHIVES"
 SERIES

Re: Colonized Planet 5, Shikasta
The Marriages Between Zones
 Three, Four and Five
The Sirian Experiments
The Making of the
 Representative for Planet 8
Documents Relating to the
 Sentimental Agents in the
 Volyen Empire

"CHILDREN OF VIOLENCE" SERIES

Martha Quest
A Proper Marriage
A Ripple From the Storm
Landlocked
The Four-Gated City

SHORT STORIES

This Was the Old Chief's Country
The Habit of Loving
A Man and Two Women
The Temptation of Jack Orkney
 and Other Stories
Stories
African Stories
The Real Thing: Stories and
 Sketches

OPERA

The Making of the
 Representative for Planet 8
 (Music by Philip Glass)

POETRY

Fourteen Poems

NONFICTION

Particularly Cats
Going Home
A Small Personal Voice
Prisons We Choose to Live
 Inside
The Wind Blows Away Our Words
Particularly Cats . . . And Rufus
African Laughter

AUTOBIOGRAPHY

Under My Skin

The Doris Lessing Reader

DORIS LESSING

IN PURSUIT
OF THE
ENGLISH

A DOCUMENTARY

HARPER PERENNIAL

NEW YORK • LONDON • TORONTO • SYDNEY

This book was originally published in Great Britain by MacGibbon & Kee
Ltd. in 1960. First U.S. edition was published by Simon & Schuster in
1961.

HarperCollins books may be purchased for educational, business, or sales
promotional use. For information please write: Special Markets Department,
HarperCollins Publishers, Inc., 10 East 53rd Street, New York, NY 10022.

First HarperPerennial edition published 1996.

ISBN 0-06-097629-2

07 08 09 10 RRD 10 9 8 7 6 5 4

Chapter One

I came into contact with the English very early in life, because as it turns out, my father was an Englishman. I put it like this, instead of making a claim or deprecating a fact, because it was not until I had been in England for some time that I understood my father.

I wouldn't like to say that I brooded over his character; that would be putting it too strongly, but I certainly spent a good part of my childhood coming to terms with it. I must confess, to be done with confessions right at the start, that I concluded at the age of about six my father was mad. This did not upset me. For a variety of reasons, none of which will be gone into here, the quintessential eccentricity of the human race was borne in upon me from the beginning. And aside from whatever deductions I might have come to for myself, verbal confirmation came from outside, continuously, and from my father himself. It was his wont to spend many hours of the day seated in a rickety deck-chair on the top of the semi-mountain on which our house was built, surveying the African landscape which stretched emptily away on all sides for leagues. After a silence which might very well have lasted several hours, he would start to his feet, majestically splenetic in shabby khaki, a prophet in his country, and, shaking his fist at the sky, shout out: 'Mad! Mad! Everyone! Everywhere Mad!' With which he would sink back, biting his thumb and frowning, into sombre contemplation of his part of the universe; quite a large part, admittedly, compared to what is visible to, let us say, an inhabitant of Luton. I say Luton because at one time he lived there. Reluctantly.

My mother was not English so much as British an

intrinsically efficient mixture of English, Scottish and Irish. For the purposes of this essay, which I take it is expected to be an attempt at definitions, she does not count. She would refer to herself as Scottish or Irish according to what mood she was in, but not, as far as I can remember, as English. My father on the other hand called himself English, or rather, an Englishman, usually bitterly, and when reading the newspapers: that is, when he felt betrayed, or wounded in his moral sense. I remember thinking it all rather academic, living as we did in the middle of the backveld. However, I did learn early on that while the word *English* is tricky and elusive enough in England, this is nothing to the variety of meanings it might bear in a Colony, self-governing or otherwise.

I decided my father was mad on such evidence as that at various times and for varying periods he believed that (a) One should only drink water that has stood long enough in the direct sun to collect its invisible magic rays. (b) One should only sleep in a bed set in such a position that those health-giving electric currents which continuously dart back and forth from Pole to Pole can pass directly through one's body, instead of losing their strength by being forced off course. (c) The floor of one's house should be insulated, probably by grass matting, against the invisible and dangerous emanations from the minerals in the earth. Also because he wrote, but did not post, letters to the newspapers on such subjects as the moon's influence on the judgment of statesmen; the influence of properly compounded compost on world peace; the influence of correctly washed and cooked vegetables on the character (civilized) of a white minority as against the character (uncivilized) of a black, indigenous, non-vegetable-washing majority.

As I said, it was only some time after I reached England, I understood that this – or what I had taken to be – splendidly pathological character would merge into the local scene without so much as a surprised snarl from anyone.

It is, then, because of my early and thorough grounding in the subject of the English character that I have undertaken to write about this business of being an exile. First one has

2

to understand what one is an exile from. And unfortunately I have not again succeeded in getting to know an Englishman. That is not because, as the canard goes, they are hard to know, but because they are hard to meet.

An incident to illustrate. I had been in London two years when I was rung up by a friend newly-arrived from Cape Town. 'Hey, Doris, man,' she says, 'how are you doing and how are you getting on with the English?' 'Well,' I say, 'the thing is, I don't think I've met any. London is full of foreigners.' 'Hell, yes, I know what you mean. But I met an Englishman last night.' 'You didn't?' 'I did. In a pub. And he's the real thing.' At first glance I knew he was the real thing. Tall, asthenic, withdrawn; but above all, he bore all the outward signs of the inward, intestine-twisting prideful melancholy. We talked about the weather and the Labour Party. Then, at the same moment, and from the same impulse – he was remarking that the pub was much too hot, my friend and I laid delighted hands on him. At last, we said, we are meeting the English. He drew himself up. His mild blue eyes flashed at last. 'I am not,' he said, with a blunt but basically forgiving hauteur, 'English. I have a Welsh grandmother.'

The sad truth is that the English are the most persecuted minority on earth. It has been so dinned into them that their cooking, their heating arrangements, their love-making, their behaviour abroad and their manners at home are beneath even contempt, though certainly not comment, that like Bushmen in the Kalahari, that doomed race, they vanish into camouflage at the first sign of a stranger.

Yet they are certainly all round us. The Press, national institutions, the very flavour of the air we breathe indicate their continued and powerful existence. And so, whenever confounded by some native custom, I consider my father.

For instance. It is the custom in Africa to burn fireguards for dwelling-houses and outhouses against the veld fires which rage across country all through the dry season. My father was burning a fireguard for the cow shed. It was a windless day. The grass was short. The fire would burn slowly. Yet it was in the nature of things that any small animal, grounded bird, insect or reptile in the two-hundred-yard-wide, mile-long stretch of fire would perish, not, presumably, without pain. My father stood, sombrely contemplating the creeping line of small flames. The boss-boy stood beside him. Suddenly there fled out from the smoke-filled grass at their feet, a large fieldmouse. The boss-boy brought down a heavy stick across the mouse's back. It was dying. The boss-boy picked up the mouse by the tail, and swinging the still-twitching creature, continued to stand beside my father, who brought down his hand in a very hard slap against the boss-boy's face. So unprepared was he for this, that he fell down. He got up, palm to his cheek, looking at my father for an explanation. My father was rigid with incommunicable anger. 'Kill it at once,' he said, pointing to the mouse, now dead. The boss-boy flung the mouse into a nest of flames, and stalked off, with dignity.

'If there is one thing I can't stand it's cruelty of any kind,' my father said afterwards, in explanation of the incident.

Which is comparatively uncomplicated, not to say banal. More obliquely rewarding in its implications was the affair with the Dutchman. My father was short of money, and had undertaken to do, in his spare time, the accounting for the small goldmine two miles away. He went over three times a week for this purpose. One day, several hundred pounds were missing. It was clear that Van Reenan, who managed the mine for a big company, had stolen it, and in such a way that it looked as if my father had. My father was whitely silent and suffering for some days. At any moment the company's auditors would descend, and he would be arrested. Suddenly, without a word to my mother, who had been making insensitively practical suggestions, such as going to the police, he stalked off across the veld to the mine, entered the Dutchman's office, and knocked him down. My father was not at all strong, apart from having only one leg, the other having been blown off in the First World War. And the Dutchman was six-foot, a great, red-faced, hot-tempered trekox of a man. Without saying one word my father returned across country, still silent and brooding, and shut himself into the dining-room.

Van Reenan was entirely unmanned. Although this was by no means the first time he had embezzled and swindled, so cleverly that while everyone knew about it the police had not been able to lay a charge against him, he now lost his head and voluntarily gave himself up to the police. Where he babbled to the effect that the Englishman had found him out. The police telephoned my father. Who, even whiter, more silent, more purposeful than before, strode back across the veld to the mine, pushed aside the police sergeant, and knocked Van Reenan down again. 'How dare you suggest,' he demanded, with bitter reproach, 'how dare you even imagine, that I would be capable of informing on you to the police?'

The third incident implies various levels of motive. The first time I heard about it was, when very young indeed, from my mother, thus: 'Your governess is not suited to this life here, she is going back to England.' Pause. 'I suppose she is going back to the smart set she came from.' Pause. 'The sooner she gets married the better.'

Later, from a neighbour who had been confidante to the governess. 'That poor girl who was so unhappy with your mother and had to go back to England in disgrace.'

Later, from my father: '. . . that time I had to take that swine Baxter to task for making free with Bridget's name in the bar.'

What happened was this. My mother, for various reasons unwell, and mostly bedridden, had answered an advertisement from 'Young woman, educated finishing school, prepared to teach young children in return for travel.' The Lord knows what she, or my mother, expected. It was the mid-twenties, Bridget was twenty-five, and had 'done' several London seasons. Presumably she wanted to see a bit of the world before she married, or thought of some smart Maugham-ish colonial plantation society. Later she married an Honourable something or other, but in the meantime she got a lonely maize farm, a sick woman, two spoiled children, and my father, who considered that any woman who wore lipstick or shorts was no better than she ought to be. On the other hand, the district was full of young farmers looking for wives, or at least entertainment. They were not, she considered, of her class, but it seemed she was prepared to have a good time. She had one, and danced and gymkhana'd whenever my parents would let her. This was not nearly as often as she would have liked. She was being courted by a farmer called Baxter, a tough ex-policeman from Liverpool. My father did not like him. He didn't like any of her suitors. One evening, he went into the bar at the village and Baxter came over and said: 'How's Bridget?' My father instantly knocked him down. When the bewildered man stood up and said: 'What the f--ing hell's that for?' my father said: 'You will kindly refer, in my presence at least, to an innocent young girl many thousands of miles from her parents and to whom I am acting as guardian, as Miss Fox.'

Afterwards, he said: 'I must not allow myself to lose my temper so easily. Quite obviously, I don't know my own strength.'

When stunned by *The Times* or the *Telegraph*; when — yes, I think the word is interested, by the *Manchester Guardian*; when unable to discover the motive behind some dazzlingly stupid stroke of foreign policy; when succumbing to that mood which all of us foreigners are subject to, that we shall ever be aliens in an alien land, I recover myself by reflecting, in depth, on the implications of incidents such as these.

Admittedly at a tangent, but in clear analogy, I propose to admit, and voluntarily at that, that I have been thinking for some time of writing a piece called: In Pursuit of the Working-Class. My life has been spent in pursuit. So has everyone's, of course. I chase love and fame all the time. I have chased, off and on, and with much greater deviousness of approach, the working-class and the English. The pursuit of the working-class is shared by everyone with the faintest tint of social responsibility: some of the most indefatigable pursuers are working-class people. That is because the phrase does not mean, simply, those people who can be found by walking out of one's front door and turning down a side-street. Not at all. Like love and fame it is a platonic image, a grail, a quintessence, and by definition, unattainable. It took me a long time to understand this. When I lived

in Africa and was learning how to write, that group of
mentors who always voluntarily constitute themselves as a
sort of watch committee of disapprobation around every
apprentice writer, used to say that I could never write a
word that made sense until I had become pervaded by the
cultural values of the working-class. In spite of all the
evidence to the contrary, these mentors claimed that not one
truthful word could ever be written until it was first bap-
tized, so to speak, by the working-class. I remember even
now the timidity with which, just as I was about to leave
Africa, I suggested that having spent twenty-five years of my
life in the closest contact with the black people, who are
workers if nothing else, some knowledge, or intimation, or
initiation by osmosis must surely have been granted me.
And I remember even now the indignant tone of the reply:
'The Africans in this country are not working-class *in the
true sense*. They are semi-urbanized peasants.' I should have
understood by the tone, which was essentially that of a
defender of a faith, that I must stick by my guns. But it
always did take me a long time to learn anything.

I came to England. I lived, for the best of reasons, namely,
I was short of money, in a household crammed to the roof
with people who worked with their hands. After a year of
this, I said with naïve pride to a member of the local watch
committee that now, at last, I must be considered to have
served my apprenticeship. The reply was pitying, but not
without human sympathy: 'These are not the real working-
class. They are the lumpen proletariat, tainted by petty
bourgeois ideology.' I rallied. I said that, having spent a lot
of my time with Communists, either here or in Africa, a
certain proportion of whom, even though a minority, are
working-class, surely some of the magic must have rubbed
off on me? The reply came: 'The Communist Party is the
vanguard of the working-class and obviously *not typical*.'
Even then I didn't despair. I went to a mining village, and
returned with a wealth of observation. It was no good.
'Miners, like dockworkers, are members of a very special-
ized, traditionalized trade; mining is already (if you take the
long view) obsolete. The modes of being, mores and manners

of a mining community have nothing whatsoever to do with the working-class as a whole.' Finally, I put in some time in a housing estate in a New Town, and everyone I met was a trade unionist, a member of the Labour Party, or held other evidence of authenticity. It was then that I realized I was defeated. 'The entire working-class of Britain has become tainted by capitalism or has lost its teeth. It is petit bourgeois to a man. If you really want to understand the militant working-class, you have to live in a community in France, let's say near the Renault works, or better still, why don't you take a trip to Africa where the black masses are not yet corrupted by industrialism.'

The purpose of this digression, which is not nearly so casual as it might appear, is to make it plain that when set on something I don't give up easily. Also to – but I must get back to why it took me so long to get started for England in the first place.

I can't remember a time when I didn't want to come to England. This was because, to use the word in an entirely different sense, I was English. In the colonies or Dominions, people are English when they are sorry they ever emigrated in the first place; when they are glad they emigrated but consider their roots are in England; when they are thoroughly assimilated into the local scene and would hate ever to set foot in England again; and even when they are born colonial but have an English grandparent. This definition is sentimental and touching. When used by people not English, it is accusatory. My parents were English because they yearned for England, but knew they could never live in it again because of its conservatism, narrowness and tradition. They hated Rhodesia because of its newness, lack of tradition, of culture. They were English, also, because they were middle-class in a community mostly working-class. This use of the word can be illustrated by the following incident. Scene: the local tennis club. The children are playing tennis, watched by their mothers. The hostess for the afternoon is a woman from the Cape, a member of an old Dutch family, newly married to a Scots farmer. She is shy, dignified, and on her guard. Mrs Mathews, a loquacious

Scots farmer's wife, attempts to engage her in conversation. She fails. She turns to my mother, and says: 'That one's got no small-talk to change with a neighbour. She's too good for us. She's real English and that's a fact.' Then she blushes and says: 'Oh, but I didn't mean ...' thus revealing how often she has made the same criticism of my mother.

My parents were, now I come to think of it, grail-chasers of a very highly developed sort. I cannot even imagine a country in which they would have been definitively ready to settle down without criticism. The nearest I can get to it would be a combination of the best parts of Blackheath or Richmond, merged, or mingled with a really large ranch, let's say about fifty thousand acres, in the Kenyan Highlands. This would have to be pervaded by a pre-1914 atmosphere, or ambience, like an Edwardian after-glow. Their Shangri-La would be populated thickly, for my mother, with nice professional people who were nevertheless *interesting*; and sparsely, for my father, with scamps, drunkards, eccentrics and failed poets who were nevertheless and at bottom *decent* people.

I would, of course, be the first to blame my parents for my own grail-seeking propensities.

England was for me a grail. And in a very narrowly-defined way. Not long ago people set foot for the colonies – the right sort of people, that is – in a spirit of risking everything and damning the cost. These days, a reverse immigration is in progress. The horizon conquerors now set sail or take wing for England, which in this sense means London, determined to conquer it, but on their own terms.

I have an anecdote to illustrate this. I had been in England for about five years, and was just beginning to understand that I had got the place whacked, when an old acquaintance telephoned to say that he had arrived in London to write a book. He had forever turned his back on his old life, which consisted of making enormous sums of money out of gold mines, drinking a lot, and marrying a succession of blonde and beautiful girls. I visited him in his flat. It was in Mayfair, furnished at immense expense in the most contemporary taste, with two refrigerators. He was very excited that at last he had had the strength of mind to cut all his profits and tackle England. I remember on the whole without regret, the strong, involuntary moral disapprobation that I radiated as he talked. Finally, and the remark welled up from the depths of my being, from the perfervid heart of the myth itself: 'Do you mean to tell me that you are going to live in a flat that costs twenty-two guineas a week, in Mayfair, *with* a refrigerator, *to write a novel*?'

Looking back, I can see that there were several occasions when I could have come to England years before I did. For instance, there was talk of my being sent to school here. That would have meant my being taken on by a section of my family which I detested – I see now quite rightly – by instinct, and without ever having met them. I used to get ill with mysterious spontaneity every time this plan was discussed. I would lie in bed and dream about England, which of course had nothing in common with that place inhabited by my cousins. That England was almost entirely filled with rather dangerous night-clubs, which had a strong literary flavour. I was then fourteen. I think the only person I would have allowed to bring me to England at that time was a father-figure in appearance like Abraham Lincoln, with strong white-slaving propensities, yet fundamentally decent, and with an untutored taste for the novel *Clarissa*. My most powerful fantasy was of how I would gently release the captives, all of them misunderstood girls of about fourteen, all of them incredibly beautiful, but full of fundamental decency. I would press enough money into their hands (willingly given me by my master for this purpose) to enable them to find themselves, and set them free. At the same time I would be explaining to my master the real and inner significance of the novel *Clarissa*, while he gently toyed with my breasts, and, kissing me on the brow, willingly handed me large sums of money which would enable me to find myself.

The other occasions when nothing prevented me from coming to England but enough energy to do it, were the same: a powerful inner voice said it was not yet the time. The time, finally, was in 1949, when England was at its dingiest, my personal fortunes at their lowest, and my morale at zero. I also had a small child.

I have it on the highest secular authority that this propensity of mine to do things the hard way amounts to nothing less than masochism, but a higher authority still, the voice of the myth itself, tells me that this is nonsense.

By the time I came, things had been satisfactorily arranged in such a way that the going would be as hard as possible.

For instance. The ships for years after the war were booked months in advance. Yet I know now – and it would have been obvious to anyone but me – that the simple process of bribing someone would have got me a passage on one of the big regular boats. Instead I decided on a much cheaper, but slower, Dutch boat for which I would have to wait in Cape Town. Of course, by the time I had hung about in Cape Town, and spent money for four weeks on that terrible slow boat, it would have been much cheaper to fly.

The moment of arriving in England, for the purposes of the myth, would be when I got to Cape Town. This is because the Cape is English, or, as the phrase goes, is pervaded by the remnants of the old English liberal spirit.

It so happened that the first people I met in Cape Town were English. This was an immediately disturbing experience. They were a university professor and his wife, who had been, the last time I saw them, bastions of the local Communist Party. That had been eighteen months before. Now they had left the Communist Party. Things have now changed so that it is quite possible to leave the Communist Party and retain a sense of balance. In those days, one was either an eighteen-carat, solid, unshakable red, or, if an ex-red, violently, and in fact professionally anti-Communist. The point was, that this *volte-face* had taken place about six weeks before, and in a blinding moment of illumination at that, like on the road to Damascus. I went into their beautiful house, which was on one of the hills overlooking the bay. I was full of comradely emotions. The last time I had seen it, it was positively the area office for every kind of progressive activity. I was greeted with an unmistakable atmosphere of liberal detachment, and the words: 'Of course we have left

the Party and we are no longer prepared to be made use of.'
Now I was hoping I might be asked to stay a few days while
looking for a room; in fact I had been invited to stay any
time I liked. I became even more confused as the conversation proceeded, because it seemed that not only had they
changed, I had, too. Whereas, previously, I had been fundamentally sound, with my heart in the right place, yet with
an unfortunate tendency towards flippancy about serious
matters which ought to be corrected, now I was a dogmatic
red with a closed mind and a dangerous influence on the
blacks who were ever prey to unscrupulous agitators. I was
trying to discuss this last bit reasonably, when I was
informed that Cape Town was overflowing, that no one but
a lunatic would arrive without arranging accommodation,
and there was no hope of my finding a room. My situation
was, in short, admirably deplorable. While my son has
always been the most delightful, amiable and easy-going
person, yet, being two years old, he needed to sleep and eat.
My total capital amounted to £47. I was informed that the
prices for even bad accommodation were astronomical. They
telephoned some boarding houses which turned out, much
to their satisfaction, to be full. They then summoned a taxi.
On my suggestion.

The taxi-driver was an Afrikaner and he had an aunt who
ran a boarding house. He instantly took me there, refused
payment for the trip, arranged matters with his aunt, carried
in my luggage – which was extensive, because I had not yet
learned how to travel – taught my son some elementary
phrases in Afrikaans, gave me a lot of good advice, and said
he would come back to see how I was getting on. He was a
man of about sixty, who said he had forty-four grandchildren, but had it in his heart to consider my son the forty-
fifth. He was a Nationalist. It was not the first time I had
been made to reflect on that sad political commonplace that
one's enemies are so often much nicer than one's friends.

Sitting in the taxi outside Mrs Coetzee's boarding house,
the mirage of England was still strong. While features like
the white-slaving father-figure and the night-clubs had disappeared, and it was altogether more adjusted to my age, it

can't be said to have had much contact with fact – at least, as experienced. The foundation of this dream was now a group of loving friends, all above any of the minor and more petty human emotions, such as envy, jealousy, spite, etc. We would be devoted to changing the world completely, and very fast, at whatever cost to ourselves, while we simultaneously produced undying masterpieces, and lived communally, with such warmth, brilliance, generosity of spirit and so on that we would be an example to everyone.

The first thing I saw from the taxi was that the place was full of English. That is, English, not South African British. Several English girls were sitting on the wooden steps, their famed English complexions already darkened, looking disconsolate. The boarding house was on one of the steep slopes of the city, and overpowered by a great many dazzlingly new hotels that rose high above it on every side. It was very old, a ramshackle wandering house of wood, with great wooden verandahs, a roof hidden by dense green creeper, and surrounded by a colourful garden full of fruit-trees and children. It had two storeys, the upper linked to the lower only by an outside wooden staircase. The place was filthy, unpainted, decaying; a fire-trap and a death-trap – in short, picturesque to a degree. A heavy step upstairs made the whole structure tremble to its foundations. My room was in the front, off the verandah, and it had bare wooden floors, stained pink walls, stained green ceiling, a wardrobe so large I could take several strides up and down inside it, two enormous sagging double beds, and four single beds. My friend the grandfather had gone, so I went in search of authority, my feet reverberating on the bare boards. It was mid-afternoon. Towards the back of the house was a small room painted dingy yellow, with a broken wood-burning stove in it, a large greasy table dotted with flies, a hunk of cold meat under a great fly-cover, and the fattest woman I have ever seen in my life dozing in a straight-backed chair. It was as if a sack of grain was supported by a matchbox. Her great loose body strained inside a faded orange cotton dress. Her flesh was dull yellow in colour, and her hair dragged in dull strands on her neck. I thought she must be the coloured cook; but when I learned this was Mrs Coetzee herself, suppressed the seditious thought. I went back to my room, where a small, thin, chocolate-coloured girl who looked about twelve, but was in fact eighteen, was engaged in replacing the dirty sheets on the biggest of the beds with slightly less dirty sheets. She was bare-footed, and wore a bright pink dress, rent under the arm. Her name was Jemima. She did all the housework of the boarding house, which had between fifty and sixty people in it, and helped Mrs Coetzee in the kitchen. She earned three pounds a month, and was the most exploited human being I have known. To watch her do my room out was an education in passive resistance. She would enter without knocking, and without looking at me, carrying a small dustpan and brush, which she dropped on an unmade bed and did not use again. She would direct her small sharp body in a straight line to my bed, while her completely expressionless round black eyes glanced about her, but unseeing. With one movement she twitched the bedclothes up over the rumpled pillows. She then smoothed the surface creases on the faded coverlet out with the right hand, while already turning her body to the next bed, in which my son slept. She twitched up the bedclothes on that with her left hand, while she reached out the other for the dustpan and brush. She was already on her way to the door before her right hand, left behind, had picked up the dustpan. She then turned herself around in such a way that at the door she was facing into the room. She used the edge of the dustpan to pull the doorknob towards her. The door slammed. The room, as far as she was concerned, was done.

Mrs Coetzee and she carried on warfare in shrill Afrikaans which I did not understand. But like all wars that have been going on for a long time, it sounded more like a matter of form than of feeling.

I got all the information I needed as soon as I approached the loaded staircase. A dozen resigned voices told me the facts. These were all brides of South African soldiers. They were all waiting for some place to live in. They had all arrived on recent ships. Mrs Coetzee was a disgusting war

14

profiteer. For horrible food and conditions she charged the same as that charged by respectable boarding houses on the beach. If one could get into them. And if they would take children without making a fuss – which Mrs Coetzee did. But the fact that she was easy about the children did not outweigh her hatred of the English, about which she made no secret.

I rang up the shipping offices who said there was no sign of the ship, which was well known for taking its time at ports around the coast. It might be next week or the week after, but of course they would let me know. I was sitting on one of the beds, waving the flies off my cheerfully sleeping child, when a crisp white envelope slid under the door. It said: 'I and my husband would be very happy if you would care to join us for a drink after dinner. Yours sincerely, Myra Brooke-Benson. (Room 7.)' Room 7 was opposite mine, and I could hear English voices male and female, from behind the closed door. A high voice, clearly at the end of its tether: 'But, my dear, I really do think that this DDT must have lost its strength.' And a low voice, firm and in command. 'Nonsense, my dear, I bought it this morning.'

Towards five in the evening I went again in search of the landlady. Mrs Coetzee was now awake, seated at the kitchen table, slicing pale yellowish slices off an enormous golden pumpkin. Her arms stuck out at her sides like wings, supported by wads of shaking fat. Great drops of sweat scattered off her in all directions. Jemima stood beside her, rapidly squeezing pale pink ground meat into flat cakes between her palms. I coughed. Mrs Coetzee nodded. She returned to her work. She had no English.

The supper was served in a room into which refinement had been injected in the shape of a dozen small tables that were covered with red tissue paper, and set with a knife, fork and spoon at each place. A coloured paper lantern was tied with string to the naked light bulb. We ate roast pumpkin, fried meat cakes, and fried potato hash. Afterwards, there were fried pumpkin fritters. Everyone was eating avidly from starvation. The portions were no larger than necessary to maintain life. I immediately pinpointed my hosts for after dinner. They were a small, fair pretty woman, looking incredibly clean and neat; and a bald, fierce-looking man with a well-brushed moustache. I smiled at them, but as they stiffened and merely nodded back, I imagined I must be mistaken. When I presented myself at the door of No. 7, however, they were smiling and full of welcome. They had been here for three weeks, and were waiting for a flat to fall vacant in Ndola, where he was to work on the copper mines. 'I will not, I simply will not stay here, Timothy,' she kept saying, with crisp plaintiveness. And he kept saying, with bluff reassurance: 'But, my dear, of course we are not going to stay here.' We drank brandy, and made small talk. We offered each other many commiserations. We said goodnight, smiling. As far as I was concerned the evening had passed without any of that vital communication essential to real human relationships. I imagined it had been a failure.

Next morning, when I woke, the double bed opposite had two elderly women in it. They were asleep. I shushed my son and we waited. They woke, good-natured, smiling and unembarrassed when Jemima came in, without knocking, and slopped down four cups of tea on the floor just inside the door. They smiled and nodded. I smiled and nodded. Conversing in smiles and nods, we all dressed, and they departed in an ancient dust-covered car in a direction away from Cape Town.

I went into the kitchen. Mrs Coetzee was slicing pumpkin. Jemima was slicing beef into pale strips. I said: 'Mrs Coetzee, I would like to ask what those two strange women were doing in my room last night.' Jemima spoke to Mrs Coetzee. Mrs Coetzee spoke to Jemima. Jemima said: 'Says they are cousins from Constantia.' 'But why in my room?' 'Says boarding house is full.' 'Yes, but it was my room.' 'Says you can go.'

I retired. Myra Brooke-Benson was just going into No. 7. She gave me a pretty but measured smile, appropriate to our having bumped into each other, with apologies, on the pavement a week ago. Nevertheless, I told her what had happened. 'My dear, anything is possible here,' she said. 'As for me, I simply will not have it. I have been trying to get her to give me a carafe for drinking water for a week, and if I don't get it, I shall report her to the city authorities.'

I gave the question of my correct relations with the Brooke-Bensons some thought, and at last hit upon the right mode, or method. I found a piece of writing paper, and a clean envelope, and wrote: 'Dear Mrs Brooke-Benson. I would be so happy if you and your husband would join me tonight after dinner for a drink. Yours sincerely.' This I pushed under her door. I was sitting on my bed waiting for her reply, in another envelope, to insinuate itself under my door, when she knocked, and said: 'Timothy and I would be delighted to accept your kind invitation for this evening. It is so very kind of you.'

Meanwhile, it was observable from my windows that a great deal of human energy was being misapplied. The deeply lush garden was teeming with small children, and about two dozen young mothers were perched on the outside stairs, on the front steps, or on the grass, each anxiously watching her own offspring. I knew that they were all waiting for that blessed moment when these children would be sleepy, so they could put them to bed and rush off down into the city in order to interview housing agents and employment agents. For my part, I wanted to look up friends. I therefore approached a woman sitting rather apart from the rest, a small, plump, dark, fiery-cheeked person, who was guarding a small girl, and said it would be a good idea if we all took turns to look after the children, thus freeing the others. 'You've just come,' she said. 'Yesterday,' I said. 'This is not a place I would leave my child alone in,' she said. 'But surely, they wouldn't be alone,' I said. She said: 'Some of these girls here I wouldn't trust a dog with, let alone a child.' I went to my room and considered this. It was only afterwards I realized she was middle-class and most of the other women were not. Believing that Myra Brooke-Benson's knock on my door entitled me to the same intimacy, I knocked on hers. She opened it with annoyance. 'Actually,' she said, 'I was trying to get the baby to sleep.' I apologized and withdrew.

After dinner, at what was the right time, I put my plan to her. She thought it was admirable. 'The trouble is, there's only one other woman here I'd trust with my poor little boy. She has a delightful little girl. Some of these women here are quite appallingly careless with their children.' I realized she meant Mrs Barnes, the red-cheeked woman in the garden. I still did not know what was the matter with the others, but suggested that in that case we three might take turns with the children. 'I should be quite delighted to keep an eye on your charming little boy,' she said, 'but I'm afraid that mine doesn't take easily to strangers.'

We spent the evening discussing the carafe. It turned out that Mrs Coetzee didn't have a carafe. Through Jemima, Mrs Brooke-Benson had insisted she should buy one. Mrs Coetzee had said, through Jemima, that if Mr Brooke-Benson wanted a carafe so badly he could buy one for himself.

We all went to bed early. The boarding house resounded until late every night with people coming in, going out, shouting good-bye and singing. Noises in the passage sounded as if they were in my room. I did hear furtive sounds in the night, but imagined they were made by some lucky reveller creeping in so as not to disturb the rest of us. As if this were likely. When I woke in the morning there was a young man asleep in the double bed opposite. My son was watching him with much interest. I got up, shook him, and demanded what he was doing in my room. He started awake, let out a furious exclamation in Afrikaans, shook his fist, exclaimed some more, and strode out to the bathroom. Luckily, the taxi-driver dropped in to see his aunt after breakfast, so I stopped him and explained what was happening. He sat on the edge of my unmade bed, picked up my son, set him on his knee and said: 'You have the best room in the house. It is too big for you and your child.' 'But I'd be quite happy to have a smaller one.' 'But there is no smaller one.' 'Well, that isn't my fault.' 'But my Aunt Marie has a kind heart and is not happy to turn away a man who has no place to sleep.' 'But you must see I can't go to bed every night not knowing who I'm going to find when I wake in the morning. Besides, it's not good for my son.' 'Ach, he is a very fine child, your son.' 'You must talk to your aunt.' 'Ya, man, but this terrible war we have had, the English started it, and now we are all suffering.' 'But please talk to your aunt.' 'Ach, Gott, she has had a hard life. Her husband – you've seen him by this time – he is no good for any woman.' I had seen a furtive little man around the back of the premises but not connected him with Mrs Coetzee. 'Ya, ya, God is unkind to many women sometimes. He could not even give her a child. Now your husband gave you a child. You should thank God for it.' 'Please will you speak to your aunt.' 'A poor woman, without a man to help her and without children. She is a brave woman and she works hard.' By this time my son was clambering all over him, and Mr Coetzee was chuckling and smiling with pleasure. 'I will tell her what you said. But it is a hard world for a woman without a man. If you are uncomfortable, I have a cousin who keeps a boarding house in Oranjezicht.' 'No, no, I'm very happy here, if you could just explain to your aunt.' 'This is a very good child you have here, and when he grows up he will be a good strong man.' With which we went into the passage, my son on his shoulder. There stood Mr Brooke-Benson, scarlet with anger, scarlet even over his bald pate. 'That bloody woman,' he said, 'she will not give me a carafe.' 'And what is this?' enquired Mr Coetzee. I explained. He nodded. 'Ach. Ya. I will speak to her.' That afternoon he came in with a carafe which he presented to the Brooke-Bensons. They were furious, and kept saying it was a question of principle. He suggested, with courtesy, that to buy a carafe was a small thing to do for a woman who had no man to look after her, and it was a pleasure for him to do things for his auntie. He gave me a great bag of peaches, and my son a pound of sweets. Then he took my son for a drive in his taxi to visit his cousin Stella.

That night, the envelope slipped under my door contained an invitation to morning tea next day. Myra Brooke-Benson was equipped with every kind of instinct for domesticity. She had a spirit lamp, a silver teapot, and some fine china teacups. Her room, every bit as unpromising as mine, had flowers, clean linen, even cushions. She said there was a most unfortunate misunderstanding which she felt bad about even having to mention. It appeared that Mrs Barnes said she was going to complain to Mrs Coetzee that I had been observed to have a man, not my husband, in my bedroom. She, Myra Brooke-Benson, had explained the situation to Mrs Barnes, but Mrs Barnes had said that if a strange man entered her room in the night she wouldn't have been able to sleep at all. Her sixth sense would have warned her. But the point was, any plan for guarding each other's children was now out of the question.

I now resigned myself. The days, and then the weeks passed. I wrote notes of invitation for after-dinner drinks and morning tea with the Brooke-Bensons, and they wrote them to me. We ate pumpkin and fried meat for every meal. Mr Coetzee came to see me and my son often, and we talked about his children and his grandchildren. I rang up the shipping agents daily. Only once was my room invaded again, and that was when a man and a wife and five children arrived, apologetically, at three one morning, explaining they were maternal relatives of Mrs Coetzee. Mrs Barnes coloured and stiffened whenever she saw me. She spoke only to the Brooke-Bensons. My son had a nice time playing in the garden. I found one of the English girls who was prepared to let her children out of her sight occasionally, and we took turns to relieve each other. The English girls continued to sit on the stairs and to talk, with bitter homesickness, about England. I was bored to death, but consoled myself by dreaming about England which I knew by now would not actually begin until the moment I set foot on its golden soil.

Suddenly I got a letter from an old friend, an Afrikaans painter, who had been out of Cape Town on a painting trip. While I was reading the letter he arrived in my room with flowers, fruit and an enormous fish, which he had just caught.

'Ya,' he said, looking at me severely, 'you must get the management to cook it for you. I can tell you, you need feeding up. I can see it. The English can't cook. They can't eat. You look very bad.'

'The management,' I said, 'is Afrikaans.'

'Wait,' he said. 'I will go and make enquiries.' I heard him stride over the bare boards of the passage. A silence. He came back, still swinging the fish by a loop of string through his forefinger. 'I can't give her this fish,' he said. 'She would not cook it as it should be cooked. And what are you doing here? This place is going to be pulled down, and instead we shall have a fine modern hotel with all conveniences for the tourists.' He laid the fish on the floor. The room was pervaded with a loud smell of salt, sea and fish. It was an extremely hot afternoon.

'Piet, I wish you'd take that fish away. People are very sensitive in this place. You'd be surprised.'

He nodded, with solemnity. 'I thought so,' he said. 'It's that English colony you've been living in. It makes people suspicious and conventional. In a minute you will be telling me not to speak so loudly.'

Piet did not look himself at all. Or rather, he was wearing his smug look, which went with his public personality. He was a tall man, rangy, with a high bounding stride. He had a long, pale portentous face. He wore his hair rather long. He also wore, for the benefit of his trade, flapping and colourful clothes. He had the ability to appear, by slightly tightening the muscles of his face, like a pale and enduring Christ. This is not at all what his character was. In fact I have never known a man who enjoyed himself more wholeheartedly than he did. He had a smile that spread, wicked and sly, from cheekbone to cheekbone, and eyes that crinkled amusement. Not, however, at the moment.

'You have come at a bad time,' he said. 'I'm not happy. I have realized that in three months I shall be forty. I have only ten years to live. I have always known that I shall die at fifty. It is a terrible thing to understand suddenly – death is approaching in great silent strides.' He smiled, slightly, sideways, his eyes narrowed, as it were listening to the footsteps of death. 'Ya,' he said. 'Ya. Ten years. So much to do, so little done.' With a great effort he prevented himself from laughing, and sighed deeply instead.

Piet is not the only man I've known who has sentenced

himself to death in advance. I know a doctor, for instance, a man of the highest intelligence moreover, who decided when he was thirty-six that he had ten years to live, and planned his life accordingly. It seems the Medical Association, or some such body, had announced that the average age for doctors to die was at forty-six, and from coronary thrombosis. Meeting this man after an interval, I pointed out that he now had only five years to live, and I trusted he was making good use of his time. But the BMA had meanwhile raised the statistical life of a doctor by ten years, and so things were not so urgent after all.

'But there will be a silver lining to my personal tragedy,' said Piet. 'When my death is announced in the Press, for the first time in her history South Africa will be united.'

'How is that?'

'Surely you can imagine for yourself? Ya, think of it. Think of that morning. It will be very hot. The pigeons will be cooing in the trees. Then the news will come. The pigeons will stop cooing. In every town, in every village, in every little dorp, there will be a silence like the end of the world. Then there will rise into the still air a single cry of agony. Then from every house will come wailing and weeping. From every house will rush weeping women, old women, young women, wives, mothers, the Mayor's daughter and the wife of the linesman. They will look at each other. By their tears they will know each other as sisters. They will run into each other's arms. English and Afrikaans, Jewish and Greek, they will weep and cry: Piet is dead. Our Piet is dead.'

'And the men?'

'Ya, the men. Well, they will be united by the inconsolable grief of the women.' He sighed again. 'I have been thinking of that day all the way back in my car. I have had a terrible trip this time, because of my new understanding of my approaching death. But I have made a lot of money this time. I have been painting pondokkies all over the Free State. Thank God, now I can pay my debts.'

Piet was a man of talent. He had even painted in Paris and London. But he had been unable to make a living in the

Cape. Therefore, whenever short of money, he drove off into the interior, his clothing subdued and his expression mournful. He introduced himself to the Mayor or some bigwig in each city, as a sound son of the Afrikaans nation, and explained that it was a terrible thing that this great people should be so uncultured as not to support its talented child. He painted them, their houses, their children, and their wives. He also painted points of local interest, which, as he explained, always turned out to consist of pondokkies. In other words, African huts, slums, broken-down villages, shabby sheds and picturesque houses.

'And why do you come on holiday to Cape Town when I am not even here? My poor child, with no one to look after you. But as it happens now I must rush off, because I must take this beautiful fish home to my wife. I shall cook it myself. No woman can cook as well as I do. I caught it in a pool where I caught its brother last year. That is probably the most beautiful pool in the whole world. I'll take you there tomorrow.'

'I can't. My son isn't the right age for fishing.'

'A child? Of course, I forgot. Where is he?'

I pointed out of the window.

'A fine child.' He almost groaned. 'Ya, ya, and when I am dead he will be a fine young man, enjoying life, and I will be forgotten.'

'No, not that one, that one.'

'They are all fine children. And all of them, they will be fishing and – painting pondokkies when I am dead. But now you have this child you will be very dull and full of responsibility. Why is it, all women have children. Sometimes I think you do it to spite me.'

'All the same. And besides, my morale is very low due to living in this Afrikaans boarding house. I am weak from malnutrition and haven't the heart for fishing.'

'And why do you put me and my nation at a disadvantage by taking a holiday in such a place?'

'I am not on holiday. I am waiting for my boat to England.'

He groaned. 'England. So that's it. Ya, that's it. Well, you'll be sorry, I am telling you. And what will you do, in a country full of these Englishmen? They are no good for women. I know this. When I arrived in London all those poor women, they rushed out with their arms extended saying: "Piet, Piet, is that you? Thank God you've come at last." '

'We shall see,' I said.

'Ya, it is a terrible thing.'

'It's a fact that men of all nations are convinced that men of any other nation are no good for women. I'm sure a statistically significant number of women would be able to vouch for this.'

'And listen to how you talk. You are bitter already. When I hear a woman use words like statistics, I know she is bitter. It is that English colony. It has very likely marked you for life. Ya. I shall come tomorrow and cheer you up. Now I shall take my fish. I have a very sensitive sense of smell, and I can tell it is time.'

With which he left, jerking the fish after him along the floor and saying: 'Come, come, little fish, come with me, come and leap into the great black pot where you will die another death for me.' Over his shoulder he said: 'And I shall bring you a real picture I have painted, to show you that all these pondokkies have not ruined my talent.'

Mrs Barnes knocked. 'Excuse me,' she said. 'I am afraid I really must ask you not to have fish in your room. This place is bad enough without fish as well.'

'It was caught this morning,' I said.

'The whole building smells.'

'I didn't invite the fish.'

'Is your friend a fisherman?' Her soft English cheeks were a clear red, and her full brown eyes, that had no whites to them, were glazed with suspicious fascination.

'He is a painter,' I said. 'He has won prizes in Paris, not to mention London.'

'How interesting,' she said.

Next day Piet arrived in a severe black suit. He looked like a predicant. His face was a solemn yard long. He carried a very large picture of a nude girl. He lifted it past the miserable English girls on the steps with an air of critical detachment. He put down the nude, and said: 'There, you see I can still paint. And what is more, this afternoon I have been furthering the cause of art in this continent. I am now, you must know, a leading representative of the Council for Art. I am very respectable. There is an exhibition on. It is by a homosexual poor boy. He wrote to me and asked for my encouragement and patronage. His pictures are all of male nudes and in very great detail. The arts teacher at the school here for nice English girls wrote to me and asked for my help and encouragement. So this afternoon I met this teacher, poor woman, at the door, wearing my beautiful black suit and an expression of cultural integrity. I lowered my voice to an official note. And I entered the hall followed by the teacher and a hundred and fifty pretty girls, all in search of artistic experience. And I escorted them around for an hour, all around those pictures on one subject only, pointing out the technique and the line and the quality of the paint. With severity. He is a bad painter. And not once did I smile. Not once did that poor English teacher smile. Not once did all those little girls smile. We were in the presence of art.' He flung himself across my bed and laughed. The whole building shook.

'For the Lord's sake,' I said, 'don't shout.'

'There, what did I tell you? Already you are asking me to lower my voice. The English will finish you, man. Ya.'

'All the same, I wish you could hurry on that boat. I've been here six weeks, and I'm very unhappy. Apart from anything else, there's an English couple across the passage and we have morning tea together all the time. And as soon as I say anything at all, about anything, they look very nervous and change the subject. It's a bad augury for my life in England.'

'Poor little one. Poor child. There, what did I tell you?' He roared with delight. I heard a door open on to the passage.

'*Piet.* And there's a woman called Mrs Barnes. She's very bad-tempered.'

'Poor woman,' he said. He took two large soundless strides to the door, opened it with a jerk, and there was Mrs Barnes in the passage. She frowned. He smiled. Slowly, unwillingly, and hating every second of it, she smiled. Then, furious, she went dark plum colour, glared at us both, and went into her room, slamming the door hard.

'It is a terrible thing,' said Piet sentimentally. 'A bad-tempered woman. It is all the fault of her husband. I suppose he's English.'

'Scottish.'

'It is all the same thing. That reminds me . . .' He told a story. By the time he had ended I was laughing too hard to ask him to lower his voice. He was rolling in an agony of laughter back and forth over the floor. The whole boarding house was hushed.

'That reminds me,' said Piet again. He talked, listening with delight to the silence of his invisible audience. Then he told his story about his visit to a brothel in Marseilles. Unfortunately it is too indecent to write down. It was not too indecent for him to shout at the top of his voice. The end of the story was: 'Imagine me, in her room, in such a predicament, and the boat was leaving. It was giving out long, sad hoots of pain, to warn us all there was no time to waste. And there I was. My friends came in. They bandaged me. And I walked down to the ship through the streets of Marseilles, cheered on by the onlookers, with a bloodstained bandage a foot and a half long sticking out in front of me. I climbed up the gangway, supported on either side by my loyal friends, watched by the captain, a very fine fellow, and at least five thousand women. That was the proudest day of my life. That afternoon they gave me the gold medal for my artistic talent was nothing compared to it.'

Mrs Barnes came in. 'I am afraid I have to tell you that I have had no alternative but to complain to the management.' She went out.

'Poor woman,' said Piet. 'It is a very sad thing, a woman like that. Don't worry. I shall now go to Mrs Coetzee and tell her I'll paint a picture for her.'

Half an hour later I went to the kitchen. Mrs Coetzee was wheezing out helpless, wet laughter. Jemima, her face quite straight, her eyes solemn, had her hand cupped over her mouth, to catch any laughter that might well up and press it

26

back again. Her narrow little body shook spasmodically. 'I told you,' said Piet. 'It is all right. I have explained to her that she must have a picture of this fine boarding house. I shall paint it for her, at a medium cost. I shall also make a copy and donate it to the city's archives, for the memory of a building such as this must not be lost to mankind. I feel it will be the finest pondokkie I have ever painted. Poor woman, she is very bitter. The war makes her unhappy.'

'She's doing very nicely out of it.'

'No, the Boer War. Those concentration camps you had. Ya, ya, the English were never anything but savages. Now, please, think no more about it. I have made everything right for you.'

He went. Almost at once Mrs Coetzee came in, with Jemima. It was a visit of goodwill. She was smiling. Then she noticed the picture, which unfortunately Piet had forgotten. Her face sagged into folds of disapproval.

She spoke to Jemima. Jemima said: 'Says will not picture her house.' 'Tell her it's not my picture.' 'Says take it away.' 'I'll tell my friend to take it tomorrow.' 'Says your picture, not his picture.' 'But it is his.' 'Says he is Afrikaans. A good boy.' 'It is a picture of his wife. She is a very good Afrikaans girl.' 'Says good boy does not make bad picture like that.' Jemima's face was expressionless, but her body shook. I tried to catch her eye. It was blank. Only her body was amused. 'Says you bad woman, says you go,' said Jemima.

That evening, the shipping agents rang to say the boat would be in tomorrow. As a favour, Mrs Coetzee allowed me to stay for the one night. Mrs Barnes came in to say she was sorry there had been this unpleasantness. *If she had known* she would not have complained to Mrs Coetzee. I have never been able to understand this. But my chief problem was to find the right way to say good-bye to the Brooke-Bensons. At last, my suppressed instinct for communication blossomed into a large bunch of flowers. I presented these, not so much to the Brooke-Bensons, as to a failed relationship. I shook hands. I noticed Myra's eyes were wet. She said, with formality: 'I will be so sorry when you've gone. I feel I have made a real friend in you.' Her husband said: 'And please keep in touch. Now that we've got to know each other.' I shook hands again and we said good-bye.

The boat was full of English. That is, South African British, going home. I had no time to meet them. My son was so excited by the experience of being on the boat that he woke at five every morning and did not sleep until eleven at night. In between, he rushed, hurled himself, bounded and leaped all over the boat. I arrived in England exhausted. The white cliffs of Dover depressed me. They were too small. The Isle of Dogs discouraged me. The Thames looked dirty. I had better confess at once that for the whole of the first year, London seemed to me a city of such appalling ugliness that I wanted only to leave it. Besides, I had no money, I could have got some by writing to my family, of course, but it had to be the bootstraps or nothing.

The first place I stayed in was a flat off the Bayswater Road. I passed the house the other day, and it now seems quite unremarkable. This is how it struck me at the time:

'A curving terrace. Decaying, unpainted, enormous, ponderous, graceless. When I stand and look up, the sheer weight of the building oppresses me. The door looks as if it could never be opened. The hall is painted a dead uniform cream, that looks damp. It has a carved chest in it that smells of mould. Everything smells damp. The stairs are wide, deep, oppressive. The carpets are thick and shabby. Walking on them is frightening – no sound at all. All the way up the centre of this immense, heavy house, the stairs climb, silent and ugly, flight after flight, and all the walls are the same dead, dark cream colour. At last another hostile and heavy door. I am in a highly varnished little hall, with wet mackintoshes and umbrellas. Another dark door. Inside, a great heavy room, full of damp shadow. The furniture is all heavy and dead, and the surfaces are damp. The flat has six rooms, all painted this heavy darkening cream, all large, with high ceilings, no sound anywhere, the walls are so thick. I feel suffocated. Out of the back windows, a vista of wet dark roofs and dingy chimneys. The sky is pale and cold and unfriendly.'

My arrangements for living here had been made with great

intelligence by a friend. The idea was, I should share this flat with another woman, an Australian, who had a small child. We should share the rent and expenses, and the children would share each other.

They took to each other at sight and went off to play.

The Australian lady and I had now to make acquaintance. She was a woman of inveterate sensibility. Her name was Brenda. She was sitting in a huddled mass in a deep chair by an empty grate. She was a large woman, of firm swarthy flesh. She had a large sallow face, and black hair cut doll-like across her forehead. She wore artistic clothes. She had been crying, and was still damp. Almost the first thing she said was, 'I do hope your child is sensitive. My Daphne is very sensitive. A highly-strung child.' I knew then that the whole thing was doomed.

Daphne was three, a strapping, lively-eyed child with a healthy aggressiveness. Peter was two and a half. They were well-matched. They began to fight, with much enjoyment. Brenda went next door, pulled Daphne to her, and said in a weak voice: 'Oh, darling, he's such a nice little boy, don't hit him.' She set Daphne in a chair with a picture book.

Then she said everything was too much for her, and so I went out and bought the rations and had some keys cut. While I did this, I reflected on the value of helplessness. During the next weeks I reflected about this often. Brenda was renting the flat for seven guineas a week. I don't know how she managed it. I've never since seen a flat of such size, class, and solid furnishing going at such a low rent. She had already let two rooms in it, at three and a half guineas each. That left four rooms. The largest room was her sitting-room, because she had to have privacy. The children had a room each, because Daphne could not sleep unless she was by herself. The largest room upstairs was Brenda's bedroom. That left one for me. She had put the dining-room table in it, where we would all eat, as she said this would be more convenient for all of us. She intended to charge me seven guineas a week. I did all the shopping and the washing-up and the tidying, because life was too much for her, particularly in England. Also I had to keep my son away from

Daphne, because they would play together, and in the most insensitive manner.

I have often wondered about that remarkable phenomenon – that for sheer innate delicacy and appreciation of the finer sides of life, one has to seek for a certain type of Colonial.

Piet for instance. Robust is the word I would use to describe him. Yet his tastes in art, save when he was painting pondokkies, were all exquisite. Corot he liked. Turner he liked. A passage of nature description in Chekhov would make him screw back the tears from his eyes. A couple of the more oblique sentences in Katherine Mansfield would send him into a melancholy ecstasy. But Balzac was coarse, and Rubens had no poetry. A letter from Piet would end something like this: . . . the exquisite veil of translucent twilight drawn gently down to the horizon, and I sit, pen in hand, and dream. The fire crepitates in the grate, and the shadows deepen on the wall. Ach, my God, and life is passing. Your old friend, Piet. P.S. – We went to the Bay this afternoon and swam and bought three crayfish for sixpence each. I boiled them till they squeaked and we ate them in our fingers with melted butter. My God, man, they were good. I bet you don't get crayfish in that godforsaken colony full of English. Christ but you're crazy, I'm telling you.

For real perception into the side-channels of British culture, one has to go to a university in Australia or South Africa. The definitive thesis on Virginia Woolf will come, not from Cambridge, but from Cape Town. Brenda was writing a thesis on: Proust – a nature poet manqué.

In short, we were temperamentally unsuited. I began looking for somewhere to live. Besides, I still had not met the English.

Chapter Two

I had already moved away from the counter when some instinct turned me back to ask: 'I suppose you don't know somewhere I could live?' The girl behind the counter shrugged profoundly, sighed and said: 'I don't know, dear, I'm sure.' I took this as a dismissal, but she looked at me shrewdly and said: 'Depends on what you're looking for, doesn't it now?'

When I had first entered the shop the girl was standing motionless, hands resting palm downwards, while she gazed past me into the street, her face set into lines of melancholy resignation. She was a small girl, her face broad under very black and glossy hair that was piled into a dense and sculptured mound. Her hair, and her thin black crescent brows, made her look like a cockney Madame Butterfly, particularly as she was wearing a loose flowered wrap over her clothes. Her mouth might have been any shape; the one she had painted was another crescent in cherry pink, as deep as the half-circle eyebrows. Her voice toned with the sad lips and eyes.

I said: 'I've been looking for six weeks.' My voice was by this time drenched with self-pity. 'I've got a small child,' I said.

Her face became shrewd as she examined me from this new point of view. Then she said, with confidence: 'I don't know whether it would suit, but my friend where I live has a flat.'

'How much?'

'I don't know, dear, I'm sure. But she's ever so nice, and she likes having kids about the place.'

'What sort of a flat?'

'It's upstairs,' she said, doubtful again. But added: 'One room, but ever such nice furniture. It's only a minute from here.'

I hesitated. My companion, who was directing this conversation with a skill I only learned to appreciate later, said, with casualness: 'You just tell her Rose sent you. She'll know it's all right if you say Rose. Besides, she likes young people. She likes a bit of life about.' She glanced at me, waited a moment, then raised her voice to shout: 'Nina, are you busy?' A woman appeared in the back. This was a jeweller's shop, very dark and crowded, and she had to push her way through trestles burdened with clocks, watches, trinkets, rubbish of all kinds. She was fat and pale, with rusty dyed hair, but her look of puffy ponderousness was contradicted by her eyes, which were calculating. After a rapid summing-up look, she stood beside Rose, with the air of one putting herself completely at disposal.

'Flo doesn't take just anyone, does she, dear?' suggested Rose, and the woman said promptly: 'That's right. She likes to pick and choose.'

'I'll give you the address,' said Rose, and wrote it down.

Seeing she had served her purpose, the pale woman pulled her lips back and exposed her teeth in a sweet smile. Then she threaded her way back to the room she had emerged from. At the door she turned back and said: 'How about that other place – you know, that you heard about this morning?'

Rose seemed displeased. She said unwillingly: 'I don't know anything about it – not to recommend.'

The pale woman's submissive helpfulness vanished. She said to me with a ferocious smile: 'I hope Rose is looking after you properly.' She disappeared. Rose was annoyed. She raised her voice to say: 'You come back tomorrow, dear, and your watch will be ready.' She had been saying this every day for the past week.

'What's the address of this other place?' I asked Rose.

'I'll write it for you. Mind you, I'm not recommending it.' Then, the desire to do her friend Flo a service dissolved into the fellowship of the suffering, and she said: 'Of course, these days, you grab what's going.'

I thanked her and left. Glancing back, I saw she had taken up her former position, and her face was all lifeless curves.

I decided to try the second address immediately. About the first I felt like the horse dragged to water. I could have said, of course, that Rose's insistence showed there must be something wrong with it. But there was more to it than that. For six weeks I had been tramping the streets with a guidebook, standing in queues outside telephone booths, examining advertisement boards. Stoicism can reach a point where, if someone says: I'm sure you'll be lucky sooner or later, one feels positively indignant. I was defensively rejecting possibilities in advance. This state of mind was not only mine. Talking to other home-hunters I learned it was an occupational disease. It means one cannot enter a house-agent's office without an air of hostility; or open the advertisement columns of a newspaper without a cynical (and consciously cynical) smile, as if to say: You don't imagine I'm going to be taken in by this, do you?

During those weeks I had formed alliances with various people I met in the agents' offices, or under the advertisement boards. I remember, particularly, a lady with a grown-up daughter and a grand piano. The daughter was talented, come all the way from Australia to study in London. For three months these women had been looking for a shelter for their piano. At the time we met they had become so bitter that on several occasions, setting out for some possible address, they exclaimed: 'What's the use, they won't have us!' – and turned aside into a café to brood over a cup of tea.

It is a curious fact that at a time when we were all short of money, when getting a place to live was essential before we could start to live at all, we would spend the larger part of each working day (for me the hours that my son was in nursery school) sitting in teashops gripped by bitter lethargy. We used to discuss the various places we had lived in, the climate of this country or that, landladies, the woman who had affronted us the day before, the harpy who had offered one room and use of the kitchen at four guineas a week provided one agreed not 'to walk on the floor before eight in the morning'. The teashop had become our home, our refuge, the bedclothes we pulled over our heads. We could no longer face another long walk, another set of dingy lodgings, another refusal. We could not face seeing our fantasies about what we hoped to find diminished to what we knew we would have to take.

I went in search of the second address with a grim and barbed gaiety. My by now highly-developed instinct told me it would be useless. Besides, the interminable streets of tall, grey, narrow houses that became half-effaced with fog at a distance of a hundred yards, the pale faces peering up from basements past rubbish cans, the innumerable dim flights of stairs, rooms crowded with cushioned and buttoned furniture, railings too grimy to touch, dirty flights of steps – above all, an atmosphere of stale weariness; had worked on me in a way I did not understand myself.

The street I wanted was not in my guidebook. I was directed back and forth by passers-by, each one saying helpfully, 'It's just around the corner,' and looking impatient when I said: 'Which corner?' This business of the next corner is confusing to aliens, who will interpret it as the next intersection of the street. But to the Londoner, with his highly subjective attitude to geography, the 'corner' will mean, perhaps, a famous pub, or an old street whose importance dwarfs all the intervening streets out of existence, or perhaps the turning he takes every morning on his way to work.

The house I wanted was a broader, taller house than most, and separated from its neighbours by a six-inch space on either side. The steps were scrubbed white; the doorknob gleamed; the wood of the door was newly-varnished chocolate brown. While I waited for the bell to be answered, a young man came out, carrying suitcases, which he left on the bottom step. Soon a young woman followed him, vehemently slamming the door, and looking to him for approval of this action. But he said irritably: 'Don't give them grounds for complaint.' She was a tall slender girl, wearing an enormous black picture hat, very high black heels, a deep black decolletage crowded with crimson roses, and furs slung over one shoulder. Because of her appearance I looked again at the man. He was as unfamiliar to me as she was. He wore a sharply-angled brown suit, and pointed brown shoes. He was tall, dark, slickly good-looking, with prominent brown eyes that were now suffused with uneasy anger. The door swung inwards, this time to show an elderly grey woman in a stiff white nurse's uniform. She looked past me at the couple and said: 'You must have all your things out in half an hour or I'll call the police.' The young woman gave a shrill laugh; the young man frowned and began to say something; but the nurse interrupted him by saying to me: 'Come in.' Her voice still held the sharpness which she had directed at the other two.

Inside there was a narrow hall carpeted with crimson. A grey satin wallpaper was sprinkled all over with small gilt coronets and harps. Small gilt-framed mirrors hung at various levels, chandelier, sprouting large electric bulbs.

The nurse left me in these surroundings of dispirited opulence, saying: 'I'll ask for the keys.' Soon a very old lady, swathed in pink and mauve wool, wheeled herself in a chair across the hall, giving me a cold stare. Then she turned herself around and rolled back, with another prolonged stare. When the inspection was over the nurse came back with a bunch of keys, and led me up one, two, three, four, five flights of stairs, all muffled in crimson carpet, the walls thick with large brownish pictures. She unlocked a door that barred our way into a more bleak corridor. The stairs were now very narrow and twisted sharply after each short flight. There was no carpet. It was dark, save when we passed the windows, which shed a pallid glow over our heads on to more pictures, so that at short intervals the gloom was broken by a confusion of dimly inter-reflecting lights.

All the way up were doors with names written on cards beside the bells. I imagined vistas of passageways, opening on to yet more rooms, more lives. It was very silent, a humming breathing quiet, like listening to someone sleep. It was as if I had become a midget and was walking up the main gallery of a large antheap.

On the top landing it was completely dark; we were standing in a closed box. 'Here we are,' said the nurse briskly, and flung open a door. There was a dim space before us, filled with jostling furniture. The colours were dull crimson and purple, with a dark plummy wallpaper, and so many armchairs, buttoned pouffes and small hard tables that it was difficult for the nurse to move in a straight line to the window, where she jerked back heavy curtains. They were red damask lined with black silk, which absorbed the filtering light so that the room became only slightly less obscure than before.

'There!' she exclaimed with pride, turning to gaze lovingly at the oppressive room. 'This used to be the old lady's room before she got too ill to climb the stairs. She liked it for the view. It's a lovely view.' At the window I saw crowding roofs, and beyond them, the tops of trees shadowed with cold sunlight.

'Has she been ill for long?'

'Thirty years,' said the nurse with pride. 'Yes, I've been nursing her for thirty years. She won't have anything changed up here, even though she can't come up herself. It was her room she used to sit in when she first got married. She used to paint. No one was allowed up here, not even her husband.'

The way she spoke, diminishing those thirty years to the scale of a long convalescence, made the fruity room congeal around us; the thick curved surfaces thrust themselves out aggressively in affirmations of changeless comfort. 'You won't find many rooms like this at the price. Not good things like this. Can't buy them these days.' She gave a proud stiff glance around her. 'She won't have just anybody up here. Except when there are mistakes.' The little foxy face stared at a point immediately before her; it was a table gleaming in the rufous light from the curtains. With an angry movement she jerked forward and picked up a brown, sticklike object which I took to be a cigar. 'Incense,' she said indignantly. 'What next!' Holding the thing between thumb and forefinger, little finger crooked away in disgust, she nosed her way warily through the angles and shoulders of the furniture like a fish at the bottom of a pool, and flung open another door. 'I suppose you'll want to see the bedroom,' she said, as if this was unreasonable of me. 'The other people aren't properly out yet, remember.' This was a tiny room, more like the usual run of let rooms. It had a large jangly bed with brass bedballs, a fireplace that was occupied by an electric fire, and a single yellowing chest of drawers. The climate of this room – a thin bleakness, with a narrow shaft of colourless light directed over the bare floor from a high window – was as if I had accidentally opened the door into the servants' quarters from a lush passage in an old-fashioned hotel. The nurse was staring down at the bed, which was in disorder, the bottom sheet stained and crumpled, a single dent in the pillow, which held several glinting yellow hairs. Furs, flowers, dresses and underclothing lay everywhere. She picked up an empty scent bottle and flung it, together with the spill of incense, into an open drawer. 'You can cook on this,' she said grudgingly, pulling a gas-ring from behind a small curtain. 'But this suite is not arranged for heavy cooking. My old lady won't have cooking in the house. You'll have to go out if you want to eat fancy.'

'How much?'

'Twelve guineas.'

'A month?'

Her face creased into suspicion. 'A week,' she said affrontedly. 'Where do you come from? I might as well say now that the old lady won't take foreigners.'

'What do you mean by foreigners?'

She looked me up and down, a practised, sly movement. 'Where do you come from, then?' She moved slowly backwards, her hand pressed against her chest, as if warding off something.

'Africa.'

The hand slowly dropped, and at her side, the fingers clenched nervously. 'You're not a black?'

'Do I look like one?'

'One never knows. You'd be surprised what people try to get away with these days. We're not having blacks. Across the road a black took to the bottle on the first floor. Such trouble they had. We don't take Jews either. Not that that's any protection.' She sniffed sharply, looking over her shoulder at the bed. 'Disgusting,' she said. 'Disgusting.' In a prim fine voice she stated: 'And I may as well say we're particular about what goes on. Are you married?'

'I'm not taking it,' I said going into the living-room.

The nurse came after me; her whole attitude had changed. 'Why not, don't you like it?'

'No, I do not.'

'It's very comfortable, only select people in this house . . .' She glanced back at the room. 'Except when there's mistakes. You can't help mistakes.' She stood between me and the door, her hands clasped lightly at her waist, in an attitude of willing service, but with a look of affronted surprise on her face. It was clear that letting this place quickly was necessary as part of her revenge on the couple she had turned out. 'If the old lady likes you she might put the rent down to eleven guineas.'

'But I don't like it,' I repeated, moving past her to the door.

'We don't have any difficulty in letting it, I can tell you that,' she sniffed challengingly, marching over to twitch the curtains back, so that now the room was absorbed back into its cavernous ruddy gloom. 'You're the second in half an hour – by the way, how did you hear of it? It hasn't even gone to the agents yet.'

'One hears of places, house-hunting.'

'I suppose you are a friend of that precious pair downstairs.' She grasped my arm, as if to pull me to the door. 'I hear the bell. That'll be someone else, I suppose, getting me up all these stairs for nothing. Come along now.' She glanced at me, stiffened, stared: '*If* you'll be so kind.' She went on staring. At last, she said: 'It's much better when people are straightforward about things, that's what I say.'

'About what?'

Looking straight ahead, her hands lying down the folds of her stiff skirt, she descended the stairs with a consciously demure rectitude, and said: 'If I'd known you were a foreigner, it would have saved me so much time, wouldn't it?

One must have thought for other people, these times.'

'What kind of a foreigner do you think I am?'

'I've known people before, calling it sunburn.'

In the hall the old lady was lurking in a doorway, leaning forward in her wheeled chair from a mist of pastel shawls. Her small beady eyes, like a bird's, were fixed on me. Her face was twisted into a preparatory smile of stiff welcome, but a glance at the nurse caused her to give me a slight toss of the head instead. Leaning back, she daintily took a grape from a dish beside her, and held it to her mouth in a tiny bony hand, her eyes still regarding me sideways, so that she looked even more like a watchful parrot.

On the steps was the young man, alone. 'How do you think I can leave when you won't let us take our property?' he asked the nurse.

'I'm not having you set foot in this house.'

'I've paid the rent, so if you take my wife's things . . .'

'Your *wife*!'

Immediately his attitude changed to one of confident challenge. 'I'll show you my marriage certificate, if that's your attitude.' His hand was already in his pocket, but she had slammed the door. There was a clinking noise, and the letterbox slit showed dark with a face hovering white behind it.

'You deserve to be in prison,' said the shrill voice through the slit.

'If you don't give me my things I'm going straight to a lawyer.'

'You tell that woman of yours to come here this afternoon and I'll have them bundled up for her in the hall.' The metal flap dropped with a clatter.

'I say!' shouted the young man in an injured way. 'Do you know that's a legal offence?' With one shoulder thrust forward, his chin stuck angrily out, he looked as if he were about to fling himself on the door.

Nothing happened. Slowly the young man straightened, letting his shoulders loosen. For a moment he stood gazing with sullen reflectiveness at the door; then he turned and his eyes came blankly to rest on me. The glowering anger

left in him from the encounter with the nurse simmered in
him, unreleased; but soon he smiled a statesman's smile,
bathing me in winning frankness. 'It's only right for me to
warn you,' he said, 'I shouldn't want any friend of mine to
live in that house.' He swung his head to glare at it before
going on. 'Don't take it. I'm warning you.'

'I haven't taken it,' I said.

Disbelief congealed the smile. 'Not fit for pigs,' he said.
'Better change your mind now, before it's too late. Better late
than never.' This aphorism pleased him so much that he
repeated it, and his smile was momentarily gratified. He
leaned towards me, his eyes were anxiously penetrating. If I
had said I had taken the rooms, he would now be as
anxiously testing me for the lie. 'Go in and cancel the
contract now, better that way.' The word *contract* in his
mouth was loaded with suspicion. 'But I haven't taken it.'
He stared at me closely. 'Mind, it's not too bad at first sight.
You see the snags when you're in. You can't call your life
your own.' I smiled. He grew uneasy. A genuine impatience
must have shown itself in my face, for at once his body
arranged itself into a new attitude, and he leaned forward
with a gentle and disarming persuasiveness. 'If you're looking for a place to live, I'm your man.'

'Do you know of somewhere?'

'It's my business. I'm an estate agent.'

'Then you're lucky. You won't have difficulty in finding
somewhere yourself, will you?'

At this he inspected me for some time, in silence, and
with hostility. Thus it was that right at the beginning, the
quality which he most valued in his victims – my naïvety –
confused him. He could not believe that I was as green as I
seemed. Looking back, I can't believe it either.

Looking back it is clear that he believed I was putting on
innocence to lead him on, to some dark goal, for reasons of
my own. Yet there were moments when I was as gullible as
a fish. I confused him. And he confused me. I disliked him
at sight, but I saw no reason not to trust him. I had never
met a con-man in my life.

'I'll have no trouble,' he remarked at last. 'I've nothing to worry about. And they can't turn me into the street, just like that – not Andrew MacNamara.'

Envying him, I walked away down the steps, and found him striding beside me, giving me calculating glances from his large treacly brown eyes. He was still tortured by uncertainty as to whether I was lying. And what was important to him was not the fact, but whether he was being made a fool of. 'If you don't believe me, I can tell you things about that crowd in there that would put them into prison. It's no place for decent people.'

'Then it's lucky I haven't taken it.'

He changed ground. 'If you don't have to count the pennies, there's flats for the asking.' A pause. 'I could fix you up tomorrow, today.'

'But I have to count the pennies.'

'That's always a good line, to start with,' he probed.

'Besides,' I said, 'I've got a small child.'

'That's bad,' he said. 'It won't make things any easier. But you can buy anything.'

We had reached a main street. Half a dozen large red buses lumbered past, concentrating all the colour and light there was in their cheerful and exuberant bodies. 'Taxi?' he suggested. 'There's a friend of mine in the rank over there.' He raised his arm to wave.

'No, a bus.'

He frowned. 'A penny saved is a penny gained,' he said.

'Can you tell me the way to – '

'It's just around the corner.'

My head was, as usual in those early days in London, in a maze. To my right and left stretched that street which seemed exactly like all the main streets in London, the same names recurring at regular intervals, the same patterns of brick and plaster. It seemed to me impossible that the people walking past the decent little shops that were so alike, and the cold stone slabs decorated with pale gleaming fishes and vivid parsley, like giant plates of salad thrust forward into the street, could ever know one part of London from another.

'I'm going that way myself,' he said. He took my elbow in the urgency of unconcluded business. I got on to a bus and

41

he leaped on to it beside me as it moved off. 'Before you go, take the name of my agency. I said I'd fix you up,' he reproved me.

'Where is it?'

'I've five rooms and a staff of nine,' he said casually. 'It's over in Holborn. But for special customers I've a little office of my own. For private talking.'

'Give me the address and I'll come when I've got time.'

'Never let the chance slip,' he said reproachfully, giving me a lesson in living. 'It might get snapped up before you get there. That's not the way to do business.'

'But I'm not doing business,' I said, throwing him off balance again. He was also annoyed. 'You want a flat, don't you? You said so, didn't you?' Automatically, he looked around for witnesses. 'I heard you say so. You want a flat.'

'Tickets,' said the conductor.

'Allow me,' said Mr MacNamara, taking out sixpence with such an air that I was surprised to find in myself the beginnings of gratitude commensurate with his having produced tickets for the front row of the stalls.

'It's a pleasure,' he smiled, pocketing the tickets carefully. 'Business. You decide what you want. You find what you want. You get what you want. You pay for what you want. Or you pay someone else to get it for you.' We were sitting side by side on the long seats at the entrance of the bus. Four working women, in respectable hats, carrying crowded shopping bags, were sitting with us. 'Pay,' remarked one of them humorously, as if to the air. 'That's the co-operative word.' Mr MacNamara flushed angrily. He struggled to ignore this woman. But vanity won. In a voice of furious hostility he said: 'What you want you have to pay for. The thing is, who wants to pay too much?'

'Not me, that's for sure,' she said. She glanced around at the other women, and winked. She did not look at Mr MacNamara. The conductor, who was leaning negligently against the steps, smiled tolerantly, and said: 'Who's for the Church?'

'That's me,' said the woman, upheaving herself from beside me. Potatoes rolled from her bag into my lap, and she grabbed at them as they scattered. 'Here,' she shouted upwards, crouched among feet, 'potatoes at sixpence a pound. Mind your great boots.'

'Now, love,' said the conductor indulgently, 'get a move on or I'll take them home to my missus.'

'Try it,' she retorted, and lurched off the bus, thrusting potatoes into her bag and her pockets. From the pavement she remarked in a detached voice: 'Still, sixpence a pound is what you pay for new potatoes, when it's right, and not like what some people I know try to get.' Where this barb was directed could not easily be decided, for she was gazing absently at the back of the bus. One of the three women who remained took it up, saying: 'That's right dear, some people have no consciences.' This exchange hung in the air as far as I was concerned, in spite of the gently-grinning faces all around me. I heard Mr MacNamara complain: 'I say!' The woman on the pavement, who must have been waiting for him to react, beamed directly at the conductor, and, indicating her bruised potatoes, said: 'I won't have to mash them now, will I?'

'That's right, love,' he said. He had his thumb on the bell, and was looking up and down the street. A few paces off a well-dressed woman was running towards the bus. He pressed the bell; the bus began to move; and the woman fell back, annoyed. Now he had held up the bus over the affair of the potatoes as if he had all the time in the world. Once again Mr MacNamara exclaimed: 'I say!' Whistling under his breath, the conductor passed down the bus. The three working women opposite surveyed us with critical eyes, in which showed a calm triumph. The bond between them and the jaunty conductor could be felt.

'It should be reported,' said Mr MacNamara belligerently. At once occurred that phenomenon which is inevitable, in an English crowd on such occasions. The women looked straight ahead of them, disassociating themselves, shaking gently with the shaking of the bus. Every face, every pair of shoulders expressed the same thing: This is no affair of mine. In this emotional vacuum, Mr MacNamara fumed alone.

My stop appeared and I stood up. 'Good-bye,' I said. At once he got up. 'You haven't got my address,' he said.

'I haven't a pencil,' I said. At this, there came indulgently pitying looks on to the faces of the women. I found a pencil in my hand. 'Try that,' urged Mr MacNamara, restored to normal by the familiar situation. 'That's a real pencil. I can get them for you from a friend in Brixton.'

'Ah, Brixton's the place for pencils now,' said the conductor.

'That's enough,' said Mr MacNamara, his eyes once more suffused with anger.

'Temper, temper,' remarked one of the women gazing out of the window. When Mr MacNamara said: 'Here, what's that?' she turned her head with a look of calm unconcern, and rose to her feet. To the conductor she said: 'Give the bell a shove for me, love.' The conductor came right down the car to help her out. To the rest of us he said: 'Hurry up now.' As I stepped off, the conductor said to me, grinning, 'Mind his pencil, lady.' The women began to shriek. The bus departed in a tumult of good humour. Mr MacNamara, his fists squared, shouted after it: 'I'll report you,' and the conductor shouted calmly back: 'A sense of humour, that's all I ask.'

'That wouldn't have been possible before the war,' said Mr MacNamara.

'What wouldn't?'

'They're all out of hand.'

'Who?'

'The working-classes.'

'Oh!'

'Of course you wouldn't know,' he said after a moment's suspicion. 'In your part of the world there isn't any trouble, is there? With niggers it's easy. I've often thought of emigrating.'

'Here I must leave you,' I said.

'Tomorrow morning at nine-fifteen.' He glanced at his watch, frowning. 'No, at nine-forty. I've an appointment at nine-fifteen.'

'I'll telephone you,' I said. For I had already decided I

would go back to Rose and take the flat she offered. I felt that this was where I would end up. Besides, it was the first time I had heard, in all those weeks of hunting, of a landlady who would welcome a child.

Mr MacNamara and I were facing each other on a street corner, while people surged past. We kept our places by sticking out our elbows into aggressive points. He was very irritated. 'I work to strict business methods,' he said. 'But I'll tell you what I'll do for you. I'll constitute myself your agent, that's what. I'll work for you. I'll get you a flat by tomorrow morning.'

'That,' I said with politeness, 'is very kind of you.' I was by now longing to be rid of him. He smiled suspiciously, 'Good-bye,' I said.

'Wait,' he said. 'The fee is two guineas.'

'What fee?'

'I know of just the place. Three rooms, kitchen, pantry, bathroom. Hot and cold and all modern cons. Three guineas a week, *inclusive*.' I thought that if this place existed it was cheaper than anything I had seen. 'I promised it to someone else, but for a retainer I'll give it to you. I got nothing out of him, all promises he was.' A look of disgusted anger came on to his face. This look was genuine: the flat, therefore, must also be genuine? But this is an excuse. I felt as if I had been stung into torpor by a predatory spider. I was being impelled to hand over the money. I began fumbling in my handbag, and as I did so, I knew I was a fool. The thought must have shown on my face, for he said: 'For you, I'll make it pounds.' The money melted into the air above the flesh of his palm. I could hardly believe I had given it to him. So strong was this feeling that I wanted to count the money I had left to see if I had given it to him.

A couple of policemen who had been standing against a wall, upshifted themselves with a stolid and determined movement and came towards us. Instinctively I looked around to see if Mr MacNamara had vanished. I was wrong, for he stood negligently beside me, gazing with impatience at the policemen. They, it seemed, had also expected him to vanish, for now they appeared uncertain. 'Anything I can do for you?' enquired Mr MacNamara efficiently. They hesitated. He turned his back and marched off.

'Everything all right?' asked one of the policemen.

'I do hope so.'

They looked at each other, communed, and moved back to their wall, where they stood, feet apart, hands behind their backs, heads bent slightly forward, talking to each other with scarcely-moving lips, while their slow contemplative eyes followed the movements of the crowd.

I walked slowly towards the jeweller's shop, thinking about Mr MacNamara. It had by now occurred to me that he was what they referred to as a spiv. But he was not in the least like any of the rogues and adventurers I had known in Africa. They had all had a certain frankness, almost a gaiety, in being rogues. Mr MacNamara had nothing whatsoever in common with them. His strength was – and I could feel just how powerful that strength was, now I was recovering from my moment of being mad – his terrible, compelling anxiety that he should be able to force someone under his will. It was almost as if he were pleading, silently, in the moment when he was tricking a victim: Please let me trick you; please let me cheat you; I've got to; it's essential for me.

But the fact remained, that at a time when I had less than twenty pounds left, and counting every halfpenny, I had just parted with two pounds, knowing when I did it that I would never see it again. I was clearly much more undermined by England than I had known; and the sooner I got myself into some place I could call my own the better.

When I told Rose I had lost the piece of paper with the address she said it didn't matter, she'd take me home with her. The pale woman entered from the back and said unpleasantly: 'Closing early, aren't you?'

Rose answered: 'Half past five is closing time, isn't it?'

'Like your pound of flesh, don't you, dear?'

'I don't get paid overtime.' She added casually: 'I worked three nights late last week. I didn't notice any complaints.'

The pale woman said quickly: 'I was only joking, dear.'

'Oh no you wasn't,' said Rose. Without another glance at her employer, she began making up her face, not because

46

there was any need to, but so she could stand negligently, back turned, absorbed in her reflection and her own affairs. Before leaving, however, she said 'Goodnight' quite amiably; and the pale woman returned, indifferently: 'Sleep tight,' just as if this exchange had not occurred.

Rose had said the house she lived in was just around the corner; it was half a mile off. She did not speak. I didn't know if she was offended because I had lost the address; or whether she was irritated with her employer. She replied listlessly to my remarks: Yes, dear; or – Is that so? Her face was heavy, despondent. It was difficult to guess her age. In the dimly-lit shop, she looked like a tired girl. Here, though her skin was spread thick with dun-coloured powder, under her eyes were the purple hollows of a middle-aged woman. Yet she looked defenceless, and soft, like a girl.

At first it was all shops and kiosks; then towering gloomy Victorian houses; then a space where modern luxury flats confronted green grass and trees; then a couple of acres of rubble. 'Bombs,' said Rose dispassionately. 'We had them around here something awful.' It was as if the houses had shaken themselves to the ground. Thin shells of wall stood brokenly among debris; and from this desolation I heard a sound which reminded me of a cricket chirping with quiet persistence from sun-warmed grasses in the veld. It was a typewriter; and peering over a bricky gulf I saw a man in his shirt-sleeves, which were held neatly above the elbow by expanding bands, sitting on a tidy pile of rubble, the typewriter on a broken girder, clean white paper fluttering from the rim of the machine.

'Who's he?' I asked.

'An optimist,' said Rose grimly. 'Thinks he's going to be rebuilt, I shouldn't be surprised. Well, it takes all sorts, that's what I say.'

We turned finally into a street of tall narrow grey houses. I understood, from our quickening steps, that we were going downhill. I was almost running. Rose was moving along the street without seeing it, her feet quick and practised on the pavement. I asked: 'Have you always lived in London?'

There was a short pause before she answered; and I

understood it was because she found it difficult to adapt herself to the idea of London as a place on the map and not as a setting for her life. There was a small grudging note in her voice when she said: 'Yes, dear, since I was born.' I was to hear that reserved, non-judging voice often in the future – the most delicate of snubs, as if she were saying: It's all very well for you . . .

Rose stopped in front of a wooden gate slung loosely between pillars where the plaster was flaking, and said: 'Here we are.' The wood of the gate was damp, and in the cracks were traces of green that I thought at first were remains of paint. Looking closer I saw it was that fine spongy fur that one finds, in the veld, cushioning the inside of a rotting tree trunk where the sun never reaches. Rose led the way down steps, along the side of the house, into a narrow gulf of thick damp brick with water underfoot. She let herself in at the door, and we were at once in darkness that smelt strongly of ammonia. A stairway led up, through darkness, to a closed door. In front was another door outlined in yellow light. There was a blare of noise. The door opened violently and out spilled puppies which scrambled and snapped around our feet. Rose said: 'Come in.' She went forward into the room, abandoning me, indicating why I was there to the other with a brief meaningful nod of the head.

It was a long, narrow room with a tall window at one end. Towards the top of the window one could see a frieze of dustbins and watering cans. A single very strong electric bulb filled the room with a hard shadowless light. The place was divided into two by curtains – or rather, curtains looped back high against the walls indicated a division. One half was the kitchen, the other a living-room, which seemed crammed with people, puppies, children, kittens. At a table under the light bulb sat two men reading newspapers, and they lifted their heads together, and stared with the same open, frank curiosity at me. They both wore very white cotton singlets, hanging loose. One was a man of about forty, forty-five, who gave an immediate impression of a smouldering but controlled violence. His body was lean and long, swelling up into powerful shoulders and neck, a strong, sleek, close-cropped head. His hair was yellowish, his eyes flat and yellowish, like a goat's, and the smooth heavy flesh of his shoulders rather yellow against the white singlet. But he was going soft; he paunched under his singlet. The other was very young, eighteen, twenty, a dark, glossy, sleek young animal with very black eyes. A woman came forward from the kitchen end. She was short and plump, with a small pointed face in a girlish mass of greying black curls. Her mouth was opening and shutting and she was gesticulating angrily at the puppies under her feet and at a small child who was grabbing at her apron. The radio was blaring and she was trying to shout through the music: the noise was so great that my eardrums were receiving it as a dull crashing roar, like a great silence. The older man reached out a hand, turned a knob, and at once a shrill voice assailed me, rising through the snapping and yapping of the dogs and the whining of the child. 'Shut up,' she screeched. 'Shut up, I tell you.' The older man rose and pushed the puppies outside into the passage with his foot. There was a sudden startling quiet. The room seemed empty because of the absence of sound and of dogs.

Rose said: 'Flo, this lady here wants to see your flat.'

'Does she, dear?' screeched Flo, who had grown so used to shouting through noise that she was unable to lower her voice. 'Drat you!' This was to the child, as she slapped down its hands. There was, in fact, only one child there, a little girl who seemed at first glance to be a dwarfed seven or eight, because of her sharp old face, but was three years old. 'Drat you,' shouted Flo again. 'Can't you shut up when I'm talking?' The husband got up and lifted the child on to his lap with the patient forbearance of a man married to a termagant. 'So you want to see our nice flat, dear?' She smiled ingratiatingly; her eyes were calculating. 'You'll be very happy with us, dear. We're just a big happy family, aren't we, Rose?'

'That's right,' said Rose, flatly.

'Dan will show you the way,' screeched Flo. 'My name's Flo. You must call him Dan. You needn't stand on ceremony with us, dear.'

'She hasn't taken it yet,' commented Rose, in her flat expressionless voice.

'She'll like the flat,' shouted Flo persuasively. 'The rooms are ever so nice, aren't they, dear?'

'That's right,' said Rose. She began smoothing down her eyebrows in front of a small wall mirror, with a forefinger wetted with spit, exactly as she had turned herself away to make up her face in the shop: she was saying: 'Leave me alone.'

'Let's all go up,' shouted Flo. But although she had conducted the interview until this point, she now gave her husband an uncertain, almost girlish look, and waited for him. He rose. 'That's right, dear,' she said to him, her voice softening, and she offered an arch, intimate, merry smile. He responded with a direct, equally intimate flash of his eyes, and a baring of very white, prominent teeth. Even at that early stage I was struck by the boy's sullen look at the couple. He was Jack, Flo's son by her first marriage. But they had already adjusted their faces, and returned to the harsh business of life. Dan picked up the little girl and dropped her into Jack's arms. At once she began to wail. Her mother grabbed her, exclaiming: 'Oh, you'll be the death of me.' She yelled even louder. Automatically the father reached for her, and set her on his shoulders where she sat smiling, triumphant. He did not do this in a way which was critical of his wife; it was an habitual thing.

All of us, the son included, filed into the dark well at the foot of the stairs. The smell of ammonia was so strong it took the breath. We began to ascend the stairs, which were narrow, of bare wood. I was at the head of the procession, and could see nothing. Flo shouted: 'Mind the door.' I came into collision with it, a hand reached under my arm, and we all moved backwards down the steep incline as the door swung in over our heads, letting in a shaft of dull light. We were now in the hall. There was a puddle near the stairs. 'Drat these dogs,' shouted Flo.

50

'Last time it was Aurora,' commented Rose.

At once Flo slapped the child where she sat on her father's shoulders. Aurora let out a single bellow and immediately became silent, and watched us all with her black sharp eyes. 'Don't you do that again,' shouted Flo. The child's mouth opened and she let out another loud roar as if a button had been pushed. Again she fell to watching us. Nobody took the slightest notice of this scene; and indeed Flo beamed encouragingly at me as if to say: Look at the trouble I'm taking on your behalf.

'Oh dear, oh dear me,' she grumbled, smiling, 'that child will be the death of me yet.'

'Perhaps it was the old people,' said Jack, regarding the puddle.

'Oh,' said Flo, 'so it must be. Dirty, filthy old swine . . .' She caught a glance from her husband and smiled guiltily. 'But they won't bother you, dear. They sit by themselves in there, getting up to their mischief and their tricks . . .' Again Dan glared at her. and she smiled. 'They won't bother you at all, dear,' she said, and hastily went upstairs. We followed her, flight after flight, past shut doors. Nearing the top of the house was a shallow grey cement sink, with a tap which was making a happy tinkling noise, like a celesta. 'This tap,' said Flo in an offhand voice to her husband. Dan frowned. He heaved violently on the tap, his great shoulder muscles bulging, and a steady splash-splashing resulted. 'Look,' said Dan to me. 'If you turn it round like this it's quite all right.' Once again he heaved with all his strength. We stood at varying heights on the stairs above and below the obstinate tap, gazing at it in suspense. Dan slowly, warily, straightened himself. A single heavy drop of water gathered weight on the lip of the tap and hung, trembling. It flew downwards to the puddle in the sink with a defiant tinkle, and at once another followed.

Flo decided to shrug. 'Anyway,' she said, 'there's the bathroom downstairs for real washing, it only costs fourpence for a real good deep bath, and you can use this just for washing up. If you turn it good and tight, it will be quite all right, you'll see.'

'She'll need some strength,' said Rose. 'It runs all over the landing some days, when Mrs Skeffington doesn't turn it hard enough. It needs a man.'

Flo nudged her to be quiet, and Rose shrugged. 'We've only just moved in,' said Flo, 'and we haven't got everything fixed right yet.' We started climbing again.

'Two years,' said Rose's voice from the flight below. 'Oh, you shut up,' said Flo in a loud whisper down past my head; as if the act of lowering her voice and directing it to Rose made it inaudible to everyone else. Then she screeched gaily to me: 'We're nearly there now.'

We climbed two more flights in silence. Flo was ascending in front of me with the phlegmatic calm of a mountaineer who has only an hour to the summit; her fat flanks moved regularly up and down; her feet were planted wide for balance; and her hands pushed down on each knee in turn, for greater propulsion.

We came to another door, which Flo opened saying: 'You'll be nice and private in here, see?' There was one more short, sharp flight, very steep, ending in an abrupt twist that brought us to a handkerchief-sized landing. 'Here we are,' said Flo, with an anxious glance at me. It was a small room under the roof, with double skylights slanting inwards for illumination. A vast double bed took up most of the floor space, with a glossy toffee-coloured wardrobe. There was a minute kitchen that held a gas cooker, and a set of food canisters ranged on the floor. They all stood around me, smiling encouragingly, even Rose, whose desire for accuracy and fairness was momentarily quenched by the necessities of the occasion. She said: 'It's ever so private up here.' She thought, and added: 'There's a lot of room, really.' She was tiny, as I've said, and as she spoke she moved in from the wall, straightening herself painfully, for she had been bent in a curve, because the roof slanted down almost to the floor. Then, having done what was expected of her, she said: 'Excuse me,' and escaped downstairs, looking embarrassed.

Flo said: 'We don't know what we'd do without Rose, and that's a fact. We get all our people through her. They come into the shop and ask if she knows, when they're stuck for a flat – like you did.' She offered me this information as if Rose's compliance was an additional attraction of the house.

'I have a small boy,' I said, with dread.

'That's right,' said Flo instantly. 'Rose said so, when she phoned us. That's nice, dear. He can play with Oar. We like kids. Don't we, Dan?'

Dan said, 'That's right,' and meant it.

'And Rose likes kids, too. We all do.'

'Is Rose a relation?'

'Oh no. She lives here, see, because she's going to marry Dan's brother.' But here Dan frowned; glances were exchanged and Dan said: 'Well, how do you like it?'

'How much?' I said. Three pairs of eyes exchanged glances. At last Flo asked: 'How much did you think of paying?'

Dan was calculating, his yellow eyes on my clothes. 'Have you got a lot of cases?' he enquired.

'Far too many.' At this, the three faces became extremely businesslike, and Flo said: 'You wouldn't think four pounds too much, would you, dear?' At once she grinned in an abashed way, when Dan glared at her.

'Yes, I would,' I said, and picked up my handbag from the bed.

'She's made a mistake,' said Dan scowling. He was furious with Flo, and she instinctively wrung her hands and appealed to him with her eyes for forgiveness like a small girl. 'The price is thirty-five shillings,' he said.

'Of course it is,' said Flo apologetically. 'I was thinking of the rooms downstairs.'

'One pound fifteen,' I said.

'Thirty-five shillings,' corrected Flo. They waited again, their eyes fixed anxiously on my face.

'I'll get my things over,' I said. 'And I'll fetch my son.'

For the next few minutes I was the passive victim of their exclamations of delight and welcome. They showed me how to use the gas-stove. And Flo kept saying: 'Look, it's ever so easy, dear,' as she pulled the shoelace that had been suspended from the electric light, 'look, it just goes on and off as you pull it, see?'

Finally they went downstairs, smiling at each other.

I heard Flo say in an offended offhand voice to Dan: 'Oh, shut up, she's taken it, hasn't she?'

I got over my luggage and stacked it in the slant under the roof. By climbing on to a trunk in the middle of the room I could see over through the skylights into a brick channel between the outer wall and the roof which was filled with damp and blackened refuse – fragments of brick, bits of paper, scraps of rag. From this channel were propped some planks which shored up the roof. Flo, who had come up with the luggage, sat on the bed watching me anxiously, and anticipating any criticism I might have been tempted to make with defensive or encouraging remarks. 'We had the blitz, dear,' she kept saying. 'We had it ever so bad. It was right through this part, because of that station, see? The Government's going to mend everything for us, when they get around to it. I don't know what they're doing, we've filled in the forms and all, over and over again.'

I fetched my son, and at once he vanished into the basement with Aurora. Later, exhausted with the warmth and the welcome of the family downstairs, he fell asleep, saying he liked this house and he wanted to stay in it.

This upset me, because in the meantime I had decided it was impossible; in spite of my having suddenly understood that this was indubitably a garret, and that I had fulfilled the myth to its limit, and without any conscious intention on my part. There was no room in this garret to put a typewriter, let alone to unpack my things. I would have to start again.

Then I remembered Flo had said something about rooms downstairs. I went down to see Rose about it.

When she opened her door to me I at first did not recognize her; she looked like her own daughter. She had just taken a bath, and wore a white wool dressing-gown. Her black hair was combed loose, and her face was pale, soft and young, with dark smudges of happiness under the eyes. Her mouth, revealed, was small and sad. She said, with formality, 'Come in, dear. I'm sorry the room is untidy.' The room was very small and neat; it had a look of intense privacy, as a room does when every article means a great deal to the

54

person living in it. Rose had brought her bed and her small easy chair and her linen from her own home. The curtains and bedcover had pink and blue flowers; and there was a cherry-pink rug on the black-painted floor. That everything she touched or wore should be perfectly clean and tidy was important to her; she was one of the most instinctively fastidious people I have ever known. Now she pushed forward her little blue-covered armchair, waited until I had sat down, and said, smiling with pleasure: 'I'm glad you came. I like some company.'

'I came to ask about the room Flo mentioned – is there another one free in the house?'

At once she looked sorrowful and guilty; and by now I knew her well enough to understand why. Her loyalties were in conflict. She said: 'I don't rightly know. You'd better ask Flo.' She blushed and said hastily: 'Of course that place upstairs isn't fit for a pet cat, let alone a woman with a kid.' She added: 'But Flo and Dan'll be good to that kid of yours. They really like kids.' 'Yes, I know,' I said. 'That's the trouble.' 'I see your trouble,' she said. She hesitated. 'If there was a room going, and I'm not saying because I don't know – it's like this, see – Flo and Dan are new in this house business, they have fancy ideas about the rent they're going to get. And they never thought they'd let that dump upstairs at all – see, at least, not for so much. Of course, you're a foreigner, and don't know yet.'

'I see,' I said. 'I'll ask Flo, then.'

'Yes, that would be better for me. I'm a friend of hers, see?'

'Of course.'

'About that other place you saw – did you see it?'

'Yes.' I began to tell her, but she knew about the house. 'I know because I get to know all sorts of things, working in that shop. But was there anything about someone kicked out?'

'A Mr MacNamara,' I said. Her face changed with rich suddenness into a delighted appreciation.

'Mr MacNamara, is he? The son of a rich lord from Ireland?'

'I don't know about the lord.'

She sat on the bed, and regarded me patiently.

'There's a lot you don't,' she said. 'If he's Mr MacNamara to you, then watch out. You didn't give him money, did you?'

I admitted it. To my surprise, she was not scornful, but worried for me. 'Then watch out. He'll be after some more. Didn't you see what he was like?'

'Yes, I did. It's hard to explain . . .' I began, but she nodded and said: 'I know what you mean. Well, don't you feel too bad. He's got a real gift for it. You'd be surprised the people he diddles. He did my boss out of twenty quid once, and to this day she wonders what came over her. And now you take my advice and have nothing to do with him. Mr MacNamara. Well I remember when he was a barrow-boy, and he knows I remember it, selling snaps and snails and puppy-dogs' tails for what he could get. But even then he had his head on the right way, for the next thing was, he had his own car *and* it was paid for. That's the trouble with him – it's not what you call a spiv; at least, not all the time. One minute he's got his hand in the gas-meter and the next he's doing real business.'

'Well, thank you for telling me.'

She hesitated. Then she said in a rush: 'I like you, see. We can be friends. And not everyone's like Flo – I don't want you to be thinking that.' She added guiltily – 'It's because she's a foreigner, it's not her fault.'

'What kind of a foreigner?'

'I'm not saying anything against her; don't think it. She's English really. She was born here. But her grandmother was Italian, see? She comes from a restaurant family. So she behaves different. And then the trouble is, Dan, isn't a good influence – not that I'm saying a word against him.'

'Isn't he English?'

'Not really, he's from Newcastle. They're different from us, up in places like that. Oh no, he's not English, not properly speaking.'

'And you?'

She was confused at once. 'Me, dear? But I've lived in

56

London all my life. Oh, I see what you mean – I wouldn't say I was English so much as a Londoner, see? It's different.'

'I see,' I said.

'You going out?' she asked, offhand.

'I thought of wandering about and having a look.'

'I understand.'

I did not know she wanted to come with me. Coming to a new country, you don't think of people being lonely, but having full lives into which you intrude. But she was looking forlorn, and I said: 'Don't you go out in the evenings?'

'Not much. Well, not these days I don't. It gives me the 'ump, sitting around.'

'Flo said you were engaged to Dan's brother.'

She was very shocked. 'Engaged!' She blushed. 'Oh no, dear. You mustn't say things like that, you'll put ideas into my head.'

'I'm sorry. Flo said you might be marrying him.'

'Yes, that's so. I *might* be, you could say that.' She sighed. Then she giggled, and gave me a playful nudge with her elbow. 'Engaged! The things you say, you make me laugh.'

Flo's voice sounded up the stairs: 'There's a gentleman to see you. Rose, tell her there's a gentleman.'

'How does she know I'm with you?'

She said: 'It's easy to think Flo's stupid. Because she is. But not about knowing what goes on.'

'But I don't know anyone,' I said.

'Oh, go on. Don't you know who it is?'

'How should I?'

'It's Mr Bobby Brent, Mr MacNamara to you. Silly.'

'Oh!' I got up from the chair.

'You're not *going*,' she said, shocked. 'Tell Flo to send him off.'

'But I think I'm interested, after what you've said.'

'Interested?'

'I mean, I've never met anyone like him before.'

She was puzzled. Then, unmistakably hurt. I did not understand why. 'Yes?' was all she said. She turned back to her dressing-table and began brushing her hair out.

Rose's *yes* was the most expressive of monsyllables. It could be sceptical, give you the lie direct, accuse you, reject you. This time it meant: Interested, are you? Well, I can't afford to be *interested* in scoundrels. Fancy yourself, don't you?

Whenever, in the future, I was interested in a person or a situation which did not have her moral approval, she would repudiate me with precisely that – Yes?

But her good heart overcame her disapproval, for she said as I left the room: 'If you must you must. But don't let him get his hands on to your money.'

Flo was in the hall with Mr MacNamara. As I came down the stairs he was saying: 'It's a little matter. A hundred nicker. And it'd double itself in a year.' He had the full force of his hard brown stare on her. She was bashfully languishing, like a peasant girl. She tore her gaze away from his face, to say almost absently: 'I told your friend. I told him for you. You've got a flat with us.'

'Yes, I have,' I said. Flo was again looking up into his face. 'Dan'd know best,' she said. 'You must talk to Dan.'

'I'll talk it over with him. But I want you to talk it over with him first, Mrs Bolt. You've got a real head for business, I can see at a glance.'

'Well, dear, I ran a restaurant over in Holborn right through the war, dear. I ought to know my way about. A real big restaurant. I had three girls working for me. Dan was in the navy. But I did all right, I can tell you.'

'I'm sure you did, Mrs Bolt. Ah yes, the war was a difficult time.'

'We carried on and did our best.'

'Excuse me,' I said, and began to go upstairs. Instantly Mr MacNamara came after me.

'There's a little matter we should discuss,' he said.

'But she's fixed up, dear. Ever so nice, with us.'

'Four rooms, kitchen and bath *and* a telephone, three and a half a week.' I came downstairs again. 'And there's another matter.'

'Can we see it now?'

'I'll take you.'

I said to Flo: 'If I can get it, I will. I really do need more room, you know.'

She nodded, her eyes, now thoughtful, on Mr MacNamara.

We two went to the door, and I heard her shrieking as we went out: Rose. Dan. Rose. Dan . . .

'You know Miss Jennings?'

'No, I don't think so.'

'You'll meet her,' he said darkly. 'You mustn't believe all you hear.'

'Rose Jennings?'

'People are not to be trusted. Not since the war.'

Now he had me on the pavement, he was thinking out his tactics, while making a pretence at examining his watch. 'My man won't be in for fifteen minutes. I'll take you to a pub near here. The best pub in London. They have nothing but vintage beers.'

'That would be nice.'

He began walking me fast down the street, into an area that had been laid flat. About five acres of earth had been cleared of rubble, and was waiting for the builders. 'Nice job, that,' said Mr MacNamara, nodding at it. 'One bomb – did the lot. All that damage. Nice work.'

We walked past it. Mr MacNamara began sending me furtive glances, sideways.

'Know where you are?' he asked casually.

I had, because Rose had walked me past here, but I said, 'No, I've no idea.' His furtiveness cleared into triumph and he said: 'These bombed areas are confusing.' We had now walked three sides of the square, and he hesitated. 'It's not so far now,' he said, and turned to complete the fourth side, which would take us back to our starting point at the bottom of the street the house was in. I walked willingly beside him, feeling him watch me. He was anxious. We had now made the full square, and he said: 'Now do you know where you are?' For a moment I did not answer; and at once a baffled angry look filled his eyes. His body was tense with violence. Nothing was more important to him, just then, than that I should not have seen through his trick.

'It seems miles,' I said.

'That's because you don't know the ropes,' he said, relaxing, the violence all gone. 'Seen that building before?' – pointing to a house a couple of hundred yards away from Flo's and Dan's house.

'They all seem alike,' I said.

He nodded. 'Mind you, I've been thinking, it might not be possible for you to see that flat this evening. But I'll telephone to make sure.' He strode into a telephone box, and went through the motions of telephoning. He emerged with a brisk air. 'My client isn't in, after all.'

'That seems a pity.'

'I'll take you for the drink I promised, in any case.' He applied a tender pressure to my upper arm; but lost interest in the gesture almost at once; his face was already dark with another pressure.

'I'm taking you to this pub,' he said, 'because it's famous.'

We went into a glossy lounge bar, and he said casually to the barman: 'I'll have two of the usual.'

'What's your usual?' said the barman.

'I'm used to service,' he began, but the barman had turned away, as if accidentally, to serve someone else. Mr MacNamara took me to a free corner table, and said, 'This is the best firm in England. Their liquors are all vintage. You know what vintage is?'

'No, not really.'

Delighted, he said: 'I do. I mix with the best people. I'm going to marry the daughter of a member of parliament.'

'Good for you.'

'Yes. Her father is a lord.'

'Rose told me your father was a lord, too, from Ireland.'

His body tensed with anger. He narrowed his eyes, and clenched his teeth. Then he controlled himself. The violence in him so strong his whole body quivered as he damped it down. 'I told you, you shouldn't believe Rose Jennings. She can't tell truth from falsehood. Some people are like that.' He thought a moment and came out with: 'Actually, my real name's not MacNamara. It's Ponsonby. I use MacNamara for business. But I'm Irish all right. Yes, from the Emerald Isle.'

'I hope you've managed to get Mrs MacNamara somewhere to sleep tonight.'

'Well of course she'd not really Mrs MacNamara. To tell you the truth, I don't quite know what to do with her. She was going to marry a client of mine. He rang me up this morning – he's off to Hong-Kong, on business. He left her in my charge.'

'Poor girl.'

'I've fixed her up for the night in a hotel in Bayswater.'

'Good.'

'But perhaps Mrs Bolt can fix her up tomorrow. She said she had a room.'

'Oh, she did, did she?'

'Of course it's not what Miss Powell is used to. But then these days we take what we can get. Like you, for instance. You could afford much better if you were offered it.'

The barman now came over and said: 'What'll you have.'

'Two light ales,' said Mr Ponsonby.

When the barman brought the ales, Mr Ponsonby said: 'I say. You're not going to serve me that? I'm used to the best.'

The barman studied him a moment, his good-humoured eyebrows raised. Then he picked up the glasses, set them on the counter, interposed his back between him and Mr Ponsonby, and after whistling a soft tune between his teeth, lifted them round and set them down again.

'That's better,' said Mr Ponsonby. He handed the barman silver, and gave him a shilling tip.

'Some mothers do 'ave 'em,' remarked the barman to the air, still whistling, as he returned behind the bar.

Mr Ponsonby was saying to me: 'I could put you on to a good thing. A hundred nicker. That's all.'

'I haven't got it,' I said.

He examined me for some time, in silence. It was extraordinary how frankly he did this, as if the necessity to do so made him invisible to me; as if he scrutinized me from behind a barricade.

'Mr MacNamara,' I said. 'You're making a mistake about me. I really don't have any money.'

This remark seemed to reassure him. 'Ponsonby,' he said. 'Well, I'll show you you can trust me.' He reached his hands into his pockets. From one he brought out military medals, about a dozen of them. From another a packet of papers. Matching one to another on the table he showed me citation after citation for bravery, etc., to Alfred Ponsonby. Among them was the DSO.

'I was in the Commandos,' he said.

'I'm not surprised.'

'Yes, they were the best days of my life.' He replaced the medals in one pocket and the papers in the other and said: 'I keep fit, just in case. Ju-jitsu. There's nothing like it.'

'I think it's time I got back.'

He examined me again. Then he leaned himself forward to me, the surface of his brown eyes glazed with solicitude. 'I would really like to see you fixed up. I can see you are a little disappointed with me. Oh, don't deny it. I could see, when I telephoned and my client wasn't in. But I've a special interest in you.' His gaze went blank while he searched for words. Then he smiled intimately into my eyes with a brown treacly pressure. 'Now I want to put something to you. I can get that flat for you tonight – just like that!' He snapped his fingers. 'But I must put something down for the landlord. It would cost five pounds and it would be worth it.'

'I must get back,' I said and got up.

Without a change of tone, he said: 'I'll take you over tomorrow night.' Consulted his watch. 'Eight o'clock.' And again, narrowing his eyes. 'No, an appointment at eight. Eight-fifteen. I'll make an appointment.'

'Good.'

To get from the pub back to the house was five minutes walking. He faced towards the house. His face was twisted with conflict. 'Know where we are?'

'No.'

Smiling with cruelty, he walked me right around the bombed space, watching my face all the time. Anxiety crept into him. At the bottom of the street he hesitated and said: 'Do you know what I've just done?'

'Not an idea.'

Half from pleasure at having tricked me, and half from anxiety I might find out, he said: 'I've taken you a long way round. You never noticed it. Got to keep your eyes open in this city. But you're all right with me. You can trust me.'

'I know I can,' I said. We were at the front door.

'I'll see you tomorrow,' he said, tenderly.

I went inside and up the stairs. Rose appeared and said, 'Are you all right, dear?'

'I hope so.'

'I hope so, too. I got ever so worried about you.' She took my arm between her hands and gently tugged me into her room. 'Listen,' she said. 'I feel real bad, what I'm doing, but you're my friend now. I must tell you. Flo's got all in a state about losing you – ' She giggled, and adjusted her face. 'Sorry, but it does make me laugh, when Flo sees the pennies slipping through her fingers. Well, because you went out with Bobby Brent, she thinks she'll let you the room. But Bobby Brent wants it for his fancy woman. So now she's all torn up, wondering who'll pay the most.'

'He will, I should think,' I said.

'You don't know our Bobby.'

'Is it true he was in the Commandos?'

'Oh, yes. A real war hero and all. But listen! I'll show you the room and you can see if you like it.' She cautiously opened the door and listened. 'No, Flo's too busy quarrelling with Dan to snoop.'

'Well, I'm sorry.'

'Don't be daft. They're in love. They've only been married three years, see? When people are in love they quarrel. Dan got real mad about Bobby. She makes him jealous on purpose, see? Then he gets mad and they quarrel and they make it up in bed. See?'

I laughed. She giggled. 'Shh,' she said. We crept into the passage outside her room, and we listened again. Downstairs a din of shouting voices and music. Rose opened a door, and switched a light on. It was a very large room, with two long windows. There was a tiny fireplace at one end. The walls were cracked and the ceiling was stained.

'Don't notice the mess,' Rose whispered. 'It's the war. The war damage people is coming in. They'll fix it. But it's a nice room, and Dan'll paint it for you. He's in the trade, and he's good at those things, whatever else you can say about him. And if you're clever with Flo, you'll get it cheap because of the cracks and all. If you don't mind me telling you, you don't treat Flo right at all. I watched you. You've got to stand up to her. If you don't, she'll treat you bad.'

'Tell me what to do?' I asked.

At this direct appeal, she hesitated. 'I do feel bad,' she said apologetically. 'I'm Flo's friend. But I'll just give you advice in general. She'll come and see you tomorrow. Don't just say yes, and thank you. You must bargain with her. I know it's not nice, how she is, but I put it down to her Italian blood. She likes to bargain.'

'All right,' I said. 'I will. And thank you.'

We crept back to her door, and she said: 'Tomorrow night, when your kid's asleep, we'll go for a walk. It'll be real nice to have company.'

'Good,' I said. 'I'd like it.'

'And I'll show you some ropes around here. You don't mind me saying it, dear, but you don't know how to look after yourself. You don't really.'

'I know.'

'Well, never mind, Rome wasn't built in a day, that's what I always say. Sleep tight.'

When I got back to my room from taking my son to nursery school next morning, Flo was standing there, with a guilty look. 'I've just put away some things for you,' she said. 'To show you how comfortable it is. It is really.'

I said involuntarily. 'It's very kind of you, Flo,' and, as involuntarily she gave a little smile of victory, and said in a cheerful voice: 'I told you you'd like it up here.'

I summoned the spirit of Rose to my aid, and said: 'But I don't want to unpack. Because if I get somewhere with more room, I'll move.'

All the life went out of her, and she sat despondently on my bed. She sighed. She looked at a pack of cigarettes lying on the bed and said: 'You've got so many lovely cigarettes, darling, aren't you lucky.' The sense of guilt which accompanied all colonials to England, in 1949, overcame me and I said: 'Help yourself.' Instantly she became happy again. She picked up the box and handled it, looking at me. Then she carelessly took out a handful, but dropping some in her anxiety lest I might be angry, and pushed them into her apron pockets. She understood that guilt very well by instinct, because later, when I learned to understand the role cigarettes played in that house she would say automatically: 'We had such a hard time during the war, dear, you wouldn't believe it.'

'I've put your things where you can find them,' she said. I looked at the top drawer, unable to discover any logic in her arrangement of it, until she said: 'You've got some lovely things, dear.' She had put the more expensive things on top, in a layer over the cheap ones. In the second drawer she had laid out six pairs of nylons, side by side, as if in a showcase. I began rolling them up and stacking them in a corner. She said quickly, over and over again, 'Sweetheart, darling, I'm sorry I didn't do them nice for you.' She was sitting on my bed, full of innocent concern; while one hand kept touching her apron pocket, to reassure her of the existence of the cigarettes. She looked like a child who has done its best to please and now expects a reprimand. 'I was only trying to help you, darling.' I said nothing, and she said: 'Please, please, darling, give your Flo some nylons.' With an enormous effort, invoking Rose again, I said: 'Now why should I give you my nylons?' Her face puckered with discouragement. Then she laughed with frank good-humour, and having lost that round of the game, she said, 'I'll go down and get my old man's dinner.' At the door she remarked innocently: 'I'm glad you're so happy up here.'

'Flo, I told you, I must move when I find something better.'

In a wail of despair, she cried out: 'But you wouldn't like the other rooms we've got . . .' She clapped her hand over her mouth; she had been instructed by Dan not to mention them. She waddled fast downstairs, with one hand nesting the cigarettes in her pocket.

That night Rose congratulated me. 'You're learning,' she

said. 'And perhaps you'll be lucky. Because Bobby Brent hasn't been back. They're arguing about it, Dan and Flo, now. About the rent.'

'How much should I pay?'

'Don't ask me,' she pleaded. 'It makes me feel bad – I've just been having supper with them, see? But when she says, bargain. Now, you're coming out with me.'

She put her two hands around my arm, and walked me away down past the bombed site I had been made to go round last night by Mr MacNamara-Ponsonby-Brent. I told Rose of the incident, and she listened, without surprise. 'He's like that,' she commented. 'He was always like that. That's why he frightens me, see? So don't you have nothing to do with him.'

'He said he was going to take me to see a flat tonight.'

She let her hands drop away from my arm. 'You didn't say you'd go?'

'Yes, I did.'

She was silent. 'Why?' she asked at last timidly. 'You don't believe what he says. I know that.'

'Well, it's because I've never met anyone like him before.' When she didn't reply, I said: 'Why don't you like that?'

She thought. Then she said: 'You talk like he's an animal in a zoo.'

'If you went to a new country, you'd like to meet new kinds of people, too.' She didn't reply. I persisted: 'Well, wouldn't you?'

'What makes you think I'm going to any new countries?' she said, with resentment. We walked on for a while in silence. Then she forgave me. She put her hands around my arm again, squeezed it, and said: 'Well, never mind, it takes all sorts. I've been thinking. The reason I like you, well – apart from being friends now, it's because you say things that make me think.'

We were in streets that differed from those behind me in a way I could not name. They were dingy and grey and dirty. There were gangs of noisy sharp-faced children. Youths lounged against corner-walls with their hands in their pockets. Here was the face, which comes as a shock to a colonial, used to broad, filled-in, sunburned faces. It is a face that is not pale so much as drained, peaked rather than thin, with an unfinished look, a jut in the bones of the jaw or the forehead. People were smaller. Rose was absorbed among her own kind and I saw her differently. I was thinking that there were miles and miles of such streets, marked only by a difference in shop-names or by the degree to which brick and stones had been stained and weathered – square miles full of deprived people. I felt alien to Rose, and as if it were dishonest to be here at all. I understood that I was dishonest because I had brought the colonial attitude to class with me. That it does not exist. I had not thought of Rose as working-class but as foreign to me. She must have been thinking me intolerably affected. Later on she said something that cleared my mind. 'When you first came to live with us,' she said, 'you just made me sick. It wasn't that you fancied yourself, it wasn't that, but you were just plain ignorant about everything. You didn't know nothing about anything, and you didn't even know you were ignorant. You made me laugh, you did really.'

Rose stopped, pulled out a purse from her bag and peered into it. We were alongside a fruit-counter that projected into the street. The man serving nodded and said: 'What are you a-doing of down here, Rosie?'

'Just off for a walk. With my friend.' She nodded at some cherries and handed over exactly the marked price for half a pound. She kept her eye on the money in the man's hand, and smiled and nodded when threepence was handed back. 'Thanks,' she said. 'And this is my friend, see? She'll be coming down here I expect, so you treat her right.'

They smiled and nodded, then she took my arm and pulled me after her. 'You go there for fruit, see? Now he knows you're my friend it'll be different. And don't you go buying stuff on those barrows. That's only for them who don't know better. I mean you have to know which barrows are honest.'

She began spitting stones into the gutter. 'See that?' she said, giggling happily. 'I used to be a winner at school every time.' Now I was under her protection. She kept herself

67

between me and the crowd, and at every moment she nodded and smiled at some man or woman leaning against a counter or a stall.

'I was a kid down here,' she said; and I saw that this part of the great city was home, to her; a different country from the street, not fifteen minutes' walk away, where she now lived. Slowly the word *slum*, which had for me a literary and fanciful quality, a dramatic squalor, changed; and at last I saw the difference between this city and the streets that held my new lodgings. Those had a decaying, down-at-heel respectability. This was hard and battling, raw and tough; showing itself in the scepticism of the watchful assessing glances from the shopmen and women, and the humour of the greetings that Rose took and gave. She was happily nostalgic. Passing these familiar places, which knew her, acknowledging her by a gleam from a lit window or the slant of a wall, like so many friendy glances or waves of the hand, reinstated her as a human being with rights of possession in the world. 'I used to get all my shoes here,' she said, passing a shop. Or: 'Before the war they sold a bit of fried skate in this shop better than anything.'

We turned into a narrow side street of short, low, damp, houses, a uniform dull yellow in colour, each with a single grey step. It was almost empty, though here and there in the failing light a woman leaned against a doorway. Rose said suddenly: 'Let's have a sit-down,' and indicated a low wall that enclosed a brownish space of soil where a bomb had burst. There was a tree, paralysed down one side, and a board leaning in a heap of rubble that said: 'Tea and Bun – One Penny.'

Rose settled herself on the wall and spat pips at a lamp-post.

'Who sold the tea?' I asked.

'Oh, that? He got hit. That was before the war.' She spoke as if it was a different century. 'You don't get tea and a bun for a penny now.' She looked lovingly around her. 'I was born here. In that house down there. That one with the brown door. Many's the time I've sat here with my little brother when he was driving my mother silly. Or sometimes my stepfather got into one of his moods and I'd clear out and come here for a rest, in a way of speaking. He used to make me mad, he did.' She lapsed into a silence of nostalgic content. A man slowly cycled down the street, stopping at each lamp-post. Above him, while he paused, a small yellow glimmer pushed back the thick grey air. Soon the houses retired into shadow. Pools of dim light showed wet pavements. Rose was quiet beside me, a huddled little figure in her tight black coat and head-scarf.

It was long after the sky had gone thick and black behind the glimmering lamps that Rose came out of her dream of childhood. She stretched and said: 'We'd better be moving.' But she didn't move without reluctance. 'At any rate, the blitz didn't get it. That's something to be glad about. And the bombs fell around here. God knows what they thought they were trying to bomb!' She spoke indifferently, without hate. 'I expect the planes got lost one night and thought this would do as well as anything. The Americans do that, too, they say – they just get fed up flying around in the dark, so they drop their bombs and nip home for a cup of tea.'

As we walked back, she said: 'I'll have to get a hurry on. I've got to help Flo with the washing-up or she'll get the pip.'

'Do you have to help her?'

'No. Not really. But I've got into the habit of it. She's like that – I don't want to say anything I shouldn't. But you just watch yourself and don't let yourself get into the habit of doing things. I'm telling you for your own good.'

At the bombed site her gait and manner changed. She withdrew into herself and became suspicious, looking into people's faces as they passed as if they might turn out to be enemies. I couldn't imagine this Rose, all prim and tight-faced, spitting pips with a laugh. In our street of great decaying houses she clutched at my arm for a moment and said, 'This place gives me the 'ump sometimes. It's not friendly, not like what I'm used to. That's why.'

Bobby Brent was coming out of the side door from the basement, a natty brown hat pulled down over his eyes. When he saw us, he frowned; then smiled. 'You thought I'd forgotten our appointment,' he said. 'Well, you don't know me.' Then it struck him: he examined his watch and exclaimed. 'I say! It's half-past nine. We agreed eight-fifteen.'

'Oh, come off it, Bobby,' said Rose giggling. 'You do make me laugh.'

He gritted his teeth; forced his lips back in a smile. 'I'll take you over now,' he said to me. 'Of course, the one I tried to get for you's gone; nobody to blame but yourself. But there's another. Just right for you.'

Rose was leaning against the gate-pillar, watching him satirically. 'Wait a moment,' she said to him, and pulled me inside the front door.

She took my handbag from me, opened it, and removed all the money from it. 'I'll keep this till you come back,' she said. 'I've left you two shillings, that'll be enough. Now, if you want this room next to me, it's a good thing you go off with Bobby. It'll make Flo nervous. And they're doing ever such a deal, the three of them.'

'What sort of deal? Why don't you stop Flo?'

'Oh no, it's like this. If Bobby wants, for argument's sake, five pounds, then don't let him have it. But if it's a hundred and it looks all right, that's different, see? Bobby's got an idea for a club, a night-club or something. Dan is going to lend him a hundred. And they're talking how to get money out of you.'

'But I haven't any.'

'Yes, I know,' she said, giggling. 'Don't mind me, but I did sort of keep my face straight, as if I thought you had money, because it makes me laugh, Flo and Dan, when they get the itch. There are two sorts of people in the world,' she concluded, 'the kind that get money, like Flo and Dan and Bobby. That's because they think about it all the time. And people like us. Well, it takes all sorts. See you tomorrow. I'll put your money under your pillow.'

Bobby Brent said as I joined him: 'There's just one kind of person that I can't stand. The envious ones. Like Rose Jennings. She's eaten up with it.'

'Where's the flat?'

'Around the corner.'

70

We walked half a mile in silence. 'How's Miss Powell?' I asked. 'I don't mind telling you, she's a real problem to me. She's got it into her head she wants to marry me.' 'Bad luck,' I said. 'The trouble with women is, they're monogamous.' 'I know. It's all very badly arranged.' 'What do you mean – my arrangements aren't crystallized.' 'Never mind, you'll feel different when you're married to the daughter of the lord.' 'I'm not so sure. Women never understand. They tie a man down. They expect him to live the same life, day after day. Well, I was in the Commandos three years, and now I expect to call my life my own.' 'Cheer up. It looks as if there might very well be a war soon.' 'You can't count on it,' he said.

We were now in a hushed and darkened square, and outside a large house. The name on the doorbell we pushed was Colonel Bartowers. The door opened to show a martial old man, with protruding stomach, red face, and an aggressive blue stare.

'We're here on business. My name's Ponsonby – Alfred Ponsonby.' He thrust a card into the Colonel's hand. The Colonel stood his ground, looking at him up and down, raising his white eyebrows in a terrifying way. 'We understand you have premises to let.'

The Colonel fell back, astonished, and we were in the hall. The Colonel looked at me, and said blankly: 'Well, come inside, now you're here. How on earth – I haven't even sent it to an agent – ' He pulled himself together. 'Well, I don't know, these days you can't even think of moving without getting in hordes of ... however, I'm very glad. Come in.'

He showed us into a living-room. It was charming. This was the England I had read about in novels.

'As a matter of interest,' said the Colonel to me, 'how did you hear about this flat?'

Mr Ponsonby strode forward and announced: 'My cousin from Africa asked me to find her a flat.' I tried to catch the Colonel's eye, but Mr Ponsonby was in the way. 'I'm in the business, as my card shows. There would be no fee to either lessor or lessee.'

'A question of philanthropy,' said the Colonel gravely;

and Mr Ponsonby fell back, spelling out the word to himself. 'Blood is blood,' he offered at last.

'Oh, quite,' said Colonel Bartowers. He sighed and said: 'Well, I suppose I might as well show you the flat, in case I decide to go abroad. You mentioned Africa?' he said to me.

'My cousin has just come,' said Mr Ponsonby, trying to get between the Colonel and me, but he was brushed aside, and the Colonel took my arm.

'I was myself in Southern Rhodesia for ten years. A little before your time, I expect. I left in 1905. Do you remember . . .' And he began reciting names which are part of the history of the Empire. 'This is the kitchen,' he said, waving his hand at it. It was equipped like an American kitchen. 'All the things one needs in a kitchen, I believe. So my wife said. She ran off with someone else last year. No loss. Not really. But I don't use the kitchen. I eat out. Now, tell me, did you ever meet Jameson? I suppose not.'

In the bedroom he absently opened one cupboard after another, all filled with lush blankets and tinted linen of all kinds, shutting the doors before I could properly savour them. 'All the usual things for bedrooms – hot bottles, electric bottles and so on. Never use the things myself. Now, tell me, did you ever go shooting down Gwelo way?' He told a story of how he had shot a lion in the chicken-run, in the good old days. 'But perhaps things have changed,' he remarked at last.

'I think they have, rather.'

'Yes, so I hear.' He threw open another door. 'The bathroom,' he announced, before shutting it. I caught a glimpse of a very large room with a black and white tiled floor, and a pale pink bath. 'A bit cramped,' he said, 'but in these days.'

'Well, I think that's all,' he said at last. 'Shall we have a drink on it?' He produced a bottle of Armagnac; then he looked at Mr Ponsonby, for the first time in minutes, and frowned. 'There's a pub round the corner,' he said putting back the bottle. In the pub he ordered two drinks for me and for him, added a third as a calculated afterthought, and turned his back on Mr Ponsonby. 'Now,' he said, his fat red face relaxing. 'We can talk.' For the space of several drinks I said yes and no; and in the intervals of his monologue, the Colonel ordered, with brusque dislike, another for Mr Ponsonby, who was reacting to this situation in a way which disconcerted me. I expected him to be angry; but his eyes were focused on some plan. He watched the Colonel's face for some time while he pretended to be listening to his talk. Then he turned away and got into conversation with a man sitting next to him. I heard phrases like 'a good investment' and 'thirty per cent' spoken in a discreet, almost winning voice.

'That Bulawayo campaign. The best days of my life. I remember lying on the kopje behind my house and taking pot-shots at the nigs as they came to the river for water. I was a damned good shot, though I say it myself. Of course, I still shoot a bit, grouse chiefly, but it's not the same. It was a good life, say what you like.' He shot a pugnacious blue glance at me and demanded: 'From what I hear they'll be taking pot-shots at us soon, getting their own back, hey? This idea seemed to cause him a detached and almost kindly amusement, for he guffawed and said: 'I used to get good fun with those nigs. Damn good fellows some of them. Sportsmen. Good fighters. Ah, well.' He sighed and put down his glass. 'Two more of the same.'

'Closing time, sir.'

'Blast. This damned country. Can't stand it. It's a nation of old women these days. It's the Labour Government. Petticoat government, that's what I call it. That's why I'm thinking of getting out again. To Kenya, I thought. I've got a cousin. I'd go back to Rhodesia, but my wife, blast her, is there with her new husband. Not big enough for both of us. The trouble is, though, once you've lived out of England, you can't really settle in it. Too small. I expect you'll find that, too. I remember I came back on leave after that Bulawayo campaign and asking myself, How the hell did I stick England all those years. I still ask myself.'

I heard Mr Ponsonby say: 'A nice little sideline for a man with a few hundred to spare.'

The Colonel, peevishly fiddling with his empty glass, listened.

'Needs doing up. But it's in good repair. All it really needs is some paint and a bar.'

'Your cousin . . .'

'He's not my cousin.'

'Of course not. Ah, well, these people have their uses, I suppose! He appears to have irons in the fire.'

'Dozens. He's a man of enterprise.'

'That's what this country lacks, these days.'

'He was in the Commandos, too.'

But the Colonel's face expressed nothing but distaste. 'Was he? I like clean fighting myself. Still, I suppose those fellows were necessary.'

'My principal needs a quick decision,' said Mr Ponsonby. 'You can give me a ring in the morning.' He got off his stool and turned to us, not immediately recognizing us, so great was his preoccupation. 'Well,' he asked. 'Everything fixed?' He spoke as if this little matter could only be kept in the forefront of his attention by the greatest concentration.

'About the rent,' I asked.

'Well, my dear,' said the Colonel, 'I know one can get anything one asks these days, but I don't like to take advantage. For you I'd make it ten guineas.'

'You could easily get fifteen or twenty,' I said.

'Yes, I know. Those Yanks'd pay that. But I don't like 'em.'

'But I haven't got the money to pay that, anyway.'

'Well, it doesn't matter, because I don't really want to let it. It's an idea that came into my head last week. But I suppose I'll have to end my days here. In the old country. The trouble is, it isn't the old country any longer. I used to be proud to call myself English. I'm damned if I am these days.'

Mr Ponsonby was examining his watch.

'This proposition you were discussing with that fellow,' said the Colonel.

'A night-club. Perhaps you might be interested?'

'A night-club?' said the Colonel, livening up. 'Well, I might be interested to have some details.'

Mr Ponsonby had by now replaced me beside the Colonel. His manner with him was quite different than with me. He looked, perhaps, like a sergeant-major in mufti, rather bluff and responsible. 'My principal,' he said, 'is very concerned about the hands it might get into. Needs decent people, you know.'

'Ah,' said the Colonel, a trifle suspiciously.

'Shall I ring you in the morning, sir?'

'Yes, you could do that.'

We parted, the Colonel wishing me well, but without much confidence, because, as he said, I should have come to England before the First World War, it had never been the same since.

Walking home, I was offered a share in the night-club. He also said that if I had four hundred he would double it for me in a month. There was a house for sale for one thousand five hundred; and he knew a man he could sell it to for two thousand three hundred. 'And what would you get out of it?' I asked.

'Your confidence in me,' he said. 'Of course, I'd charge a small commission. There's nothing in it. I can't understand it, people slaving away, when it's so easy to make money. All you have to do, is use your intelligence.'

'All I want at the moment is a flat.'

'You'll never find another flat like the Colonel's, at that price.'

'But he didn't want to let it.'

'That's not my fault.' We were now at the house, and he said: 'I'll tell you what. I'll drop around tomorrow and take you to another little place I know about.'

'Goodnight,' I said.

'I like a person like you, who thinks twice about risking their money. I'll be in touch,' he said.

Chapter Three

Next day I began to look for a job, and the attitude of the household changed. Rose said: 'Now you're going to be a working girl like me. I'm glad.' But Flo was disappointed in me, even offended. 'You should have told us, shouldn't you,' she said. 'Told you what?' 'Now you're nice and comfortable up in that little flat that's so nice.' 'Flo, I'm looking for a real flat, I told you.' 'Ah, my God!' I heard her complain, as she descended the stairs. 'Ah, my Lord, she'll be the death of me yet, they all will.'

'You just stick it out,' said Rose 'And I've told Flo, I'm not having that dirty Miss Powell in the room next to me. Either her or me, I said to Flo.'

Next day negotiations began. Flo took me into the big room and said I wouldn't like it, not really, not with all those cracks in the walls. I said I would like it. There was a small room on the landing below, with a concealed cooker in it. My son could sleep in that. The two rooms would suit me very well.

'And what,' asked Flo, 'were you thinking of paying?'

'But it's the landlord's business to fix the rent,' I said.

'Oh dear,' said Flo. 'Oh dear, oh dear! Drat it. Oh, my Lord, and Dan's at work, too, and I'm on my own.'

'Well, you could discuss it with him.'

'Poor Miss Powell, she needs a big room for herself.'

'If a single woman wants a big room, then a woman with a child surely does?'

'But you wouldn't call her single,' said Flo. She began to laugh. 'Oh, that Bobby, he's a case. And those great big eyes of his. When he looks at me, I go all funny where Dan would kill me if he knew.'

'Well, I'm quite sure his beautiful eyes make it easy for him to get a room for Miss Powell.'

'Ah, that poor Miss Powell. The landlord where she is is being ever so nasty. I'm not nasty, am I, dear? And look how nice my Oar and your Peter play.'

'Yes, I know. He loves being here.'

And you do, too, I can tell. Ah, my Lord, what shall I do, I shall have to talk to Dan.'

'That would be a good idea.'

For a week I stayed at the top of the house, hoping for the room next to Rose, waiting for my job to start. Under the roof I was cut off from the rest of the house. The two rooms under me were empty. They were still full of rubble and mess from the bombing. The plan now was that Dan should clean them out and distemper them, and then either I or Miss Powell would take them. I said I didn't like them. Flo said that was because I couldn't imagine them cleaned up and painted. Dan was going to start work, in his evenings. Then I would see. I said, either the big room or nothing. It was a war of nerves.

Under the roof it was like sitting on top of an anthill, a tall sharp peak of baked earth, that seems abandoned, but which sounds, when one puts one's ear to it, with a continuous vibrant humming. Even when the door shut, it was not long before the silence grew into an orchestra of sound. Beneath my floor a tap dripped softly all day, in a blithe duet with the dripping of the tap on the landing. Two floors down, where the Skeffingtons lived, was a radio. Sometimes she forgot it when she went to work, and, as the hours passed, the wavelength slipped, so that melodies and voices flowed upwards, blurring and mingling. This sound had for accompaniment the splashing water, like conversation heard through music and dripping rain. In the darkening afternoons I was taken back to a time when I lay alone at night and listened to people talking through several walls, while the rain streamed from the eves. Sometimes it was as if the walls had dissolved, and I was left sitting under a tree, listening to birds talking from branch to branch while the last fat drops of a shower spattered on the leaves, and a ploughman yelled encouragement to his beasts in the field over the hill. Sometimes I put my ear to the wall and heard how, as the trains went past and the buses rocked their weight along the street, shock after shock came up through brick and plaster, so that the solid wall had the fluidity of dancing atoms, and I felt the house, the street, the pavement, and all the miles and miles of houses and streets as a pattern of magical balances, a weightless structure, as if this city hung on water, or on sound. Being alone in that little box of ceiling board and laths frightened me.

At last Flo came up and said that the two rooms beneath me were ready, and I could move down when I liked. I examined them and said no. They were very small. She said: 'You can have the big room for five pounds a week.' She sounded offhand, because of her fright at my probable reaction.

'Don't be silly,' I said.

She laughed and said, 'Then you say.'

Two pounds,' I said.

'Ah, my Lord, are you laughing at me?'

'You say,' I said.

'Four pounds fifteen.'

'Two pounds ten.'

'Darling, sweetheart, you're laughing at your poor Flo.'

'You say, then.'

At last we settled for three-ten, a sum which caused Rose to be angry with me. 'You could have got it for three-five,' she said. 'You make me cross, you really do.'

'Well, I shall be next to you, and Peter will be very happy that we're staying.'

'All the same, why throw five bob a week into the dust-can? Well, you make Flo clean your room for you, then.'

'Is it likely?'

'Well, I'm not going to, and someone must – where was you dragged up, I'd like to know, you don't even know how to clean a floor?'

'We were spoiled. We had servants.'

'You had something. Because to watch you sweeping is enough to make a cat laugh.'

Flo and Dan and Rose and I stood in the empty big room that evening. 'It's such a lovely room,' said Flo. 'And you can hardly notice them cracks.'

'What we're here for, is furniture,' said Rose.

'You can have that lovely bed from upstairs.'

'She'll want somewhere for her clothes,' said Rose.

'You can have that lovely cupboard from the landing.'

Rose said: 'You make me sick.'

'But we want to furnish her nice, dear.'

'You do, do you? Then I'll show you how.' With which Rose ran all over the house, marking out pieces to be put in my room. Dan did her bidding, silently; while Flo stood, unconsciously wringing her hands as one bit of furniture after another came to rest in my room, and the little room downstairs. Rose told me afterwards that she had said in the basement that if they didn't treat me right, she'd be so ashamed she'd leave. Since Rose did half of Flo's work for her, this was effective. When the rooms were ready, Rose said: 'That's a bit more like.' Dan gave her a grudging look of admiration. By this time we were all in good humour. Flo saw Dan looking, and said sharply, but laughing: 'And you keep your eyes off poor Rose. I know what you're thinking. Can't look at a woman without thinking of it!' Dan gave her his bared-teeth grin. Rose said: 'Oh, shut up. And now I'll help you get the supper, Flo.'

'I should think so,' said Flo. 'Dear me, oh, dear me, life is so hard these days.'

Rose gave me a wink as she went out, and whispered, 'Now you settle yourself, and don't you let Flo take any of this stuff back tomorrow. I'm telling you for your own good. I'll be in after supper for a nice chat.'

Now I was in the heart of the house. Immediately above me, in two large rooms, were the Skeffingtons. I had not yet seen them. He was away most of the time. She left for work before I did, and once she was in her rooms, seldom came out. I knew about them from Flo, through a succession of nods, winks, and hoarse whispers. Her: 'She's ever such a sweet woman' – made, as these remarks always were, as if a sweet tenant were something I was getting extra, thrown in, for the rent, was sometimes: 'Poor thing, she's brave, and she pays her rent so regular.' And sometimes: 'What she has to put up with, no one would believe. Men are all the same, beasts, every one.' On the other hand, she often observed with lip-licking smile that Mr Skeffington was just like a film star, and Mrs Skeffington didn't appreciate him. These two states of mind were determined by whether we got a good night's sleep or not. Usually not. There were few nights I was not woken by the persistent frightened crying of a child in nightmare. The words 'I'm not naughty, I'm not naughty', were wailed over and over again. I heard the sharp release of bedsprings, bare feet sliding on the floor, then several loud slaps. 'You're naughty. You're a naughty girl.' The voice was high and hysterical. This duet might keep up for an hour or more. At last the child would fall asleep; soon afterwards an alarm clock vibrated; and I would hear Mrs Skeffington's voice: 'Oh, my God, my God,' and the tired release of a weighted bed. The kettle shrieked, cups clattered, and her voice: 'Crying half the night and now I can't wake you. Oh, goodness, gracious me, what shall I do with you, Rosemary?'

I knew all the tones of her voice before I ever saw her; but I found it impossible to form a picture of her. As soon as she had the child inside the door, the tussle began: the high, exasperated weary voice, and the child nagging back. Or sometimes there was exhausted sobbing – first the woman, and then the child. I would hear: 'Oh, darling, I'm sorry. I'm sorry, Rosemary. I can't help it.'

Once I heard her on the stairs, coming home from work in conversation with Flo. Her voice was now formal and bright: 'Really I don't know what I shall do with Rosemary, she's so naughty.' She gave a fond, light laugh.

From the child, sullenly: 'I'm not naughty.'

'Yes, you are naughty, Rosemary. How dare you answer me back.' Although the voice was still social, sharpness had come into it.

From Flo, a histrionically resigned: 'Yes, I know, dear. Mine's the death of me, she drives me mad all day.'

From Aurora: 'I don't drive you mad.'

'Yes, you do. Don't answer your mother like that.' There was the sound of a sharp slap.

Flo's exchange with Aurora was an echo of Mrs Skeffington's with her child, because Flo could not help copying the behaviour of whoever she was with. But the burst of wild sobs from Aurora was quite unconvincing; her tears were displays of drama adapted to the occasion. From one second to the next she would stop crying and her face beamed with smiles. Her crying was never the miserable frightened wailing of the other little girl.

One morning I met a woman on the landing who I thought must be new to the house. She said brightly: 'Gracious me, I'm in your way, I'm so sorry,' and skipped sideways. It was Mrs Skeffington – that 'gracious me' could be no one else. Under her arm she balanced a tiny child. She was a tall slight creature, with carefully fluffed out fair hair arranged in girlish wisps on her forehead and neck. Her large clear brown eyes were anxiously friendly; and her smile was tired. There were dark shadows around her eyes and at the corners of her nose. The baby who sounded so forlorn and defiant at night was about fifteen months old. She was a fragile child, with her mother's wispy pretty hair and enormous brown eyes.

'Get out of the lady's way,' said Mrs Skeffington to the baby, which she had set down – apparently for the purpose of being able to scold her. 'Get out of the lady's way, you naughty, naughty girl.'

'But she's not in my way.'

'I do so hope Rosemary doesn't keep you awake at nights,' she said politely, just as if I did not hear every movement of her life, and she of mine.

'Not at all,' I said.

'I'm so glad, she's a real pickle,' said Mrs Skeffington, injecting the teasing fondness into her voice that went with the words. She tripped upstairs, and as her door shut her voice rose into hysteria: 'Don't dawdle so, Rosemary, how many times must I tell you.'

'I'm not doddling,' said the baby, whose vocabulary was sharpened by need into terrifying precocity.

Mr Skeffington was an engineer and he went on business trips for his firm. He was nearly always away during the week. According to Rose: 'He's just as bad as she is, and that's saying something. Their tempers fit each other, hand and glove. You wait till he comes back and you'll hear something. He reminds me of my stepfather – pots and kettles flying and both of them screaming and the kid yelling its head off. It's good as the pictures, if you don't want to get some sleep.'

Rose's stepfather haunted her conversations. She would sit moodily on my bed, listening to Mrs Skeffington nagging at the child overhead, saying from time to time: 'You wait till he comes, you haven't heard nothing yet.' And, inevitably, the next phrase would be – My stepfather.

'Wasn't he good to you?'

'Good?' A word as direct as that always made her uncomfortable. 'I wouldn't like to say anything against him, see.' Then, after a moment: 'He was a bad-tempered, lying, cheating swine of a bully – God rest his soul, I wouldn't say bad things of the dead,' she would conclude, apologetically.

She had no pity for Mrs Skeffington at all. I could never understand why Rose, who was so tender-hearted, shut her sympathy off from the threesome upstairs. Once I suggested we should tell the NSPCC, and she was so shocked that she could scarcely bring herself to speak to me for days. At last I went to her room and asked her why she was so angry. 'I didn't know you was one of them nosey-parkers,' she said.

'But, Rose, what's going to happen to that poor baby?'

'They'll take it away from her, most like, and send her to prison. Not that it's not a good place for her.'

'Perhaps they might help her.'

'How? Tell me? What she needs help for, is against her husband and what are they going to do about him? Not that she doesn't deserve what she gets.'

'All that's wrong with her is she's overworked and tired.'

'Yes? Well, let me tell you, my mother brought up six of us, and she had no sense for men, real sods they were, but she never carried on like my lady upstairs.'

Meanwhile Miss Powell had moved into the two small

rooms above the Skeffingtons. She came down to see me about the child. She wore a red silk gown, trimmed with dark fur, and looked like a film star strayed on to the wrong set. She was very sensible. She suggested we should talk to Mr Skeffington when he came home and tell him his wife needed a holiday.

As soon as she had gone, Rose came in to demand what I though I was doing, talking to that whore.

I said we had agreed to tax Mr Skeffington, and Rose said: 'You make me laugh, you do. At least the Skeffingtons are decently married, they aren't a whore and Mr Bobby Brent.'

Flo said to me, her eyes dancing. 'Mr Skeffington's coming back tomorrow. You wait till you see him,' she urged – for it was one of the days she did not like Mrs Skeffington. 'You just lean over the banisters and have a look. Like a film star, he is. He's got eyes that make me feel funny, just like Bobby Brent.' For some days Mrs Skeffington was saying to the child: 'Your daddy will beat you if you aren't a good girl.'

'I am a good girl.'

'You'll see, he'll beat you. For God's sake, keep quiet now, Rosemary.'

When he did come, I heard the following dialogue through the floor: 'It's always the same. As soon as I come home, you start complaining.'

'But I can't keep a home going on what I earn.'

'I told you before I married you, I've got to pay alimony. Sometimes I'm sorry I ever did. Can't you keep that kid quiet?'

'I can't help it if Rosemary's a naughty girl.'

'I'm not a naughty girl,' wailed Rosemary.

'Don't start,' he said aggressively. 'Now don't start, that's all.'

The child wept. Mrs Skeffington wept, and Mr Skeffington went out, slamming the door, five minutes after he'd come home.

Rose came in. 'You heard?' she asked.

'Yes.'

'You still think you're going to talk them into sense?'

'No, not really.'

'I told you. You've got a lot to learn. . .'

'All the same, what about the baby?'

'What you don't know yet is, there's some people you can't do nothing about.' She offered me a cigarette, as a sign she was forgiving me. 'I've been thinking about you, dear. Your trouble is this. You think, all you've got to do is say something, and then things'll be right. Well, they won't be. You leave that pair of love-birds upstairs alone. Because I tell you what's going to happen. He's left one wife with kids already. He's not one to stick. And he'll leave her, too. And then she'll be better off and her temper'll improve. You'll see.'

Later Mr Skeffington came in. Soon we heard her plead: 'Oh not tonight, not tonight, Ron. I'm so tired. I was up with Rosemary all last night.' Rose grinned at me, nodding, as if to say: There. I told you. He said: 'I've been away two weeks and that's what I get when I come home.' 'Oh, Ron, darling.' A comparative silence. We heard his voice, adjusted to tenderness. Complete silence. Then the child started to cry. Mrs Skeffington wailed: 'Oh, Rosemary, Rosemary, can't you ever stop?' She must have been up most of the night. At seven the alarm shrilled so long that most of the house was aroused. Finally there came a shock and a crash as the clock was flung across the room. 'Oh, Ronnie,' said Mrs Skeffington, 'now you've woken Rosemary.'

He was a slight, fair, dandyish young man, with a jaunty moustache. If any of us women, Rose, Flo, myself, Miss Powell were carrying something on the stairs, we could not take two steps before we found him beside us: 'A pleasure,' he would say, assisting us on our way. His wife carried all her own burdens. She got up at seven every day, washed and dressed and fed the child, and took it to the council nursery school. She came back at lunchtime to cook her husband his meal. She finally collected the little girl at six, having spent her day cooking in a nearby café. Her evenings she spent cleaning and cooking.

At nine in the morning, Ronnie Skeffington, smelling of shaving soap and hair lotion, would emerge from the bathroom in a silk dressing-gown, and proceed upstairs with the newspapers. His breakfast had been cooked for him and was waiting in the oven. At ten he went off to work, and came back at one, expecting to find his lunch ready. He usually did not come home until late at night.

'Say what you like,' said Flo, 'that Ronnie, that Miss Powell, they give the house class. Imagine now, if you was to open the door and there was Mr Skeffington, all polite and brushed, you'd think this house has got nice flats in it, now wouldn't you?'

'Don't start putting up the rents yet,' said Rose, dryly, after one such flight.

'Rents, I didn't say nothing about rents, dear.'

'No, I'm just telling you not to start.'

There were two rooms beneath mine and Rose's. An old couple lived there. I never heard them. I never saw them. When I asked Rose about them, her face would put on the sorrowful guilty look which meant that over this matter her loyalty was to Flo. She would say: 'Don't worry about them. There's nothing to tell.' When I asked Flo, she said: 'They're filthy old beasts, but they don't worry you, do they?'

About a week after I moved down beside Rose, Flo came in to ask me down to supper that night. I thanked her. She lingered, looking hurt. 'Don't you want to come, darling?' 'But of course I do. I'd love to.' She embraced me, saying: 'There, I knew you would. I told Dan.'

My trouble with Flo was that she was uneasy unless she got exaggerated reactions of delight, complaint, or shock to her own dramatized emotions. If I did not at first react suitably, she would prod me until I did. 'There! You're laughing,' she would say, in relief. 'That's right. Laugh.' Or, hopefully: 'Aren't you shocked? Of course you are. I knew you would be.'

Rose said: 'It's no use your being all English with Flo. It gets her all upset.'

As for Rose, she could communicate a saga of sorrow with a slight droop of her mouth; the climax to a tale about her stepfather would be indicated by the folding together, in resignation, of her two small hands in her lap, not a word spoken. Her single syllable, Yes? could silence anyone in the house.

Rose made Flo uneasy, too. When she wanted to punish Flo she would sit, impassive, listening, refusing to register emotion, offering me the faintest of malicious smiles, until Flo said: 'Ah, my Lord, you're cross with me. Why are you cross with your Flo?'

I knew that the invitation to supper meant more than I understood. I had to come to know that a complicated ritual governed what went on in the house. I did not at first think about it, out of an emotion which I now realize was a middle-class hypocrisy about the value of money, the value of time. But Rose made it impossible for me not to think.

About the supper invitation she said: 'I thought she would. She feels bad about getting too much for your rooms. She was expecting you to make her clean your rooms.'

'I asked her to.'

'She doesn't like housework.'

'Who does? But she came up and gave me a lesson about dusting and cleaning and ironing.'

'I'd like to have seen it,' said Rose. 'What was your mother thinking of, sending you out into the world so ignorant?'

'That's what Flo said, too.'

'Yes. Well, now she thinks she'll make up by inviting you to eat sometimes. And, believe you me, it's better that way, because she's a cook better than anyone, even my mother.' But just before we prepared ourselves to go down to supper, she became uneasy, and said: 'You mustn't mind Flo when she gets dirty-mouthed. Just laugh to please her and take no notice.'

On weekdays, the family did not eat together until the men came in from work, about six. This meal was called tea. No one went to bed until late, after midnight. At about eleven was another meal, called supper. At both Flo served a rich variety of foods. There was always a basis of salads, cake, different kinds of bread and cheeses and fruit. Flo always cooked a different, fresh main dish for both meals. It might be spaghetti, some kind of meat, a pie, or chicken. The late meal, just before everyone went to bed, was the one they most enjoyed and lingered over. Besides, it was by tradition what Flo called a dirt session.

On that evening when Rose and I went downstairs, the men were already waiting to be served at the table. They wore, as always after work, clean white singlets. The basement was always steaming hot from the stove and from the electric fire which was never turned off. Flo was making a cauldron of spaghetti which filled the steamy air full of the odours of garlic and olive oil and meat and cheese. We sat around the table, sprawling, our elbows resting, while Flo heaped our plates. Aurora, who never went to bed before her parents, was sitting on Dan's lap. She had on a white tight nightgown, over which her black curls, Flo's pride, cascaded to her waist. She had her arm around Dan's thick neck, and was sucking her thumb. Although there were blue bruises of fatigue beneath her eyes, she continued to observe everything that went on, sleepily blinking, and nodding off, then forcing herself awake. Her smile seemed as full of sharp knowledgeable enjoyments as Flo's.

Dan's attitude to me was the same as his to Rose: he watched us appreciatively, savouring our possibilities, but with caution. Flo kept a sharp eye on his every glance.

She served herself last, and sat down, sighing, saying: 'After all that gammon I ate before I haven't room for a bite.' We all ate enormously and praised Flo's art from time to time, which she took as her due with a modest and satisfied smile. Dan chewed in ferocious mouthfuls, his white teeth glistening through the sauce, strands hanging from the corners of his lips. From time to time he pushed a spoonful into Aurora's mouth, but she always made a face, chewed once or twice, and sat with the food, unswallowed, in her mouth.

'That kid's too sleepy to eat,' Rose said.

'It's no good putting her to sleep until we go,' said Flo. 'She'll just scream and scream.'

'She needs a good spanking,' said Rose. There was always a touch of sullenness in her voice when she mentioned Aurora. She disapproved of how she was brought up.

'But I spank her, I do,' said Flo eagerly, with a warm loving smile at Aurora, to which the child responded, like an accomplice.

When we could eat not another mouthful of spaghetti, or salad or cake, Flo took away the plates, and sat down again, her eyes bright and black, looking for an opening.

'Look at your belly,' she said suddenly to Rose, who had loosened her waist-band.

Rose gave me a glance which said: This was what I meant, don't take any notice. She said to Flo, with careful unconcern: 'What of it, after all that food?'

'You look seven months. Doesn't she, Jack? Doesn't she, Dan?'

Dan grinned; Jack's smile was eager and timid. Flo drew our attention to Jack, and said: 'Look at him. He'd like to have a little bit with Rose.' Jack blushed and looked eagerly, in spite of himself, at Rose. Who said good-naturedly: 'Who, me? I don't want a little boy in my bed.'

'He's got to learn sometime,' Flo said.

'Yes?' said Rose. 'Then why pick on me? I've got to learn, too.'

'That's what I keep telling you,' Flo said. 'How old are you now? And as innocent as a baby.'

'She's twenty-three,' said Dan to me, nodding and winking.

'You shut up,' said Rose to him, 'you're as old as you feel.'

'It's time you did feel,' said Flo. 'I keep telling you, Dan's brother is like Dan, he likes a woman who knows a thing.'

Rose, who was suffering because of the long quarrel, which I still knew nothing about, with Dickie, Dan's brother, looked annoyed and put a stop to this hare – 'Then if Dickie wants it, regardless, he can pay for it.'

Jack sniggered. He sat listening, shocked, delighted, suffering, turning his eyes from one to another. Against the open, savage sensuality of Dan and Flo, and the heavy immobile good-nature Rose put on for these occasions, he looked defenceless and pathetic.

'Yes. And he will, too, if he can get better.' Suddenly she

screamed at Dan: 'Go on, Dan, tell her. Tell Rose about that dirty French girl. Tell what she did to you, the dirty beast.'

Dan smiled, and sat silent. Flo, aroused and angry, yet delighted; screamed again: 'Well, tell her, go on.'

'I don't want to hear,' said Rose primly, who had heard it often before.

'Oh, yes you do. And you do too, don't you, darling?' – This to me, in a hasty aside. 'Go on, Dan.'

Dan began. At first he kept his eyes on Rose, who sighed continuously with prepared digust. But soon he turned his glistening yellow gaze at his wife, who glanced back at him, terrified and squealing with delight.

'And now you two had better go to bed,' commented Rose, heavily, when the story was over.

'What for, darling, we're not sleepy, are we, Dan?' Flo said, very innocent, catching our eyes one after another around the table.

Dan remained, heavily sitting and smiling and watching his wife, while Aurora sat smiling sleepily in his arms.

'For God's sake, put Aurora to bed,' said Rose, disgusted. 'Put her to sleep at least.'

Flo said: 'Yes. Poor little girl, she's sleepy.' She whisked Aurora out of her father's arms. Aurora let out a single howl of routine protest, and let her head fall on her mother's shoulder.

'Yes, she's sleepy all right,' said Flo, looking down at the child with a sort of malicious satisfaction. She took Aurora next door, while Rose grimaced at me, the corners of her mouth turned down, her eyebrows raised. Dan, now Flo was gone, was openly inciting both of us, grinning at us, his yellow eyes flaring.

Flo came back and saw him. 'Ah, my Lord,' she said sighing, 'it's a crime for a man like him to be wasted on one woman.'

'Lend him to me tonight,' said Rose, smiling and full of mischief at Dan.

'Yes,' said Dan. 'Listen to you. And what would I get if I even so much as touched Rose?'

'You try it and see,' said Flo, giggling. She yawned, dramatically, and said: 'Oh, I'm ever so sleepy. And there's all that washing-up.'

'I'll do it,' said Rose.

'Then I'll just pop off into bed,' said Flo, lingering in the bedroom door, her eyes on Dan. She went in and shut the door, while Dan sat a moment, smiling in appreciation. Jack was breathing heavily, looking at his stepfather with resentment, with wonder, with admiration, with hate. After a moment Dan rose and said to Jack: 'You turn off the lights. Don't forget now.' He followed his wife into the bedroom, loosening his belt.

Jack, Rose and I remained. Now Rose's attitude became brisk and maternal, encouraging no nonsense. She whisked through the washing and drying, while I helped her, and the boy sat despondently at the table, caressing a puppy, smiling at us, hoping for Rose to soften. He even made a sad little attempt to restore the sexy atmosphere by saying: 'You do look seven months gone, Rose, like Flo said.' But she said calmy: 'And what do you know about it?' When we left him, she patted his shoulder with triumphant patronage, and said: 'Sleep tight. And keep your dreams clean.'

He slept in the kitchen on a stretcher, beside a box full of puppies. He was like a puppy himself – sleek, eager, and wistful.

I thought Rose treated him badly. When I said so, she gave me her heavy-lidded look, half-triumphant, half-sardonic, and said: 'And why's that? He's a kid.'

'Then don't tease him.'

She was indignant. She did not understand me. I did not understand her. She was shocked because Jack, later, wandered in and out of my room, to talk about a film he'd just seen, or about his boxing. She was shocked when Bobby Brent dropped in at midnight with a business proposition before going upstairs to Miss Powell. No man was ever allowed inside her room. But she would go down to the basement in a waist slip and brassière, and if either Dan or Jack looked at her she would say scathingly: 'Nothing better to polish your eyes on?' in precisely the same way a fashionable woman might pointedly draw a cloak over her naked arms and shoulders at an over-direct stare from a man. I remember once Jack knocked on my door when I had a petticoat on, and I put on a dressing-gown before answering the door and letting him in. Rose said, amused: 'You think he's never seen a woman in a slip before?' and teased me about being prudish. One night she was sitting in front of my fireplace in her nightgown, and Jack was lying on the floor turning over the physical culture magazines he read, when she unconcernedly lifted a bare arm to scratch where her brassière had left a red mark under her breast. Jack said bitterly: 'Oh, don't mind me, please. I'm nothing but a bit of furniture.'

'What's biting you?' she enquired, and when he blundered to his feet and slammed out of my room, swearing, she said to me, with perfect sincerity: 'He's a funny boy, isn't he, all full of moods.'

'But Rose, how can you tantalize him like that?'

'Well, I don't know, dear. I don't really, the things you say, they'd make me blush if I didn't know you. I can see I'm going to have to tell you about life.'

She had now taken my education over. It had begun over money, and when I got a job with a small engineering firm as secretary. I was earning seven pounds a week. I said something to Rose about living on seven pounds a week; and she gave me her heavy-lidded smile. 'You make me laugh,' she said.

'But I do,' I said. I was paying the fees for the council nursery, the rent, and the food out of that money. I found it hard, but it gave me pleasure to be able to do it.

'For one thing,' said Rose, settling down to the task of instructing me. 'For one thing, there's clothes. You and the kid, you have all the clothes you brought with you. Now suppose there was a fire tomorrow, what'd you use for money for clothes?'

'But there isn't going to be a fire.'

'Why not? Look how you live. It's enough to make a cat laugh. You say to yourself, well I'm having some bad luck just now, so you pull your belt a bit tighter, while it lasts.

That's not being poor. You always go on as if you'll win the pools tomorrow.'

'Well, I hate having to worry all the time about what might happen.'

'Yes?' said Rose, silencing me.

'All right, then, you show me.'

'Yes, I'm going to. Because you worry me, you do really. Suppose you don't get married, suppose that book of yours isn't any good?'

I was ready to listen, because this was one of the times when I believed I might not write again. I found I was too tired at night to write. My day, for some weeks, went like this. My son woke early, and I dressed and fed him and took him to the nursery before going to work. At lunchtime I went to the shops, took food home and cleaned the place out. I picked him up from the nursery at five; and by the time he was fed and bathed and read to, and he was ready for sleep, it was about nine. Then, in theory, was my time for writing. But not only could I not write, I could not even imagine myself writing. The personality 'writer' was so far removed from me, it was like thinking about another person, not myself. As it turned out, after two months or so, I got an advance from a publisher on a previously-written book, and my troubles were over. But during that time, I was ready to listen to Rose's strictures.

'No,' she would say patiently, as she took the match from my fingers and replaced it carefully in the box. 'Not like that. Why, when there's a fire burning?' She tore a strip of newspaper, made a spill, and lit her cigarette and mine.

She would say: 'I have a friend, you don't know her. She went into the chemist at the corner for a lipstick. But she could have got the same lipstick along the road for tuppence less. There's no sense in that. She's got no sense at all. She dropped some tea on her skirt. Well, round the corner there's a cleaner would've done it for one-and-nine. But she just goes into the nearest and pays two-and-six. Where's the sense in it? Can you tell me?'

Rose earned four pounds a week. She was underpaid, and knew it. The managers of shops in the neighbourhood were always offering her better-paid jobs; but she wanted to stay where she was because Dickie, Dan's brother, worked in a cigarette shop across the street. Nor would she ask her employer for a rise. 'I do all the work in that place,' she said. 'She just runs off to shop and carry-on, leaving me there alone. That husband of hers, all he knows about is the inside of watches. If a customer comes in, he diddles about, and loses everything and then shouts Rose, Rose. And I know how much money they make because I see the books. Well, if they don't know the right way to behave, the way I look at it, it's their funeral. Let them enjoy their guilty consciences. They know I'm worth twice that money to them. Well, if they think I'm going down on my knees to ask for it, I'm not going to give them that pleasure, they needn't think it.'

Rose lived well inside her four pounds a week. What it cost her to do it were time and leisure, commodities she knew the value of, but which she did not consider to be her right. Half an hour's skilled calculations might go into working out whether it was worth taking a bus to another part of London where she knew there was a nail varnish at sixpence less than where we lived. She would muse aloud, like this: 'If I go by bus, that's three-halfpence. Threepence altogether. I'd save threepence on the varnish. If I walk there's shoe-leather, and what repairs cost these days, it's not worth it. I know,' she concluded, triumphant. 'I'll wear those shoes of mine that pinch me, and then it won't cost nothing at all.' We would walk together to the shop where the nail varnish was sixpence cheaper, and she would snatch up her prize from the rich market of London, saying: 'There, see, what did I tell you? Now I'm sixpence to the good.' But walking back she would stop on an impulse to buy half a pound of cherries from one of the despised barrow-boys, against whom she was continually warning me, so that the saved sixpence was thrown to the winds; but that was different, that was pleasure. 'I'll have to go easy on cigarettes tomorrow,' she would say, smiling delightedly. 'But it's worth it.'

All her carefully handling of money was to this end – that she might buy pleasure: that once in six months she could take a taxi instead of walking, and tip the taxi driver threepence more than was necessary; that she could buy a pair of good nylons once a week; that she could throw money away on fruit when the fancy took her, instead of walking down to the street markets and getting it cheap.

Inside this terrible, frightening city, Rose had created for herself a sort of tunnel, shored against danger by habit, known buildings, and trusted people. Rose's London was the half-mile of streets where she had been born and brought up, populated by people she trusted; the house where she now lived, surrounded by *them* – mostly hostile people; and the West End. She knew every face we saw in the area we lived in, and if she did not, made it her business to find out. She knew every policeman and plain-clothes man who might pounce on her if she did not do right; she would nudge me and point out some man on a pavement, saying: 'See 'im? He's a copper in civvies. Makes me sick. Well, I wonder who he's after this time.' She spoke with a melancholy respect, almost pride.

Rose's West End was a fixed journey, on a certain bus route, to a certain Corner House and one of half a dozen cinemas. It was walking back up Regent Street for window shopping.

Flo's London did not even include the West End, since she had left the restaurant in Holborn. It was the basement she lived in; the shops she was registered at; and the cinema five minutes' walk away. She had never been inside a picture gallery, a theatre or a concert hall. Flo would say: 'Let's go to the River one fine afternoon and take Oar.' She had not seen the Thames, she said, since before the war. Rose had never been on the other side of the river. Once, when I took my son on a trip by river bus, Rose played with the idea of coming too for a whole week. Finally she said: 'I don't think I'd like those parts, not really. I like what I'm used to. But you go and tell me about it after.'

On the evenings when Rose decided life owed her some fun, she would say to me: 'You're coming with me to the West End tonight, whether you like it or not.' She began to dress a good hour before it was time to start. I could hear her bath running downstairs, and the smell of her bath powder drifted up through the house. Soon afterwards she came in, without make-up, looking young and excited. I never found out how old she was. She used to say, with a laugh, she was twenty-three, but I think she was about thirty.

'Rose, I wish you wouldn't put on so much make-up.'

'Don't be silly. If I don't wear plenty, Dickie says to me, what's up with you, are you flying the red flag?'

'But you haven't seen Dickie for weeks.'

'But we might run into him. That's one of the reasons I'm taking you. He always takes me where we're going, and if he's got another woman, then I'll catch him out and have a good laugh.'

Soon she had painted her daytime face over her real face, and had moulded her hair into a solid mass of black scrolls and waves. When Rose was dressed and made-up she always looked the same. She was conforming to some image of herself that was not the fashionable image for that year, but about three years ago. She took fashion papers, but the way we were supposed to look that year struck her as being extreme. She used to laugh at the pictures of fashion models, say: 'They do look silly, don't they?' and go off to her room to make herself into something that seemed to her safe and respectable, because she was used to it.

'Come on, get yourself dressed.'

'But I am dressed.'

'If you're coming out with me, then you've got to dress up.'

She pulled out the dress she wanted me to wear, and stood over me till I put it on. She knew I did not like the Corner House, but tolerated my dislike. She was only exerting her rights as a neighbour, exactly as I might go into her and say: 'I'm depressed, please come and sit with me.' At such times she put aside whatever she was occupied with, and came at once; she recognized a tone in my voice; she knew what was due to communal living.

We always walked to the bus-stop, and it had to be the same bus-stop, and the same bus, though there were several which would have done. She kept pulling me back, saying:

'No, not that bus. That's not the number I like.' And if the bus did not have seats free, downstairs, on the left-hand side, she would wait until one came that had. She made me sit near the window. She liked to sit on the aisle, and she held her exact fare in her hand, watching the conductor until he came for it. She handed it over with a firm look, as if to say: 'I'm not trying to get away with anything.' And she put away the ticket in a certain pocket in her handbag – one could not be too careful.

But this ritual was for when we went out, because on ordinary occasions she would take the first bus that came, and sit anywhere and was not above diddling the company out of tuppence on the fare if she could. Pleasure was different, and part of pleasure was to pay for it.

At the Corner House there was always a queue. I might say: 'It'll be half an hour at least.' I regarded queueing as tedious. Rose did not. On one occasion, after we had been twenty minutes in the queue, and were nearly at its head, a woman tried to push in front of us. And then Rose the meek, Rose the resigned, Rose, who would spend a whole evening on her knees with a bucket and a brush because she could not say No to Flo; Rose who would stay up till two in the morning ironing and washing Dickie's shirts, and then re-damp and re-iron them if there was the slightest crease in the collar – and all this devotion at a time when she was not even seeing him; this patient and enduring woman suddenly set her feet apart, put her hands on her hips, and allowed her eyes to flash. 'Excuse me!' she began in a belligerent voice, glancing at the rest of the queue for support. Every one was, of course, on her side; every one had been schooled by years of practice in queue-ethics, and had been watching, just as she had, with ox-eyed impassivity for some imposter to push forward. Rose pulled the offender by the elbow and said: 'Here, you haven't queued, get to the back.' The woman smiled in uncertain bravado, opened her mouth to fight, saw the hostile faces all around her, and then, with a pert shrug of her shoulders, went to the back of the queue.

Rose said loudly: 'People trying to get away with things.' And she stood triumphantly, standing up for her rights.

When at last our group, which had stood on the fringe of the table-packed space for at least ten minutes, were waved forward by a waiter like a policeman directing traffic, Rose tipped him and whispered, and we were taken to a table immediately by the band. Rose liked to sit just there; it meant she could lean over and ask for the tunes she wanted. She said: 'You can get the music you want without tipping the waiter to ask for you.' But that was not the reason. It was that it gave her a feeling of homely satisfaction to be able to smile at the drummer, and get a nod and a smile back again.

She did not like the food much. She used to say: 'Flo's spoiled me, she has really.' But she always ordered the same: beans on toast, with chips and spaghetti. I could not understand why until she said: 'That's what we used to get during the war in the canteen. It reminds me, see?'

We used to stay for about two hours, eating and submitting to the music. Then she stretched herself and said: 'Thanks for coming, dear. I haven't seen that so-and-so Dickie, but I've enjoyed it ever so much.'

Then we walked up Regent Street, very slowly, stopping at each window, criticizing every dress or pair of shoes. Rose had a different standard for these clothes than for the ones she wore herself. She judged these against the current fashions and was critical. She chose dresses for film stars she liked, not for herself. Sometimes we went the whole street without her approving of anything. She would say: 'Lot of rubbish today, isn't there? Not anything I'd like to see Betty Grable in. Sometimes I think those fashion-men think we're fools, with more money than sense.'

Going home on the bus we played her favourite game – spending the money she was going to win in the football pools. She never had less than ten thousand pounds to spend. She was going to buy herself a mink coat, some expensive clothes, and a little restaurant for herself and Dickie. She had chosen the house she wanted. It had a garden for the children she intended to have, and was about ten minutes from where we lived, with a 'For Sale' sign on it. We often went there in the evenings to look at it. 'I hope it won't be sold too soon,' she'd say, 'not before I win the pools.' And then – 'Listen to me, talking silly. Still, someone's got to win it, haven't they?'

'When autumn comes,' she said, 'I'll teach you about the pools. I look forward to the pools all the summer. It gives you some excitement in life, doing the pools every week and waiting to hear who's won.'

She paid Flo thirty shillings a week for her room. It was understood that for this sum she could eat Sunday dinner with the family. It was also understood that if she was invited to another meal during the week, she must pay for it in washing-up or scrubbing or ironing. Her rent included an early morning cup of tea. Rose never drank this, because she slept till the last minute before rushing off to work, so that the tea, left outside her room by Jack, who left for work an hour before she did, was always cold. But if he forgot to leave it there, she made a state trip downstairs, to say: 'I like people to keep their word. If I pay for a thing, then it's my affair what I do with it afterwards.' So every morning the cup of tea cooled outside her door, and was later emptied into the sink by Flo, who grumbled good-naturedly: 'Some people!'

Rose did not eat breakfast. 'Why waste money eating when you're still full of sleep, anyway?' She ate a sausage roll or a sandwich at midday. These odd snacks during the day cost her ten shillings; she did not eat seriously unless invited by Flo. Two pounds left out of her earnings. She smoked ten cigarettes a day – another ten shillings.

That left her thirty shillings. On pay-day she arranged this balance on her dressing-table and played with it, frowning and smiling, talking of how she might spend it.

She did not plan for holidays: when she had time off she went down to stay with her mother. Nor did she go to parties. Sometimes she dropped down to the Palais at Hammersmith on a Wednesday evening, and came back dispirited: 'None of them were as good as Dickie, say what you like. They just make me laugh.'

In the end, the money always went on clothes. And in a way which was richly satisfactory to Rose, because she seldom bought in shops, only things like gloves and nylons. She got her clothes from her employer. That fat pale woman spent a great deal on her clothes, and luckily for Rose had only just put on weight. Her cupboards were full of things she would never wear again. Rose would haggle over a dress or a suit she coveted for months, until at last she came in, victorious, saying: 'I've got it for twenty-seven-and-six, there go my cream cakes for a month, not to mention the pictures, but look, this dress cost that fat bitch twenty-five guineas.' So it was, when Rose was dressed to go out, she looked as if what she wore had cost her six months' wages. She would stand for a long time in front of the tall looking-glass in my room, surveying herself with grim satisfaction. Finally she would say: 'Well, it only goes to show, doesn't it?' a remark into which was concentrated her attitute towards the rich and the talented, an attitude without envy or sourness, but which was full of self-respect, and implicit in everything she said or did.

And yet, although she dressed herself through these means, she was upset when I said I was going to sell some of my clothes to the second-hand shops. 'You don't want to do that,' she protested.

'They're too big for you, or you could have them.'

'And what would I be doing with all those evening dresses?' She examined them, and said: 'Well, you must have had a good time where you came from.'

'Everyone dances there. It's a place where people dance a lot.'

'Yes?'

'It's not expensive to dance.'

'Yes?'

'But it's true.'

'Yes? All I know is, dancing is floor-space and a band and things to eat and drink. That's money. Who pays for it? Someone does.'

'All the same, I want to sell these things, they're no good to me.'

'Well, don't sell them around here, that's all.'

'Why not?'

'It's not nice, is it. People might see, and say things.'

'Why should I care?'

'Yes? Well, I do. People see you and me together. Then they see you selling clothes, to those old shops. Yes, I know – you'll go off one of these days, but I'm living here. So to please me you can just take a bus ride and sell them somewhere else.'

When I had sold them, she enquired: 'And how much did you get? Enough for cigarettes for a couple of weeks? Oh, I know, don't tell me. And so you've gone and lowered yourself in those dirty old shops, just for that. It's all right for film stars and models, it stands to reason, everyone knows they can wear a thing once, but not for people like us. You'd do better to keep them and look at them sometimes and remember the good times you had than sell them for cigarette money.'

'You can talk about cigarettes, going without food to smoke.'

'And who's talking, I'd like to know?'

Both of us suffered over cigarettes. I came from a country where they were cheap. I had always smoked a lot. Now I was cut down to half my usual allowance. Rose and I made complicated rules for ourselves, to keep within limits. We tried to smoke as few as possible in the day, to leave plenty for our long gossip sessions at nights. But our plans were always being upset by Flo. There was more rancour created in that house over cigarettes than over anything else. Rose might grumble a little if Flo had forgotten to ask her to supper on an evening when 'she felt like eating'. She would say: 'All very well for her, licking and tasting away all day over her stove,' but shrug it off. For food was something one could do without. But if Flo borrowed a cigarette and forgot to pay it back, Rose would sulk. And, of course, with Flo it was never a question of one cigarette. She would cadge from me, from Rose, from Miss Powell, beg from the milkman or the gas-man. 'I'll give it to you next time you come,' she would say, anxiously grabbing at the offered cigarette.

She could afford to buy as many as she liked. But she never bought enough. Five minutes after she returned from

100

a shopping trip she would come up to Rose's room, and say: 'Give your Flo a fag, dear.'

'But you've just gone out shopping.'

'But I forgot.'

'I've got four left for the evening.'

'I'll pay you back tomorrow.'

'What you mean is, I've got to do without this evening.'

'I'm dying for a smoke.'

'You owe me nine cigarettes as it is.'

At which Flo hastily thrust into Rose's hands her sweet coupons for the week.

'I don't like sweets, you know that,' said Rose, handing them back. 'Why don't you ask Dan – he'll be in in five minutes.'

'Oh, but he gets so cross with me, he gets so he won't talk to me, if I ask. I owe him so many already.'

'Flo. What you mean is, I've got to go without, then?'

'Look, darling! Look, sweetheart, here's one and six. That's nine cigarettes. I had it in my pocket all ready. You thought I'd forgotten. Well, I don't forget like that. Here, take the money.'

'I don't want the money. I'm not going to get dressed and go out again just because you get more fun out of cadging than out of buying them, straight and sensible.'

'Oh, my God, you're cross with me, darling, you're cross with your Flo.' A few seconds later, a knock on my door.

'Darling, sweetheart, give your Flo a cigarette.'

I used to give her cigarettes. That is, I used to at the beginning. But I could not withstand Rose's fury. She would get beside herself with rage when Flo had helped herself, and crept out, victorious, flushed with guilt, trying to get past Rose's door without being heard.

Rose came into me. 'You mean, you gave her some?'

'It's only some cigarettes.'

'What do you mean, only? She can afford to smoke eighty a day if she wants.'

'Don't be so angry, Rose.'

'I am angry. You make me sick. I hate to see somebody getting something for nothing. And you let her get away with it. Did you know, she even borrows from that dirty Miss Powell upstairs?'

'The cigarettes are clean enough.'

'If you think that's a joke . . . don't you let me catch you handing out free smokes to Flo again. What's right is right.' She began to smile, her anger all gone. 'Do you know what?'

'What?'

'I paid Dickie out again today. I bought my cigarettes from the kiosk and not from him.'

All through this long period of estrangement, Rose had been going into the shop, as always, to get her ten from Dickie. He would see her come in; lift his eyebrows, hum a tune, to show indifference, and lay her favourite brand on the counter. She would lay the money beside the packet, wait for the change, and go out, like a stranger.

'Do you know what? Dickie made me laugh today. I paid for my cigarettes with a pound note today. Of course I had change, but I pretended not to. And I knew he wouldn't because it was first thing Monday. And we're not speaking, see? So he couldn't say, he didn't have change in the till. And I was standing there, waiting. So he took the change out of his pocket, and gave it to me. But I just took it all for granted, and sailed away, not even saying thanks.'

On days when she felt black-hearted, she waited until Dickie's counter was clear of people, and he was looking out, to make an entrance into the kiosk next door. It was run by a good-looking youth who wanted to take Rose out. She would make a point of staying in there talking and flirting for as long as possible. At evening she would say: 'I paid Dickie out today. But I think it hurts me more than it hurts him. Because I look forward to getting my fags from him. And I'm so soft, I don't like to think he's hurt, if he thinks I like Jim. Jim's the one at the kiosk, see? Well, I don't like to hurt him. And so when he sent his shirts and socks into my shop for me to do for him, I just slipped in a new pair of socks I knew he'd like.'

'I'm damned if I'd wash and iron for a man who's stood me up.'

'The point is, I don't care about nobody else, even if I try, like when I go to the Palais. But the way I think is, he'll feel different when we're married and he settles down.'

'But, meanwhile, he's taking out someone else?'

At this her face hardened; she had the look of a deaf person, listening to his own thoughts. 'He'll be different when we're married,' she repeated, with anxiety.

Meanwhile, she was getting more and more depressed. Night after night, when she had had her bath, and was ready for bed, she would knock on my door and say: 'I've got the 'ump. I've got to be with someone.' And she sat, without waiting for me to speak.

I was depressed, too, because I was not writing. We weren't good for each other. Flo might come in at midnight, to find out what the citizens of her kingdom were up to, and find us sitting on either side of the fire, smoking and silent. 'God preseve us,' she would say. 'The Lord help me. Look at you both. Sorry for yourselves, that's what.' Rose would raise her eyes, and sigh, without words.

'Yes,' Flo said, examining her, good-natured and disapproving, 'you think I don't know. But I do know. What you want, Rose, is a man in your bed.'

'Maybe, maybe not,' commented Rose, blowing out fancy smoke patterns and watching them dissolve.

'Maybe not, she says,' said Flo to me. 'Well, I'm right, aren't I, darling? If you was a friend of Rose's you'd tell her right. You can't keep a man by playing hiding-pussy the way she does.'

Rose continued to puff out smoke. 'We have different ideas,' she said. 'It takes all sorts.'

'Your ideas'd be ever so much more better if you treated Dickie right.'

'Huh – Dickie!' said Rose, so that the message might be communicated to Dickie.

Flo said shrewdly: 'You think you're going to starve him into kissing your hand. Kiss your arse more likely.'

Rose sighed again, and shut her eyes.

'Well, aren't I right, dear?' – to me. 'And that goes for you too – if you don't mind me saying it. A woman's got no heart for sobbing and sighing when she's got a man in her bed.'

'We're not in the mood for men,' said Rose. 'They're more trouble than they're worth, and that's the truth.'

'Trouble!' said Flo. 'Ah, my Lord, and I know it. But I know if you two was tucked up nice and close with a man you fancied you'd not be sitting here all hours, looking like death's funeral.'

'We're talking,' said Rose. 'We're talking serious.'

'Don't you fancy a little bit of supper, Rose?'

'I'm not in the mood for doing your washing-up,' said Rose, ungraciously, breaking all the rules of the house.

'My God, who said anything about washing-up?'

'I am.'

'You're not cross with your Flo?'

'I don't feel like talking dirty, that's all.'

'Dirty, she says?'

'You know what I mean.'

'Oh, my God! Well, I hope you will come to your senses and then you'll be more pleasure to your friends. Give me a cigarette, darling.'

'No.'

'Give your Flo a cigarette?'

I gave her one.

'That's right,' she said, satisfied. 'And you come down on Sunday for dinner, you two, it'll do you good.'

She went, genuinely concerned for us both.

'She means well,' Rose would say. 'The thing is, now she's got her man all safe, she's not serious. Many's the good times she and I had together, just like you and me now, before Dan came along. They just took one look and began to quarrel. Well, you can always tell by that, can't you? Look at my mother and my stepfather. Fight, fight, fight. And in between they were warming up the bed.'

'Well, you must be depressed if you're on to your step-father again.'

'You can say that. I think of him often. Now I tell you what. You make us both a nice cup of tea, I could do with one, and then I won't have to go down and listen to all that sex, it just gets me mad for nothing.'

When I had made the tea, she would watch me pouring, and say: 'And now the sugar.'

'But I keep telling you, I hate sugar in my tea.'

'Yes? It's no good trying to tell you anything, sugar is food, see? And it costs nothing to speak of it. I don't like it either, but it's food. I learned that from my mother. She'd pile the sugar into my tea and say: 'That'll keep you warm, even though the money's short this week.' Because that old so-and-so he was always out of work. And my mother, she'd go out charring, seven days in the week, to earn the money, but it was never enough, not for my lord, her husband.'

Rose at night, was so different from how she was in the day that I never tired of watching her. As she sat, dark hair loose around her face, eyes dark and brooding, her face soft, fluid and shapeless in her loose white dressing-gown, she was a dozen women. With each turn of her head, each movement of her hands, she changed, and races and peoples flowed through her. When she spoke of her mother, who had spent her life cleaning other people's houses, she unconsciously smoothed down an imaginary apron; or she would fold her hands in a gesture of willing service, and she looked twenty years older – she was a working woman, with a tired body and ironic eyes. Then she would talk of Flo; and her whole pose changed, and became sceptical and knowing: Flo represented something she must fight, and so she was combative and watchful. Or she would speak of her mother's parents, who had lived in the country, and whom she had visited as a child, before they died. At such times she assumed a sturdy and vigorous pose, placing work-thickened hands on her hips, and it seemed as if she might tie on a bonnet and step out into the country past which lay such a short time behind her. 'My Gran,' she would say, 'she lived to be ninety, and I can remember her to this day, standing on a whacking great ladder as tall as a tree to pick cherries, and she was eighty then if she was a day. Well, none of us are going to live to be ninety, I can tell you that. The sorrow of the city'll kill us off before her time.'

'Would you like to live in the country?'

'Me? Are you mad? I'm from London, as I told you. That's what I mean when I say I'm not English. Not really. When I talk of English, what I mean is, my grandad and my grandma. That's English. The country. They were quite different from us – I mean my mother and me. I liked visiting with them, but they didn't really understand, not really, not what living was like. They were shut off, see? But I like to think of them when I get the 'ump. It cheers me up. And it cheered my mother up, too. When her man got her down, she'd go off to see her mother. And my stepfather got cross every time.'

'Rose, he's dead. Don't go on about him all the time.'

'I see what you mean. But I can't help it. I had him around all the time I was growing up. I think of him often and often. Sometimes I think Dickie's his living incarnation, as you might say.'

'Then that's not much good, is it?'

'But I love him. Not that I loved that old so-and-so. You know what? He used to wait for me when I'd gone out with a boy, and if I was after ten o'clock he'd take the broom handle to me. He'd lay about me until my mother came at him. She stood up for me. She stood up for us all. I must say that for her, though he was mostly good to the boys. They didn't get under his skin. Not that it makes sense, because they all upped and left home and they're scattered all over now, one Liverpool, one Glasgow, and one away off in Reading and we never see them. But I stayed, beatings and all. It was me he had it in for, all the time. But my mother was used to so-and-so's. She go so-and-so's every time. My own father was as bad. He was good to me, mind you, he used to take me driving with his fancy women, and all that, and then he used to beat my mother. Guilty conscience, as you might say. And then she went and married my step-father – a real home from home, he was. And now he's dead, and there's an old stick hanging about, sugar and spice and presents, but, mark my words, if she marries him he'll have his fists about her like the rest. She's got no eye for a man. I've told her she can't marry him, she won't have my blessing if she does. But she will, and then Rose-the-mug will be down there, pouring oil and taking the consequences.'

'But if Dickie's the same, why go on waiting for him?'

'I've thought of that, believe you me. I've tried to like the others. But it's no good. And you upset me, saying that, because I don't like thinking why. I give myself the 'ump. I do really.'

Her mood, for a few weeks, was so dark she dragged herself around work, the house, her shopping, and scarcely heard if I spoke to her. She made an impatient gesture, like someone listening to music, and said: 'Don't talk to me, dear, just let me sit.'

One evening I was reading, while Rose smoked and worried opposite me. Rosemary began to cry. Rose instantly lifted her head to listen, although she had not heard the last remark I made.

'Leave her alone,' said Ronnie Skeffington. 'She'll go to sleep again.'

'I've got to stop her. Mrs Bolt'll be complaining.' Her feet dragged across the floor. 'Oh, Rosemary, Rosemary,' she said, as the child wailed.

'Come to bed and leave her alone, she'll be all right,' said Ronnie Skeffington, in an efficient voice. 'Let her cry.'

'But where are we going to live, if they turn us out?'

'Oh, we'll find somewhere.'

'*We* will? That's good. Who wore their feet out for months trying to find a place that would take a kid?'

'Don't start that now.'

Rosemary cried herself to sleep again, and Mrs Skeffington crept back to bed.

'Oh no, leave me alone, I'm so tired.'

'Come on, don't make a fuss.'

'But, Ronnie, I'm so tired.'

'Oh, come on.'

'No, I won't.'

'Oh, so you won't!' He laughed, and she cried miserably while the bed creaked. Rose said: 'Listen to that! Just listen to it.' At last, silence; and Rose said: 'Thank God for that, perhaps we'll have some peace.' But she sat listening tensely.

A few minutes later Rosemary began crying again. We sat

still while the thing repeated itself. But when Mrs Skeffington got back into bed she cried out in hysteria: 'No, I won't, Ronnie. Don't make me.'

'Oh, come on, what fun is there in life?'

'Fun for who?' Then she screamed out: 'You've bitten me.' Rosemary and her mother wailed together.

Rose got up, her lips narrowed into a vindictive line.

'Where are you going?'

'You'll see.'

'Leave them alone.'

'They don't leave us alone, do they?'

Rose went up and hammered on the door. 'Let me in,' she shouted.

'Who's that?'

'Let me in.' The door opened. 'You ought to be ashamed of yourself,' said Rose. 'Have you got to bite your wife just because she won't sleep with you fifty times a night? You dirty beast. And what about Rosemary? What's it like for her hearing all this nonsense. Give her to me.'

'We'll keep her quiet, we will really.'

'Give her to me,' said Rose again.

Rosemary began sobbing, as a child does when it finds a refuge.

'Now you go to bed,' said Rose. 'You leave your wife alone. Anyway, why do you have to make love tonight? Friday and Saturday's for making love. Everyone has to work tomorrow, and you just go on and on.'

Husband and wife crept into their bed. Rose took the child into the other room and covered her up on the sofa. She was upstairs a long time. When she came down her eyes were red.

'Yes,' she said. 'If I had a kid I'd know what to do. But who gets them? Dirty beasts like them Skeffingtons.'

'You're hard on them.'

'Now don't you start on your talk. Just don't talk. I don't want to think about nothing at all. Because when I start thinking I begin to think about what might happen. Suppose I don't marry Dickie, what then?'

'You'll marry someone else.'

'Yes? They're all the same, when you get down to it.'

'Things are different from they used to be. You don't have to get married.'

'They might be different for you, but they're not for me.'

This was how she always put an end to our discussions about socialism. 'You're different,' she had concluded, listening to me exhort about the system. 'You're middle-class – you don't mind me saying it, I've got nothing against you personally, see? So if you want to talk about socialism, you're welcome.'

'Rose, socialism is for the working people, not for us.'

'Yes?'

'Yes. You won't get it until you fight for it.'

'Yes? I'm not going to waste my time getting excited. Things will last out my time. In the newspapers they're always talking about a new this and new that. Well, there's one thing I know, my mother worked all her life, and I'm no better off than she was.'

'Yes, you are. You won't starve, for one thing.'

'Starve? Who's talking about starving? She never starved either. There's always someone to help you out if you're in trouble. You would, if I was in trouble. But I know her life and I know mine. And I know the difference, not much.'

'It's your fault, because you won't fight.'

'Yes? Well you talk, if you enjoy it, I'll think my own thoughts.'

'We're supposed to have a new society.'

'Yes?'

'Do you get angry because there are still rich and powerful people when all that is supposed to be finished?'

'Who said it was?'

'A lot of people.'

'Well, if you want to believe all them lies, who's stopping you?'

'I didn't say I believed it.'

'Then you're talking sense for once.'

'All the same. The reason they are saying it is they want to put something over on you.'

'Yes? Well, they're not. As for them with their parties and their good times and their money here and their money here, I say, good luck to them. They've either got brains, which I haven't, or they've done something dirty to get it. Well, I don't envy their consciences. Would you like to be Bobby Brent or Dan or Flo?'

'Much rather, than being virtuous and poor.'

'Then you're not my friend. Excuse me for saying so. I don't like you talking like that. Then why don't you put money into their dirty deals?'

'Because I haven't any.'

'Don't give me that talk. I don't believe it, for one. And for another, I don't like to hear it. And I'll tell you something else. Sometimes I'm sorry you're my friend, because you make me think about things.'

'Good. That's what friends are for.'

'Yes? But not if it makes you unhappy. I've told you before, there's one thing wrong with you. You think it's enough to say things are wrong to change them. Well, it isn't. I'll tell you something else. My stepfather was Labour. Well, it stands to reason, he had unemployment and all that. And who's Labour Party in this house? The Skeffingtons upstairs.'

'Good for them,' I said.

'Yes? That pair of no-goods? They have everything bad, and so they vote Labour.' Suddenly she giggled. 'It made me laugh. When we had that election, Flo and Dan, they had Tory posters all over. Well, that makes sense, they're doing all right. And the Skeffingtons stuck a Labour in their window. Flo went up and tore it down. So the Skeffingtons made a fuss about their rights. They make me laugh. Lucky they pay the rent regular. He said to Flo: All right, then we'll leave. And she said: All right, then leave. Then she thought about the rent, and her heart broke. So for weeks, you can imagine how it was, all the house plastered up and down with Vote for Churchill, and just one window, Vote for Labour.'

'And you?'

110

'Me?'

'You have the vote.'

'Don't make me laugh. I know what's what. I just watch them at it and laugh to myself.'

'Well, you make me angry.'

'Yes I know I do, and I don't care.'

'For one thing, you make me cross because you hang about waiting for Churchill to speak. What has he ever done for you?'

'Whoever said he had?'

Rose would listen to Churchill talk with a look of devotion I entirely misunderstood. She would emerge at the end of half an hour's fiery peroration with a dreamy and reminiscent smile, and say: 'He makes me laugh. He's just a jealous fat man, I don't take any notice of him. Just like a girl he is, saying to a friend: No dear, you don't look nice in that dress, and the next thing is, he's wearing it himself.'

'Then why do you listen to him?'

'Why should I care? He makes me remember the war, for one thing. I don't care what he says about Labour. I don't care who gets in, I'll get a smack in the eye either way. When they come in saying Vote for Me, Vote for Me, I just laugh. But I like to hear Churchill speak, with his dirty V-sign and everything, he enjoys himself, say what you like.'

Similarly she would listen to programmes about the war and say: 'Well, to think all those exciting things were going on all the time. They didn't happen to us. Did I ever tell you about the bomb we had on the factory?'

But there were programmes she refused to listen to at all. Or she would return from the cinema sometimes in a mood of sullen rage, saying: 'They make me sick, they do.'

'Who?'

To begin with she was vague, saying, 'I don't know.'

But later on, when she knew me, and we had begun to fight about what we thought, she would say: 'Oh, I know what I say'll be grist to your mill, but I don't care. Those films. They make fun of us.'

There was a certain wireless programme that I thought

was funny, but if Rose came in when I was listening she would say politely: 'You think that's funny, do you? Well, I don't,' and go out until it was over.

'I don't think it's funny people talk in different ways,' she said to me at last. 'That's what that programme is, isn't it? Just to make people feel above themselves because they talk well and people like me don't. Listen to them laughing, just because someone uses the wrong grammar. I'm surprised at you, dear, I am really.'

I have seen her return from a film so angry she would smoke several cigarettes before she could bring herself to speak about it.

'They make me sick. It was a British film, see. I don't know why I ever go to them sometimes. If it's an American film, well, they make us up all wrong, but it's what you'd expect from them. You don't take it serious. But the British films make me mad. Take the one tonight. It had what they call a cockney in it. I hate seeing cockneys in films. Anyway, what is a cockney? There aren't any, except around Bow Bells, so they say, and I've never been there. And then the barrow-boys, or down in Petticoat Lane. They just put it on to be clever, and sell things if they see an American or a foreigner coming. "Watcher, cock," and all that talk all over the place. They never say Watcher, cock! unless there's someone stupid around to laugh. Them film people just put it in to be clever, like the barrow-boys, it makes the upper-class people laugh. They think of the working-class as dragged up. Dragged up and ignorant and talking vulgar-ugly. I've never met anyone who spoke cockney. I don't and no one I know does, not even Flo, and God knows she stupid enough and on the make to say anything. Well, that's what I think and I'll stick to it. And the bloody British can keep their films. I don't mind when they have a film about rich people. You can go and have a nice sit-down and take the weight off your feet and think: I wish that was me. But when they make pictures for people to laugh at, then they've had me and my money. I'll keep my money for the Americans. You don't take them serious, and anyway they don't laugh at people with different voices in America. That's because

America is all foreigners, the way I look at it, and they can't all laugh at each other, can they? Sometimes when I've got the 'ump I think I'll go to America and to hell with England, that's what I think, anyway.'

'You'd hate it in America,' I said.

'How do I know? Well, the way I look at it is, America must be like England was during the war.'

Rose, now she was depressed, talked about the war all the time. At this distance — it was 1950 now — those six years of hardship meant to her warmth, comradeship, a feeling of belonging and being wanted, a feeling she had never been given before or since. She could talk about the war for hours and never mention death, fear, food shortages or danger.

'Eight hundred people we were, in the factory. We got to know each other, by face, anyway. It was funny, everyone not knowing what'd happen next day, if their house was still standing or not, by the time they got home at nights, but at least we were all together, if you know what I mean. I used to be sorry for myself, with all the night work and everything. I used to say: When will the war be over — and not think it'd ever be over. But now I wish it was back. I don't mean the killing part of it, but I didn't know anyone who was killed, much, not much more than in peacetime — I mean, I know they were killed, but I didn't know them. But then people liked each other. You could talk to people, if you felt like it, even upper-class people, and no one would think the worse. You got to know people. You'd think about some lardyda person, they're not so bad, when you get to know them, they can't help it, poor sods, it's the way they're brought up. I remember when I got scared and raids were bad, I used to go down to the shelters and the air was foul, and I couldn't sleep and the ground was shaking all around, and I wished it would all end. But it was nice, too. You could talk to the man sitting next to you in the Underground at night, and share your blanket with him if he hadn't got one, and he never thought the worse. You'd say good-bye in the morning and you'd know you'd never see him again, but you'd feel nice all day, because he was friendly, and you was friendly too. See? And if I got real shook-up and frightened and I couldn't take the shelters, I used to go home to my mother. My stepfather was giving her hell, because he was dying of tuberculosis, only he was keeping it quiet, and we didn't know he was so ill, otherwise we'd have had more patience with the old so-and-so, but he wouldn't have me in the house, he said I was a bad girl, because of being out at nights after ten o'clock – he just made me laugh with his dirty mind. So I'd creep all quiet into mother's room and she'd lock the door and say she had a headache and we'd get under the bed on a mattress because of the bombs and we'd talk. It was company, see, with the Germans overhead and the bombs. And I'd hear that old so-and-so crying for my mother, and I'd think, sod him. Of course if I'd known his lungs were rotting on him with TB, I'd not have grabbed my mother when I had the chance, but I didn't know. If someone had told me I'd be glad to have the war back, I'd have laughed in their face. Now I think: That was a good time, say what you like. I earned eight pounds a week. Where am I going to earn eight pounds a week now? Lucky I had the sense to put some in the post office for my old age. Not that it'll be worth anything by then, the way money's melting to nothing week by week as we live. But I like to think I have something there. Without the war, I wouldn't. Yes, I know, dear, it's funny you can only get something nice these days when there's a war, but that's how things seem to me. People liked each other. Well, they don't now, do they? And so don't talk to me about your socialism, it just makes me sick and tired, and that's the truth.'

Chapter Four

I had come to England with pounds of tinned food in my trunk as to a starving country, prepared to tighten my belt and to suffer, as the newspapers back home continually assured us the British people were suffering. But I will always think of that house in terms of good eating. Not only was the whole place perfumed with the smells of feasting every evening. On Sundays there was a real feast, the emotional climax of the week.

On Sundays Mrs Skeffington cooked a roast and two veg for Mr Skeffington. On the floor above the Skeffingtons Miss Powell cooked a roast and two veg for Bobby Brent.

But in the basement preparations for Sunday dinner began on Saturday afternoon when Flo went to the market, assisted by Jack, and came back with baskets laden with food. By now she had appropriated my meat coupons and Rose's. It was understood we should all share Sunday's food. 'It's only right,' Flo said. 'All them cigarettes, and I'll never get round to paying you back, sweetheart. I don't know why it is, but there's something about cigarettes that's too much for me. Well, you just give me your meat ration, and you'll not be sorry. I swear it.'

On Sundays we all slept late. About twelve Flo knocked on my door and on Rose's, and said, smiling with pleasure: 'We're starting now. Come on down.'

In the basement, the children played on the floor among the puppies and the kittens, the men sat in their white singlets over the Sunday newspapers, and Flo and I and Rose began work.

'That Mrs Skeffington, that Miss Powell, they're cooking their roasts again,' Flo said. 'That's their week's ration gone and where's the sense. I've told them. I've told them over and over. But Mrs Skeffington, she says her husband kills her without he gets his roast Sundays. And Miss Powell's the same. Ah, my Lord, it's enough to make you cry, the waste of it.'

Meanwhile, Rose and I were preparing vegetables and beating butter and sugar.

'Ah, my Lord, but say what you like, I talk and I talk, but what can you do with this Government, no eggs, no meat, no fat, nothing but flour and water, and you expect me to cook with that?' Rose winked at me; Dan smiled over the edges of his paper.

'Yes, and look—' Here Flo flung open the doors of her food cupboard. 'See that? See that butter, for a whole week? The grocer couldn't give me extra, well, it's not my fault, is it now, if the food tastes of nothing at all.'

Flo had 'cooked English' until the year her Italian grand-mother came on a visit. It so happened that her mother had to go off unexpectedly to visit a relation in hospital. Flo and her grandmother were alone in the house together.

'And no sooner had she set foot on our soil, the old cow broke her leg. There she was, propped up stiff as a dead rabbit with her bum on one chair and her heels on another, groaning and carrying on, and saying: "I'm going to die." Die, my fanny. She'd the energy for a fifty-year-old, though she was seventy-nine and she'd lived out two husbands and one or two men on the side. She said: You look after me, my girl, or I won't give you permission to marry. I said: I'm married already, you old witch – that was my first husband, what died all those years ago – but I'll look after you. I wouldn't see my worst enemy die of starvation. We liked each other, see?' Flo interrupted herself in an explanatory way. 'Well, I put on my apron and cleaned up for her and cooked her dinner and she began to wail like a baby with a pin stuck in it. She said: I don't mind dying of a broken leg, if that's God's will – she was a Catholic, see? You mustn't mind that, everyone is in Italy, so she said, it's just a habit with them, like we have a Labour Government in with us. But I'm not going to die of your English cooking, she said.

116

You must learn to cook or your husband will die of it.'

'And what had you cooked?' asked Rose, playing her part in the tale.

'Fish and chips, like always.'

'What's wrong with fish and chips?' asked Dan, obediently, as Flo looked at him, waiting for him to contribute.

'What's wrong? Why, that's all I knew.'

'Best food in the world,' said Dan grinning.

'Yes, but you know better now, don't you, sweetheart?'

'You've just broken me in,' he said.

'My God, the ingratitude,' Flo said to me. 'Do you hear? When we started courting, he knew nothing but fish and chips. And when I cooked real food, like my granny taught me, he'd grumble, grumble, grumble, grumble. He'd come to the back of my kitchen in Holborn, and I'd feed him all the best bits, and he'd carry on like he was being poisoned.'

Dan nodded, and went on with the *News of the World*.

'But now he knows.'

'Eat what I'm given,' he said, grinning.

'Ah, my Lord, listen. Well, you can talk if you like, but I know you wouldn't go back to the old ways. Just as I wouldn't, once my granny had taught me. When she left to go back to Italy, hung in between two great black sticks with the gammy leg all crooked, like a witch she was, she said: Flo, she said, now you're fit to get married, she said. And I was married all the time. She didn't like my first husband and I don't blame her.'

Meanwhile, pots were bubbling all over the stove, and the oven was crammed.

'It's not going to be enough,' Flo said, anxiously, counting the dishes on her fingers.

'Don't be silly,' said Rose. 'We'll burst as it is.'

'No, it won't. I think I'll just run up a little pie, and if there's no room for it, it'll hot up for supper.'

At about half past two, the men cleared the long table of newspapers and laid places. The two children were sat up side by side, with napkins around their necks. 'Yes, that's right,' Flo would say. 'Make Peter sit by Oar. Perhaps the way he eats'll be an example to Oar. Oar, you see how Peter eats his food so nice? You do, too. Ah, my God, that I should be punished with a kid that won't eat.'

It was true, Aurora did not eat. She sat through the long feasts, watching everyone else eat. When one of her parents pushed some food into her mouth, she let it stay there, until they shouted at her, when she might swallow it, but more often spat it out again.

We began with rich vegetable soup, flavoured with herbs. Flo never used a recipe book. Her soups were always invented out of whatever materials lay around. Then we ate great mounds of spaghetti, or ravioli, or giant macaroni sticks stuffed with meat and herbs. By then we were all groaning and saying we could not eat another mouthful.

'There's no hurry,' Flo said, beaming with pleasure because of our enjoyment. 'No hurry in the world. We'll have a little rest now.' We leaned our elbows on the table and smoked a while, while Flo cleared the table for the next course. That would always be a small piece of roasted meat, because as she said: 'It's a waste of good rations, but just once a week we must remember what Sunday dinner is.' We all ate small herb-flavoured slices of meat; a kind of vestigial reminder of the traditional British Sunday meal.

Then came a great bowl of fresh salad.

'Yes, you eat plenty of that, dear,' Flo said. 'There's nothing like salad for emptying your stomach so there's more room for what's coming next.'

At the right moment, she whisked off the salad, and served delicate flaky pies, filled with creamed spinach, or leeks, or onions. These went with the weekly ration of tasteless corned beef, which she had cooked up with chips of potato and rich blackened onions. Or she would stuff cabbage and lettuce leaves with a paste made of rye bread and herbs and gravy and serve it with mounds of rice cooked so subtly flavoured one could have eaten it alone.

'And now stop it, Flo,' Rose said. We had all loosened our belts or undone our waist hooks, and sat helplessly, unable to move.

'Ah, my Lord, but it's Sunday – and, Dan, what's that smell? You tell me.'

118

Dan would obediently sniff. 'Rosemary? Thyme? Saffron? Garlic? Coriander?'

'Ah, you make me laugh, that's mint. Look I've got these new potatoes fresh from the market yesterday.' And she would slide in before us a flat dish with tiny new potatoes, swimming in butter and mint. 'Have some. Yes, you must. When'll we see new potatoes like that again in our lives? What with this Government there might be no food at all, at any minute.'

Then, another lull. The smell of strong coffee began to overpower the other smells. The table was cleared for the coffee cups, and as Flo filled our cups and handed us cream, she put proudly before us her fruit tart that her grandmother had taught her. No English fruit tart this, but a flat base of rich buttery biscuit, piled high with raspberries, strawberries, redcurrants and sliced peaches.

'Ma, I'm dead,' Jack would announce, stuffing in fruit and gulping down coffee.

'Well, Flo, you'll never better today,' Rose would say, caressing her stomach with both hands.

'Flo, you're the best cook I've ever known,' I'd say.

And Dan would finally get up and stretch himself, and say: 'And now for some real food. Where's my fish and chips?'

'Ah, get along,' Flo said, delighted, absorbing our grateful admiration and smiling. 'Get along with all of you. If you like what I cook, then that's all I ask. And there sits Oar, all this time, not a mouthful taken, what shall I do?'

This would be the signal for either Rose or Dan to take the child on to their laps, and try and fill her mouth by force. Aurora sat, quite passive, watching her mother, who stood across the room, hands on her hips, anxiously watching this operation. When her two cheeks were bulging out like a monkey's, she leaned over and emptied her mouth on to a plate; then shut her lips tight against the invading spoon wielded by her father or by Rose.

'Well, I don't know, dear,' Flo would say helplessly to me. 'How do you acount? After all, I cook nice, don't I?'

'Flo, you're the queen of cooks.'

'Then why doesn't my Oar ever eat a mouthful?'

'Just don't bother. If you don't bother, she'll eat.'

'Ah, listen to you. Don't bother, she says. Oar'd let herself die of starvation and not even notice. Oar, have a little mouthful of something, darling, sweetheart, just to please your mother, please, Oar.' Aurora, already on the floor with my son and the puppies, would frown, stiffening up her mouth. If Flo persisted, she would let out her routine roar of protest, and go right on playing, her lips pinched together against the threat of food.

'Oh, leave her,' Rose said.

'Then we'll wash up.'

We women washed up. It was now about four or five in the afternoon. The men were putting on overalls and getting tools and paint out. Sunday was a hard-working day for everyone. Dan and Jack went off to paint the walls of the stairs, or fix a door. Meanwhile, Flo and Rose got out buckets and brushes and began scrubbing.

'We're too full to move,' Flo said, every Sunday. 'But all that food. We've got to work it off. That's right, Rose. You clean out the oven. Because it's not fit to cook in, the way it's full of grease and smells, and how can I cook supper for tonight the way it is?'

'You don't think we're going to eat again today?' Rose said.

'Those men'll be down, you see, seven or eight, and they won't say no to my fish stew, with my garlic and my onions, you'll see.'

And later that night, about eleven, there would be a second meal, and again we ate, and ate, and ate.

'That's right,' Rose would say, as we staggered upstairs to bed. 'You eat what's offered. And besides, we've got to eat proper just once in the week. Though, of course, now you're here all the time, I suppose Flo feeds you up in the week, too.'

'No, she doesn't. She doesn't cook for herself.'

'Then what does she do with herself, I'd like to know. Because if she's not cooking, she's too stupid to live.'

Rose was bitter about Flo at this time, on two counts. For

120

one thing, because she herself was miserable and self-punishing, she was allowing herself to be exploited badly. Flo would come up the stairs at ten at night, and although Rose had bathed and was clean for bed, she would go down and scrub and wash for Flo when asked – grimly, silently, but without protest. 'If she hasn't got any conscience, making me slave for her, then that's her lookout, not mine.'

The more Rose was depressed, the more she sank under Flo's thumb.

The second reason was that now I had given up my job and was spending my time writing. Or trying to write; for I was discovering that coming to England had disturbed me, and it was going to take some time to get started again. But I was in the house with Flo. And Rose said: 'So now it means you'll be Flo's friend, not my friend.'

'I don't see why,' I said.

'It stands to reason. Before you worked. You were like me. But now you're like Flo, sitting around at home and talking.'

'But I'm trying to work.'

'Yes? Well, it's not your fault. But all the same, it makes me sad. I used to like our talks at night, but now you're not tired any more and you go off to the theatre.'

'Why don't you come too? I don't like going by myself.'

'Yes? Why should I go to the theatre? Yes, I know, I went to a play once. Dickie took me. Well, you can keep it. It had what they called a working woman in it, carrying on and making everyone laugh. Well, if you want to go and laugh at things you should know better about, I'm not stopping you. Besides, if I come with you. I might be out some evening when Dickie comes around to see me.'

'It'd do him good to find you out.'

'You think so? Well, I'm working on a plan for making him jealous, proper. When I've fixed everything I'll tell you. But, meantime, don't you let Flo turn you against me, I'm warning you.'

'She never tries to turn me against you.'

'Yes? I know the kind of thing she says. It makes me blush even to think.'

'There's no need.'

'Yes? I know Flo.'

'Well, I know Flo, too, and she's very fond of you.'

'There you are, you're on her side already. Fond! the words you use.'

'But Rose, you know she is.'

'Well, never mind. All I know is she makes me sick and so does everybody. Take no notice of me, dear. I just wish I was dead and buried and when she starts all winking and grinning out of the wrong side of her mouth about Dickie I wish I could hit her.'

Flo's life was spent in the basement. She and Aurora were confined there, with the doors and windows shut, the fire burning winter and summer, the lights burning even at midday. The radio poured out words and music at full blast. When I turned the radio down, Flo became uneasy, although she never actively listened to any programme. I had understood by now that she was lonely; something hard to accept when one looked at these houses from outside, knowing them to be crammed with people.

But here she was, alone all day with the radio and Aurora. She took the child out every afternoon to do the shopping, but for the rest, they relied on each other for company. When I lived in similarly crowded places in that other continent, where every family, no matter how poor, has black servants, the woman and children flowed together like tadpoles the moment the men left for work; and the family units were only defined again by their return.

In the mornings I crept downstairs with my rubbish-can, hoping that the din from the radio would prevent her from hearing me. But it was not a question of hearing. Flo knew by instinct exactly what was happening everywhere in the house, and she flung open the door, spilling out cats and dogs like articles from an over-full cupboard and said, with the dramatic expression of one who expected to see a burglar: 'Oh, it's you, dear, is it? Come and have a nice cup of tea.' If I said I was busy she looked so disappointed, I gave in.

Aurora was always standing on the table in her night-gown, crying with temper, with a plate of food at her feet.

'You can stay up there until you eat it,' Flo yelled. 'I'm not having any of your nonsense.' That was about ten in the morning, the time Flo got out of bed. Aurora, who had gone to sleep at eleven or twelve the night before, was still blinking and drowsy in between her fits of screaming. 'It's driving me nuts,' Flo said every morning. 'This kid never eats.' And she would grab Aurora and hustle her into a chair. 'Eat! Eat!' she commanded, glaring down, her hands on her hips. The food was left over from the night before; warmed-over spaghetti perhaps, or a bit of meat pie with cold chips. Flo explained it was no use cooking anything proper for a child who didn't eat it in any case. This daily scene once over – both sides took it as a necessary routine – Flo handed Aurora a bottle; and until mid-afternoon, when they went out to shop, the three-year-old child would wander about the basement in her night-gown, hair in curlers, sucking at her bottle, and taking no notice at all of her mother's screams: 'Get out of my way. For God's sake, get out of my way.' The place was so crowded that Aurora was in fact always 'under Flo's feet'. This pair of prisoners were bored to the point where they exploded several times a day in a violent scene, Flo cuffing and slapping Aurora and Aurora biting and scratching in self-defence so that the screams and yells reverberated through the building. Yet it seemed that this violence was of a different quality from Mrs Skeffington's with her child; because beneath the apparent mutual hatred was a sub-stratum of something warm and friendly. Flo would look down at his scrap of humanity for whom she was responsible with a look of comic bewilderment, as if she were thinking: 'What sort of trick has fate played on me?' And she'd say: 'I don't understand it, I don't really. All those years I was running that restaurant, no trouble at all, but this kid beats me and that's a fact.'

It seemed to me that Aurora understood quite well this process that Flo herself referred to as 'letting off steam', because at one moment these two females would be screaming and tussling, and the next, exhausted but amicable, they rested in each other's arms, Aurora grinning with a tear-smeared face; and Flo, a cigarette drooping from the corner of her mouth over the child's head saying over and over again: 'Oh, my Lord, it's all too much for me, Oar, I wish you'd grow up a bit and then we'd get on better, I'm telling you.'

At regular intervals a women referred to by Flo as 'that interfering busybody from the Welfare' would descend, to find Flo, bland as butter, serving tea and her wonderful cake, and Aurora dressed to kill in organdie and white ribbons. If anyone was there, Flo would direct, over the woman's head, a profound and cynical wink. 'Yes, dear; oh, yes, I know, dear,' she said in response to every piece of advice from the expert. 'I did what you said, but she's so naughty . . .' Her hand extended automatically towards a slap, and withdrew itself again; for Flo sensed that Welfare would not approve of slapping.

'You don't have to let her in,' I said, watching her frantically getting herself and Aurora ready, for the enemy had been observed going into a house three doors down to visit the child whose name was on the list before Aurora's.

'What do you mean? She's Government, isn't she? It's the Labour that inflicted all these bitches on us.'

'The Tories, too, when they get back.'

'Lord let me see the day. But they'd never want to wear us out with all them nosey-parkers.'

'You wait and see. And, besides, aren't you pleased about the Health Service?'

'I never said anything against that, did I?'

'That was Labour.' She was sceptical. 'It was, too.'

'If you say so, dear,' she said at last, with the weary good nature which meant she was going to humour me.

When we knew Welfare was on the way, Flo always waited until the last moment in her bedroom, clutching Aurora by the hand, so as to make an entrance while I opened the outer door, from a room which was the apotheosis of a bedroom. The suite had cost nearly two hundred pounds, was being paid for on hire purchase, and was all beige-coloured varnish, highlighted with gilt. As Flo said, it would give Welfare a nice impression, to see her and Oar, all in their best, coming out of a fancy room. 'And I'll leave the door so she can fill her eyes with our new eiderdown. That'll show her.'

The eiderdown was electric-blue satin and about a yard thick. It was never used to sleep under. At nights Flo wrapped it in an old blanket and put it away until she made the bed next day.

When I had opened the door for Welfare, I was expected to excuse myself and go upstairs. 'It makes me nervous,' Flo said, 'with you there, and me trying to keep her happy. The Lord knows what she'll think up next. Do you know, she said it was wrong for Oar to sleep in the same room as Dan and me?'

'Perhaps she's right.'

'Are you laughing at your Flo? My Lord, the things they think up. And she said last time Oar's teeth had to come out, they were rotting in her head.'

'Well, they are.'

'Yes, dear, but they're baby teeth and they'll fall out of themselves, the trouble they give themselves these people. Well, she's got to earn a living, hasn't she, I don't hold it against her.'

Once she asked Welfare if Aurora could go to a council nursery. But the reply was that Flo had a nice home and it was better for small children to be with their mothers. Besides, the council nurseries were closing down. 'Women marry to have children,' said the official when Flo said she was trained for restaurant work and wanted to go back to it – the truth was she planned to help with Bobby Brent's night-club.

'Women here and women there,' said Flo, when Welfare had gone. 'She's a woman herself, so you might think, only if she's got a pussy I bet she wouldn't know what to do with it; and there she is, talking about women. Sometimes I wish there was another war, I do really. All sugar and spice then, they don't talk about *women* then. Not them. Red-tape-and-scissors would be talking different. Are you doing your bit for your country, dear? she'd be saying to me. Don't worry a little bit about your dear little baby, she'd say. We'll look after her. I'd like to have her shut up here seven days a week

125

with a saucepan in her hand and a brat driving her mad with not eating, and a husband at her day and night. Mind you, a man'd do her good. Take some of the starch out of her tongue, for one thing.' She giggled, clapping her hand over her mouth. 'Ah, my Lord, can you see her with her nice little voice and her nice little face all prim and straight telling her husband – Women get married to have children, poor man, well, I'm sorry for him.'

But as Flo could not get a place in a nursery, Welfare's remark became ammunition against Mrs Skeffington. If Flo wanted to be unpleasant, she would climb the stairs to the Skeffingtons' flat and say: 'Some people get rid of their kids into a nursery. A decent woman looks after her children herself.'

Inside the flat immediately fell a defensive silence, the silence of the tenant who fears more than anything else in this world, a week's notice.

Flo would then descend the two flights, fling open my door and say: 'I didn't mean you, darling. You're different.'

'I don't see why.'

'It stands to reason. Did you see Mr Skeffington's dressing-gown this morning? All purple and silk and everything?'

When I had finished drinking tea with Flo in the mornings I would begin the fight for my right to work.

'I was ever so glad when I knew you were stopping working,' she said, every morning, with sorrowful reproach. 'I thought I would have some company for a change. Everybody works in this house, except that Miss Powell, if you can call that work.' Here she grinned, delightedly. 'I wouldn't mind if that was my only work, would you, dear?' But Flo did not waste her gifts in the mornings. For enjoyment she must have a larger audience. There had not only to be someone capable of being shocked – and for that purpose I was useful, for when I didn't show shock, she'd say impatiently: Now I've upset you, dear, I know it – go on, blush! – but there had also to be an accomplice with whom she could share amusement at the innocent's discomfort. So now she contented herself with murmuring: 'If someone would pay me for kicking up my heels.'

'But now I really do have to work.'

'Who's to make you?'

Flo was incapable of understanding that ordinary people, whom she might know, could write something which would in due course become a book. She would finger a pile of typescript and say: 'You say this is a book, dear?' Then she fetched a pile of women's magazines and said: 'You mean a book like this?' 'No, a book like this,' showing her one.

'Well, I don't hold it against you.'

When at last I got a book printed, she compared the lines of print with the words in a heap of typescript and crowed delightedly, 'Why darling, it's the same.' 'But, Flo, I kept telling you.' 'I don't hold it against you, don't think that.'

At first I thought the phrase 'I don't hold it against you', was the same as the middle-class 'Not at all', or 'Very well'. But I was wrong, because at that time I failed to understand the depths of her disapproval and disappointment in me.

Every morning when I had finished my tea, and was fighting my way backwards to the door, kicking puppies out of my way and defending myself with both hands against Flo's imploring hands, which sought to grasp and hold me like a shield against the long day's loneliness, she would eventually sigh out: 'Well, I don't really blame you.' Whenever it was a question of me or anyone else working, even Dan, she didn't really blame us. If I went to the theatre she didn't hold it against me. But going to the library twice a week earned a long, incredulous silence and the words 'I don't blame you' were brought out with real difficulty. But at last she forgave me for the books, because she took to fingering the books on my shelf and saying: 'I suppose you've got to have all this rubbish to find plots. I wouldn't have it in my place, it just collects dust, but I don't hold it against you.' In the course of the year I stayed in that house I went into most of the houses in the street, and there was not a book in one of them. That is not quite true. Two houses down on the opposite side lived an old man on the old-age pension, who was reading for the first time in his life. He was educating himself on the *Thinker's Library*. He had been a bricklayer, his wife was dead and he was now half-crazy with loneliness and the necessity to communicate what he had so slowly and belatedly learned. He lingered on the pavement at the time people were coming home from work, made a few routine remarks about the weather, and then whispered confidentially: 'There's no God. We aren't anything but apes. They don't tell the working man in case we get out of hand.'

Once it was Dan and he stared suspiciously and remarked: 'There's no God, you say?' 'That's right, that's right, I read it today.' 'Well, who cares, I don't.' Once it was Rose, and she said with good humour: 'Well, if you want to be a monkey, I'm not stopping you.'

A sternly shut door was no protection against Flo. If I stopped typing for longer than five minutes, there were steps on the stairs, then a loud 'Shut up, Oar!' and then Flo's face appeared around the angle of the door, Aurora's face just beneath it, two faces, wreathed in smiles and apparently without bodies. Flo ran forward saying: 'Don't be cross, darling, I know it must be lonely for you here. Just give me a cigarette and I'll sit and watch.'

At last I learned to work while she was there, or while Aurora played on the floor. She played differently from the normal child of her age. All her games were centred around the long mirror. She made faces at herself, sticking out her tongue and rolling up her eyes; or smiled sweetly, or with a leer. She took a cushion and held it to her stomach, or laid it to her behind and minced up and down the room, watching her reflection. She tried on my shoes, wrapped my clothes around herself, or took off her dress and stood examining her scrawny little body. She would take a pinch of flesh between thumb and finger on her chest and say to herself: 'Titties, where are my titties, I can see them, yes.' Or she would pull her long black corkscrew curls out one by one, like springs, and watch them leap back into position. This game she could play for an hour at a time, standing quite still, frowning with steady concentration at her image, watching the black curls lengthen, straighten, and spring back, again and again and again.

I tried to get her to eat, but without success. No matter

how casual my preparations were – fetching tea and cake for us both, cooking eggs, handing her her plate without comment, she would stiffen up and watch me, with the small, knowing grown-up smile which was so disconcerting.

Or she would sit on the floor, sucking her thumb, without moving, her black, sharp eyes fixed on me. Once I came into the room and caught her mimicking me. She was sitting at the typewriter, frowning absorbedly, smoking an imaginary cigarette. When she saw me she smiled, a wise, amused smile, as if to say: We both know you're funny. She jumped politely off the chair, and sat on the floor again, sucking her thumb, watching me.

It was through Aurora that I first understood Jack's position in the family. I had taken him for granted, I suppose, because Rose did.

He used to wander in and out of my room like Aurora, or like the puppies and the cats. He took very little notice of me, or I of him. The only person he responded to was Rose, outside his parents. He was totally self-absorbed – that is, absorbed in fantasy, like Aurora; and, like her, spent a great deal of time in front of the looking-glass. He was very good-looking, sleek, smooth-fleshed, swarthy. His shoulders and arms were heavily muscled, but he was dissatisfied with his chest and with his legs. There was every opportunity of seeing all of him, because he never wore anything but a singlet and running shorts, once he was out of working clothes, even in the coldest weather. He wandered about the house, flexing and stretching himself, accosting people with remarks like: 'If I got another half-inch on my calves I'd do all right, do you think so?'

He spent a good deal of time in Miss Powell's room. She tolerated him, but took care Bobby Brent did not catch him there; he was, of course, very jealous of her. When Miss Powell was busy, he came to rest on my floor, surrounded by physical culture magazines. He never paid for these. If Jack said he was going to the fish-and-chips this had nothing to do with food. He leaned on the counter of the shop, calm-eyed, gum-chewing, until the man turned his back to take the chips from the fat, and then Jack slipped out the physical culture magazines from the pile of old papers which were kept for wrapping the fish-and-chips. He paid threepence for a cornet of chips, and came home with a week's reading matter.

When Rose was in my room he alternately watched her, with a despondent hopefulness, and read his magazines. Or he stood in front of the mirror measuring himself all over with a tape-measure, repeating: 'If I had thirty shillings I could buy myself some weights.'

'Who do you think's going to give you thirty bob?' Rose would say.

'I only said, if I had thirty bob, that's all, why do you pick on me, everybody does?' he grumbled.

He went a great deal to the pictures, and came straight back to tell me the plots. Sometimes he saw two or three films in one evening. If the film was a musical, he sang the lyrics and showed me the steps of the dances. He was a natural dancer and had a good voice. Whether it was a musical or a gangster picture, he always ended: 'And that showed she loved him, see?' Or, with a pathetic look at Rose: 'And then it was time for bed.'

Then he complained about his parents: Flo's temper frightened him, she was a bad mother to him. And Dan hated him and wished he was dead.

The only person Aurora admitted to her fantasies was Jack. She would arrange a cushion on a chair in a convenient position, find some hard object, and stab to or beat it over and over again. 'Dead. Dead. Dead,' I heard her murmur viciously.

'Who's dead?'

She had the deaf look all the people in the house seemed to assume at such moments.

'Dead. He's dead. Dead. Jack's dead. My daddy's happy. Mommy's crying. Jack's dead.'

Once Rose came up at midnight, and said: 'My God, are those two at it downstairs?'

'What about?'

'Jack. Dan's silly about him. He says Jack doesn't earn enough money.'

Jack was a sort of errand-boy for a big local shop. He earned five pounds a week. He referred to the firm as 'my company'. He wanted to be a professional footballer. He had played football for 'his company' and for the army, too. He could get ten pounds a week as a professional, he said. If he became a swimming coach, then he could earn eleven, he knew a place. Or he could be a physical instructor. The sky was the limit for them, he said, all the money you liked.

'It's like this,' said Rose. 'Dan earns all that money, and he can't see why Jack can't. He doesn't see, some people can earn money like other people breathe. Well, Jack just pays Flo thirty shillings, the way I do, and spends the rest on the pictures. But Flo keeps slipping him money when Dan's not looking. And so they quarrel all the time. You should hear them. Dan says it's a matter of principle. Ha, Dan talking about principles, its enough to make a queen laugh.'

Dan worked for the local gas board. But he regarded the money he earned there as peanuts. Going into people's houses and flats to fit appliances or fix the gas was useful to him, and that was why he kept the job. The way he made his money was not exactly illegal – 'Not really illegal, darling,' as Flo said, anxious I should approve, 'not so much that as using your intelligence.' He went into bombed houses and stripped them of anything saleable, working at night, so as not to be noticed, and disposed of what he found. He would say casually to a householder: 'That wash-basin, that bath, it's not up to much, is it? – not for a house of this class. Now I tell you what, I can get you a new bath, three pounds cheaper than what you'd pay.'

He had connections with the building trade, because he had worked in all branches of it at various times. It was easy for him to get a bath, a wash-basin, a lavatory pan at cost price. This new object would be installed, and he'd make a small profit. 'This old bath's no good to you,' he'd tell the householder, 'you'd have to pay to get it taken away.' The backyard was always full of baths, wash-basins, cisterns, lavatory pans, and tangles of piping. Then, while fixing a gas leak or mending a refrigerator, Dan would say: 'That old bath of yours, it's not up to the standard of the rest, is it? I tell you what, I'll get you another. Just as good as new – a factory reject. It got a bit scratched in the enamel, and I'll do it two-thirds of the usual price.'

One week I know for a fact Dan earned fifty-odd pounds in this way, over and above his wage and the rents for the house.

'Do you know what?' Rose said. 'That Dan, he's just working-dirt like me, and I know his mum and his dad live on the old age pension and nothing over. But he's the new rich. Well, isn't he? I don't envy him his conscience and that's the truth.'

For a week the quarrels in the basement were so bad that Jack and Rose spent all their evenings with me. Sometimes Jack went out to lean over the banisters and listen. 'Still at it,' he said, settling himself back on my floor. Rose went down on occasional reconnaissance trips and came back to say: 'Hammer and tongs. Well, they've only been married three years, so what can you expect.'

'It's still about me,' said Jack, with satisfaction.

'Don't flatter yourself. It's about Bobby Brent. Flo wants to put Oar in a paying nursery, since they can't get a Council nursery, but Dan says a woman's place is in the home.'

At this we all laughed, even Jack.

'The way I look at it is this. When married people quarrel about something, they're usually quarrelling about something else they don't like to mention, if you understand me. I bet I know what's eating Dan.'

'I know, too,' said Jack. 'All he wants is to kill me, but he can't understand he wants me for witness for his case.'

'What case?' I said.

'I spoke out of turn,' said Rose. 'I promised Flo. She'll tell you in her own good time. And what makes it worse is, Flo's flying the red flag this week, and so they can't make it up in bed. So there's no peace for any of us the next three days, the way I reckon it.'

'Ah, shut up,' said Jack.

'And who's talking? Prim and proper. Well, who was knocking at my door last night just because Flo set him on?'

A couple of days later the quarrels had got so bad that Jack was white-faced, and Rose softened enough to put her arms around him. 'Poor little boy, poor baby,' she said, half-derisive, half-tender. 'Don't cry. Peace will reign any minute now, you'll see.'

It was a Sunday morning. Suddenly, from one moment to the next, silence fell downstairs, save for the sound of the radio.

Aurora came in. She was sucking her bottle.

'You're working,' she said.

'That's right.'

'Mommy and Daddy are working, too.' She helped herself to a large handful of sweets, exactly as her mother helped herself to cigarettes, with a quick guilty look and a smile of triumph she could not suppress. 'They're working on the bed. Like this.' She began bouncing up and down on her stomach on the floor. After a minute she turned her head to watch herself bouncing in the long mirror. 'Like this,' she murmured.

In about an hour Flo appeared. Her eyes were red with past crying, and she was laughing. 'Why, is Oar with you?' she exclaimed in beautiful surprise. But she couldn't keep it up. She sat down, taking a cigarette, and said: 'Dan and me nearly split up, but now it's all over. Don't go, I said to Dan. The trouble with you is, you're not used to a decent woman and her ways. I'm not like the women you're used to – he's had black, white, green, pink, and yellow, all over the world, being in the Navy, dear. But I'm different, see? I said to him: If you shout at me, and use your fists, I'll just go right out and get a job and leave you to manage Oar. That'd fix you, that would.'

Aurora seemed pleased at this possibility. 'Is my Dad going to look after me,' she enquired.

'Oh, you,' said Flo, slapping at her vaguely. Aurora sucked philosophically at her bottle and listened.

'Give the bastards what they want, that's all. He's a hot one and no mistake. Have it every night if he could. But I play tired. Even when I wouldn't mind. I think to myself, laughing away in the dark: Let the sod wait, do them good, or they take you for granted. I learned that with my first husband, not that he was much good, not a patch on Dan. Dan gets so mad I hear him wriggling and growling away on the other side of the bed.' She laughed out loud, like a young girl, clapping her hands to her kneecaps. She noticed Aurora suddenly, and flung her arms out and gathered the child to her. 'You love your mummy, darling, don't you, sweetheart.' Aurora went on sucking at the bottle. 'Of course you love your mother,' said Flo, firmly, letting her go again. She sat loosely, hands dangling, smiling peacefully to herself. 'Well, and so now Dan and I are already laughing at ourselves for quarrelling. Now, if Rose had any sense . . .'

'You tell her yourself.'

'Oh, she won't listen to me. She's so grumpy these days, I can't say a word. But Dickie's Dan's brother. They're like as two peas, for all that Dickie's a civilian, so to speak, just selling things behind a counter and my Dan's from the Navy, and that makes a man, say what you like. But I keep telling Rose, when she's listening, if you want a man you've got to go about it proper. She plays cold with Dickie so he gets fed-up. Now you tell her, any real friend of hers would do right and tell her.'

'She doesn't like talking about it,' I said.

'She doesn't know anything, let alone talking. I know. Many the times I've gone to bed early with Dan and left them alone and sent Jack to the pictures, but all I hear is a giggle and a slap, and he goes home with his hands in his pockets. So she's only got herself to blame he's got another woman.'

Now although Rose made jokes about Dickie's having another girl she believed that he was being as faithful to her as she to him.

'You'd better not tell her that,' I said.

'No. With her ideas she'd throw him over, I wouldn't be surprised. Mad. Well, if Rose wants to get him she'd better make up her mind to . . .' She watched my face. 'Now you're shocked,' she said. 'That's right, dear.' And she added another juicy image like a chemist dropping a precipitant into a test-tube. 'Go on, you must have the 'ump tonight. You are shocked, aren't you?' And she automatically glanced around for the necessary person to make this particular pleasure really satisfactory. But there was only Aurora. 'What are you listening for?' she demanded, slapping the child across the mouth. Aurora stretched her mouth across her face in a scream, and immediately fell silent, sucking at the bottle.

'That girl doesn't know nothing about life. A friend is what she needs to tell her. You don't think that bastard downstairs'd've married me if I'd hidden it, do you? Not he. They like to know what they're getting. Beasts. That's what they are. They're not like us at all, dear, not really.' She began to roar with laughter, holding both her hips and rocking side to side. 'Well, it's just as well they're not – oh, don't mind me, I like to laugh, and sometimes I think there's nobody but me in the house knows how to, there's you, all working and serious, and there's Rose, like a wet rag, and there's Jack, well, I really don't know, so I like to laugh and make you happy.'

At this point Dan bellowed up the stairs for his dinner, and exactly as if I could not have heard him, Flo murmured politely: 'Well, I can see you want to go on working. I don't blame you, dear, not at all.' She grabbed Aurora by the arm and demanded: 'What are you doing here stopping the lady from working?' Aurora went quite limp, and Flo shook her like a rag doll, saying: 'Ah, my Lord, and who would have a child?' She pulled the unresisting child, who was still sucking at the bottle, along the floor and out of the room. Aurora took her bottle out to grin at me as she was pulled round the side of the door.

Rose came in. 'What did Flo say about me?'

'You know what she said.'

'So what did you say?'

'I told her to tell you herself.'

'I suppose you agree with her. Well, I'm telling you both that if that's all he cares about me, then he can lump it.'

'Meanwhile, you haven't seen each other in weeks and everyone takes it for granted you'll get married.'

'Well, so I should think. If he doesn't I'll take him to court for breach of promise.'

'I bet you wouldn't.'

'I bet I wouldn't either. I wouldn't give him that satisfaction. The trouble with him is, he doesn't know what's good for him. No one with sense likes living in a furnished room when they can have their own home. There he is, sharing a room with two other men, playing poker and never eating proper. That's really why he cooled off, see? I told him it was time we got married. Flo with her dirty mind, she thinks it's because I wouldn't give him what he wanted.'

Rose's unhappiness had now reached the point where she could not rouse herself to go down to the basement to eat. She drank cup after cup of tea in my room, heaping in the sugar and saying it was food. When hunger assailed her so that she really couldn't ignore it, she went out for sixpence-worth of fish and chips. Even in this low condition her natural fastidiousness stayed with her: she was a connoisseur of fish-and-chip shops, knowing every shop within a mile. She would take a bus to a place that used good oil, and fried the fish the way she liked it. But having taken all this trouble, she would push across the packet to me, and say: 'I don't fancy it.'

'But you've got to eat sometime.'

'What for, I'd like to know?'

She had grown so thin that her skirts were folded at the back with safety-pins, and her face was set permanently into folds of grief, so that she looked like a woman of forty.

Meanwhile, Flo had worked on Dan, who had told Dickie that Rose was pining for him. One dinner time Dickie marched into the jeweller's shop with a covered plate of salad and salad cream, which he knew Rose liked, and placed it aggressively on the counter in front of her. He told Dan afterwards he intended this as a peace-offering; but Rose, without looking at him, carefully wrapped plate and food in newspaper, and went to the back of the shop where she slid it into the rubbish bin. She then returned to the counter where Dickie was waiting, and resumed her former position, palms resting downwards, staring past him into the street. At which he swore at her and went out again.

That evening my radio was playing: 'Try a Little Tenderness' and she burst into tears. 'Men are all mad,' she told me. 'What's he think he's doing, throwing food at me like I was something in the zoo.' She went into her room and tossed Dickie's photograph into the waste-paper basket. Half an hour later she put it back on her table, saying: 'Well, I suppose you're born stupid, you can't help it.' Rose talked to that photograph as if to Dickie himself. When I went into her room, she might be sitting with a towel pinned around her shoulders, making up, chatting softly to him thus: 'Yes. And here I sit, wasting my time powdering my nose. Do you even notice if I put a new dress on? Not you. All you notice is, if I don't look well, you complain about that fast enough.' The photograph was of a hard-faced, arrogant man – Dan without Dan's good nature.

Night after night Rose sat slumped into my big leather chair, sometimes until long after everyone else had gone to bed, which in that house was very late. She would not hear if I spoke to her. She lay back with her eyes closed, and under her eyes were heavy black bruises. If she spoke, it was to grumble steadily in a monologue: 'On my feet all day with that blasted Jewess. I said to her today, Look who does the work, you or me? Then get off that chair. Or buy another chair. Can't you afford five bob for a chair? Can you believe it, she won't get another chair into the shop in case I sit on it. She likes to think of me wearing out my feet for the money. And as for that husband of hers . . .' Rose was always anti-Semitic, in a tired tolerant sort of way. She was convinced that 'the Jews' were all like her employers, who were the only Jewish people she had ever met. But now she was depressed, she talked like a minor Goebbels, and it was queer and frightening to hear the violent ugly phrases in Rose's flat, good-natured, grumbling voice. 'But I got even with him today. I called him a dirty Jew to his face. He didn't like that. I said, I know about you, don't think I don't. You eat babies, you do, if the Government doesn't keep an eye on you.'

'You don't really believe that, do you?'

'I'll believe it if I want to. I'd believe anything of that pair.'

'Then I'm not going to listen.'

'Please yourself. But I'll sit here a bit, if you don't mind. I've got the 'ump.' Incidentally the aitch in 'ump was the only one she ever dropped; the radio had made her self-conscious. She even said: 'I've got so silly, listening to those lardy-das on the wireless, if I drop an aitch I go right back and pick it up again.' But having the 'ump was a recognized spiritual condition; Rose dropped the aitch humorously, as a middle-class person might.

I began to read. Rose watched me. I suggested it might be better if she read, instead of worrying about Dickie.

'What I want is a book to tell me how to get sense into a man's head.'

A few evenings later we were walking back from the pictures when she stooped to pick up a paperback that had been dropped on the pavement. 'Oooh, look,' she said derisively. The picture on the cover was of a woman in a low-cut white satin dress, leaning back against a table in a state of urgent defence, clutching at the folds of her dress. 'Look at that,' said Rose. 'She's as good as being raped, but she's got time to worry about keeping her clothes clean.' The man in the picture looked as if he were biting the woman's ear. 'That's a man all over,' Rose said. 'He's going to bite her ear off if she doesn't give him what he wants. That's love all right. I'm going to read it.' She read the book as we walked home, remarking 'Just push me the way I should go. I can't keep my eyes off this, and that's a fact.'

At home she arranged herself in my big chair and said: 'Just make a nice cup of tea and don't talk. I want to see if Lady Godiva gets into bed or not.' From time to time she'd look up to say: 'He's just given her a watch with diamonds. He loves her for herself, he says.' 'Now she's his secretary. She wants to help him with his career.' Late that night she left my room saying: 'We're up to page 97, and he's already given her chocolates, a watch, a car and a mink coat. She'd better watch out. Well, I'll finish it tomorrow night, so don't you decide to go out. I like to have company when I read.'

Next evening she snuggled herself into my chair with the book. I said: 'If you like those books, why don't you buy some?'

'What, waste money on this silly stuff? No, it came my way, as you might say, so I don't mind. Besides, it's giving me ideas about putting sense into Dickie's head.' At midnight she put the book down with a yawn. 'Well, believe it or not, they got married in the end. They didn't get into bed until the last page either. He said, your beautiful body, and she said: I want to feel your strong arms about me. I could do with a pair of strong arms myself, after all that. But I tell you what, I've got an idea. You remember I said about my policeman? But it's all right thinking about it, when it gets to saying yes to going out with him, I can't bring myself. But if I get off a little with Jack, Flo'll tell Dickie, and no harm done. I can handle Jack.'

'Don't you be too sure.'

'He's a kid. But I've learned a thing or two from this book. She got diamonds and mink coats all right, but no ring, not until she played him up proper.'

Rose descended thoughtfully to the basement. A few minutes later there were yells and raucous laughter from Flo. Rose ran upstairs, chased by Jack.

'Go on,' he said, 'what're you scared of?'

'Think I'd go to bed with a kid like you?'

'Then why were you kissing and hugging me just now?'

Rose slammed the door. He swore. A few minutes later he scratched softly on my door and came in. 'Lend me some money,' he said in an offhand way, not from rudeness but because he was hardly aware I existed. He took a pound, thanked me perfunctorily and crept out, his terrified little-boy eyes fixed on the door where his stepfather might emerge.

Rose came in. 'Flo'll tell Dickie,' she said, 'so that's all right.'

'Not if she tells him the truth.'

Rose giggled. 'Dan'll be mad now. He always goes on and on about never having paid a woman yet, as an example to Jack, so as to keep down the cost of living.'

Next day Jack and Rose would not speak to each other. Flo watched the aloof faces with an appreciative grin. She kept winking at me and at Dan, and when Dan did not respond, raised her eyes and shrugged at the ceiling. She had not yet realized that Dan was really angry, particularly because she had taken her son aside and made him tell her the details of his night's adventures. 'Children have got to grow up,' she kept saying, but Dan scowled and moved his feet under the table like a bull pawing at the earth. He sat in grim silence, his great powerful arms resting on the white cloth, and his heavy head turned to watch his wife, who flitted as usual at the stove end of the room, looking like a shaggy little dog with her bright inquisitive eyes under the tangle of hair. When he looked at Jack he was murderous. But Jack apparently did not notice, or pretended not to; he was glistening with triumph, taunting Rose, saying with an aggressive but pleased laugh: 'Who's a kid now?'

At last Rose, who had been quiet and listless, said: 'I'm going out to get some fresh air.' She went out without looking at Jack. Flo ran after her and kissed her with a simple affection rare in her and said: 'Rose, don't take on so about everything. You take everything so serious.'

'I'm going to the pictures,' said Jack. It was much too late for the pictures and Dan raised his head loweringly to ask: 'And who's paying?'

Jack said: 'She lent me a pound.'

'Who, Rose?'

Jack looked at me and laughed.

'More fool you,' said Dan to me. And to Jack: 'If you do that again, you know what'll you get.'

'You're not my father,' said Jack, defying him.

Dan got up and slammed out of the basement. 'I'll kill the pair of you yet,' he said.

Flo began to cry. 'Oh, my God, he's gone, he's left me, and it's your fault,' she said to Jack.

'We'll do all right without him,' said Jack.

'My God,' said Flo. 'My God. And I'll kill you if you upset him again.'

Later Jack came to knock on my door for some more money. I refused. He had expected this, and now knocked on Rose's door.

'Get away,' came her muffled voice: she was crying.

'Lend me a pound,' said Jack, shaking with triumphant laughter.

'Go and hang yourself.'

Next morning Flo was so angry she smashed a cup on the draining-board setting it down. 'That kid. Last night he pretended to go to bed as usual, then he took my coal money and went out. I'll give him women. But don't tell Dan, darling. Please don't. He'll hit him again and then Jack won't be a nice witness for our case.'

'What is this case you all keep talking about?'

'Oh, my Lord!' said Flo, putting her hand over her mouth. 'Dan'd kill me if he knew I'd said anything to you.'

'Now you have, why don't you tell me.'

'Oh, don't ask me. We'll tell you. Really we will. But don't ask me. There's enough trouble with Jack and Dan without Dan's getting angry with me for opening my mouth when I shouldn't.'

That evening Rose asserted her rights as a neighbour by saying: 'I'm going for a walk. And you're coming, too.' Her mood had changed. She was aggressive and challenging. 'We're going to take a bus, and then we'll see.'

She got off the bus at the Bayswater Road. It was summer, and it was lined with dusty trees and so thick with prostitutes they stood in groups along the pavements. 'I don't like coming here most times,' said Rose. 'But tonight I feel different.' We walked slowly along, and Rose glared angrily into the faces of the waiting girls until she got a defensive stare back.

'What's this for?' I said.

'They make me sick,' said Rose. She was trembling with rage.

I tried to turn her off into the Gardens, but she held my arm tight and made me go with her. 'Dirty beasts,' she said. 'Look at them, hanging about, a pound a time, when I think I want to vomit.' At last she got tired, and turned spontaneously off into the Park. We went to the Round Pond, which was nearly deserted: a few small boys waded along its verges with nets and tins full of tiddlers. It was dusk now; the pond lay in a dull leaden sheet; the trees stood quiet and leafy; and Rose stared into the water and said: 'Sometimes I think I'll throw myself in.'

'Better go down to the river,' I said. 'You'll only hit your had on the bottom here.'

I'm not going to laugh. I don't feel like it.' She began walking around the edge, leaving me to follow. She walked right round the pond, until she got back to where she had started.

A policeman came sauntering towards us. 'There's a cop,' said Rose. 'Well, he needn't think I'm scared of him now. Can't they ever leave us alone? I suppose he thinks we're those dirty beasts. Well, I know about cops now, since that one that's chasing me, and they're just like everyone else.' When the policeman came up and looked keenly into our faces, Rose said, 'We're just having a walk, dear,' and slipped him a shilling. 'There go my cigarettes again,' she said, as he remarked: 'Good night, miss,' and sauntered off again. We could see him standing in the dark under the great trees, watching us while we made another complete circuit of the pond. 'Can't ever leave us alone, can't ever leave us in peace,' Rose was muttering. 'A shilling. Well, Jack can throw a pound away two nights running and what for ... did I ever tell you about my Canadian?' she enquired suddenly, as the policeman, deciding we were harmless, wandered off through the trees. 'No. Well, I'll tell you now. I've been thinking of him the last few days, thinking about life as you might say. Love, it's all nonsense. I was really in love with him, too. I thought I'd never get over it when he got himself killed by those Germans. But I did get over it, and so what am I wasting good salt over Dickie for?'

'What was he like?'

'He was a sweet boy,' she drawled, her voice changing. 'He used to take me out every time I had a free evening from the factory or the blitz. If I said I was busy he'd hang about the house until I'd finished washing and ironing for my mother. Then he'd take me for a walk. He'd even do the ironing for me – can you believe it? – a man doing washing and ironing. He'd come right across London to wash and set my hair for me. He was a hairdresser in Canada. He'd go down on his knees to tie my shoelaces for me. Yes, it's true. I used to unfasten my shoes sometimes before he came to watch him do it. Well, Dickie may be a bastard, but he'd never go down on his bloody knees to tie my shoes.'

'You must have been in love.'

'Oh, if you're laughing, it's your mistake. I was, too. I was so miserable when he was killed I committed suicide. First I cried and cried, and my stepfather said he'd beat me if I didn't stop. That was before he threw me out. Well, I thought I might as well die, with my boy dead, so I put my head in the gas-oven but the gas ran out, and they found me and poured cold water on me. Then my stepfather said I was no good and threw me out.'

'Lucky the gas ran out.'

'Lucky nothing. I only put sixpence in. Well, it made that old so-and-so my step sit up and take notice, didn't it? But what I mean is, I was so in love, just like the films, I even committed suicide, well nearly, and now I'm in love with Dickie, so what's the sense in anything, can you tell me that? And so now I've decided. I'm going out with that bloody policeman. Still, I suppose someone has to be a policeman, I'm not going to hold it against him.' By now the wind was stirring black branches, and pale clouds streamed across a black sky; it was not at all the domestic little pond of the daytime with small boys and toy boats. Rose gave a fearful look back as we left it and said: 'So now that's all done. I'm finished crying, and you're not catching me committing suicide again for any bloody man, and I'm going to be hard-hearted and on the make, just like that silly bitch in that book with the picture on it, well, it's not my fault if men like to be treated bad, now is it?'

Next evening she spent two hours dressing herself, and came into my room to show off. She was wearing a new grey suit she had bought from her boss's wife, high black ankle-strap shoes, and heavy brass jewellery on her wrists and ears. 'Look at my bosom,' she said. 'I've stuffed it all out with cotton wool. Dickie hates it when I do that, but this one's not going to get near my bosom, so it doesn't matter.'

She crept to the window and looked over. 'There he is,' she said. 'Come and see.' A very tall spindly youth with a sad frog's face stared up at the house. 'You mustn't laugh,' she said accusingly, stuffing a fist against her mouth and giggling. 'I know he's nothing to look at, but he's sweet.' She took another look and reeled back, laughing. 'When I compare him with Dickie . . . but I mustn't say that. At least, he's a proper gentleman. That's what I like. When I first met Dickie and Dan I decided to go for Dan – that was before Flo. But Dan messed me about, and Dickie kept his hands to himself, for the first evening, any rate. So I decided to like Dickie instead.' She began whirling around on her toes singing: 'Kiss me sweet, kiss me simple,' and dropped laughing on to a chair.

'He's waiting,' I said.

'Let him wait. I told you, I'm not going to treat any of them right from now on. I'll wait until 7.15. I said seven. He's a fool, like they all are, so he'll think the more of me.' At a quarter past seven she went downstairs, adjusting her face to languid boredom.

As soon as she had gone, Flo darted up the stairs to ask: 'Is he good-looking?'

'But I didn't see.'

'He'd better be, or Dickie won't be jealous. Rose came down to me and said if I was a friend I'd got to go up to the shop tomorrow morning and tell Dickie, all casual, that Rose had another man. She's coming on, isn't she?'

When Rose came in that night, she was thoughtful. 'I've got used to Dickie, that's what it is,' she said. She handed me five cigarettes. 'Might as well take what's going. He gave me twenty cigarettes. When a man starts giving you things it's time to watch out. Except with the Americans and Canadians, they're in the habit of giving girls presents, it's different with them. This one says he'll take me to the Pally tomorrow, but I'm not so sure.'

After work next day she was singing. 'Dickie was standing at his door tonight giving me dagger looks, so I suppose Flo did her stuff the way I said. He said: Have a good time last night, and I said: What's it to you? Believe it or not, he's started liking me again. Can you beat it? Lot of kids they are, they make me laugh, imagine me crying over a stupid like that.'

She put on her only dance dress, pink with frills and artificial flowers. It did not suit her at all. She kept glancing at herself in a dissatisfied way, and at the last moment took it off and flung it in a crumpled heap into the corner of my room. 'Time marches on,' she said grimly; and in a few moments appeared in her suit. She watched the clock until she was exactly fifteen minutes late, and then went downstairs, swinging her hips.

At three that morning I was awakened by a dim white shape creeping across my room to the window. 'Hush,' said Flo, 'it's me, dear. I didn't mean to wake you.' She craned out of the window. 'Quick, come here,' she said. Below, under the plane tree on the edge of the pavement, in a patch of moonlight, stood Rose and the policeman, closely embraced. 'Look at that,' said Flo, delighted. 'I tried to see out of the basement, but all I could see was their feet all mixed up and wriggling like they was doing a dance. Shhhh.' She fell back from the window, laughing. 'They look so funny. He's about four feet taller than she is, and look he's got to bend right over to kiss her like a man who's had it too often.' She looked again, then, unable to stand it, said abruptly, 'I'm cold,' and rushed off downstairs to her husband.

Next day Rose was uneasy. She had begun by wanting to make Dickie jealous, but now she was half in love with love. 'We was cuddling for hours last night,' she said. 'Nothing like cuddling, say what you like. It was ever so nice. He kisses nice, too. But not as nice as Dickie. There's something about the way Dickie kisses that gets me. But there, I'm just silly. A kiss is a kiss, when all's said and done, the beasts, all tongue and slobber . . . I'm getting upset, dear. After all that, believe it or not, I'm worried about Dickie being unhappy. Can you beat it? Men don't understand, do they? It's no good telling a man that something doesn't mean anything, the way I look at it, it must always mean something for them, but it doesn't for us, not unless we love a man. If I told Dickie that I kissed my policeman last night just because of him he wouldn't see it that way at all. Well, I'm going out with him again tonight. He's a bit soft, just like my Canadian boy that was killed, but he's not bad, I suppose.'

Rose went out with her policeman for several weeks. Flo pestered me, almost in tears, for details of this affair, but even if I had been willing I couldn't have obliged her, for Rose had withdrawn into silence. The trouble was, the policeman had one almost overwhelming attraction: his parents owned the house they lived in, and had promised half of it to him on his marriage. He wanted to marry Rose at once, and she longed for a home almost as much as she longed for a husband. But the more she tried to persuade herself she cared for the policeman and had forgotten Dickie, the sadder she became. She returned from the nightly embraces under the plane tree looking embarrassed and guilty, and sat staring into my fire until I told her she must go to bed. When I tried to talk to her she said: 'It's no good, dear. I know you mean well, but you're here with us just because you're hard-up for a time and because you like living here and living there. But it's the rest of my life I'm thinking of. Yes, all right, I know I'm getting you down, well, I get myself down, but I don't care about nothing at all, except to decide what's the right thing to do.'

She was getting Flo down, too. This conscience-ridden romance was too much for her. 'For the Lord's sake,' she said. 'If you are going to have some fun with a man then have it, but Rose'd cry at her own wedding.'

'From what I've seen of people married, I'd cry with good reason,' said Rose.

'But if Dickie said, come to church, you'd go.'

'More fool me.'

'But long faces don't get the marriage bells ringing.'

'Some people like my face long or short, if others don't.'

'Then make your bed and lie in it,' said Flo, finally getting bored. She was now spending time with her enemy Mrs Skeffington. For two reasons. One, she needed her as a witness in the famous court case about which at last I was managing to get some details in the face of the apparent determination of everyone in the building that I should be kept in the dark. The other I understood when Flo came to my door, vivid with excitement, to ask in a hoarse whisper: 'Have you any pills, dear?'

'Don't tell me she's pregnant.'

'Ah, my Lord, yes, poor thing. And now we must all be good to her.'

'But she keeps herself to herself so much.'

'She'll be different now she's in trouble.'

'How far has she gone?'

'Three months.'

'Why did she leave it so long?'

'I expect she was hoping the Lord would provide, but He doesn't, does He? And Rosemary was a mistake, too. She says she can't have children, not with her husband still supporting his first wife and her kids.'

I knew Rosemary was a mistake because I had heard Mrs Skeffington say so, in front of the child herself, not once, but again and again, and with each repetition Rosemary appeared more fragile, more hesitant, her eyes growing wide and anxious, as if she doubted her own right to live.

That night we heard Mrs Skeffington and her husband:

'What the hell are you complaining about? You send Rosemary to a crèche, don't you?'

'Oh, but I'm that way, how can you, now?'

'Why not, you did before?'

'But I'm so tired, and those pills I took. And I was awake all night with Rosemary.'

'She keeps me awake as well as you, doesn't she?'

'Who gets out of bed to her? You've never got out of bed to Rosemary once in your whole life.'

'Oh, shut up.'

'Yes, Rosemary starts crying and then you wake up and you can only think of one thing.'

'Don't you love me, then? Well, if it's like that I know where to go.'

Silence. Then the woman's tired anxious voice: 'I didn't

say I didn't love you. But I get so tired. Surely you can see that.'

'Then show me you love me.'

Next day Mr Skeffington went on a business trip and we never saw him again. One morning I heard a crash outside my door. Mrs Skeffington had thrown herself down one flight of stairs, was on the point of flinging herself down a second. 'Leave me alone,' she muttered, and before I could stop her, she launched herself into space again. On the landing below she picked herself up, slowly, slowly, gasping and pale. 'That ought to shift it,' she said, with an attempt at a smile, and dragged herself, breathing heavily, up the stairs to Rosemary.

Flo and I went on a delegation to insist she should try a doctor.

'Goodness gracious me,' said Mrs Skeffington, 'those doctors don't care at all for us.'

'Not all doctors are silly,' said Flo. 'Some are nice and kind.'

'Show me one, then. I tried before, over Rosemary. He didn't care. Besides, it's too late for doctors. And I think I'm all right, because I've got a bad pain.'

She went to bed, and Rose and I took Rosemary for the night. That was the one time Mrs Skeffington permitted anyone to help her. Before and after that day, when we offered to take the child, she would say: 'Goodness gracious, whatever for, I can manage quite well.'

Next day she looked very ill, but she went to work as usual. She was sent back at midday by her employer. I fetched Rosemary from the nursery, and when her mother saw her she opened her arms, and the two lay cuddled together on the pillow. They both looked extraordinarily frail, defenceless, pathetic. 'And now how about a doctor?' I asked.

'You're very kind,' she said formally, 'but Rosemary and I'll manage.'

Flo said: 'My God, what if she's still sick for the case?'

'That's all you think of,' said Rose.

'But it'll be to her advantage, too, to get rid of those filthy old people.'

'Yes? They don't bother nobody but you and Dan. I never hear them.'

'Oh, my Lord, you're not going to say that at the case?'

'I'll say the truth. I always told you, I'll tell the truth and that's all.'

'The truth is bad enough, sweetheart, darling, isn't it?'

'And that's a fact.'

'I'll tell you, darling,' said Flo to me 'I'll tell you all about it. I swear.'

'I'll tell her,' said Rose. 'But just now I've got something she must do for me.'

'But, sweetheart, the case, and time's so short, and poor Mrs Skeffington so ill.'

'Yes? Time enough. Come along,' said Rose to me. 'We'll go into your room and you can make me a nice cup of tea.'

In my room she said: 'Dickie and I have made it up. He was hanging around when I came out of the shop tonight. He said, Have you got a date tomorrow, and I said all casual, Yes, why?' Rose thrust forward one hip and began patting at her hair, staring with studied indifference at a wall. 'Why, yes, I said, not looking at him at all. He was so upset. You know I've told you, I can't bear to see him unhappy. But I hardened my heart, because it was for his good, really, and I teased him, and then he said, would I break my date with my policeman? So I said No, I wouldn't do a thing like that!' Rose acted virtuous indignation for a moment, but it dissolved into simple good-heartedness: 'I didn't care to tease him any longer, so I said I'd go out with him.'

'And how about the policeman?'

'Oh, him?' She let out an unscrupulous chuckle. 'They can all go and pickle themselves for all I care, except for Dickie. And you can tell my policeman a nice little lie for me.'

'I can?'

'Yes. It won't hurt you. You can type out what I write on your typewriter. It makes it look more official, doesn't it, and besides, my spelling's awful.'

'So are you,' I said.

'Yes? But I don't believe you think that because you're laughing. All the last times you've been yawning and fed-up with me. Well, I don't blame you, I was fed-up with myself. And now here's the letter.'

She handed me a piece of paper on which she had written: 'Dear Froggie, I'm sorry you had a spot of inconvenience over last night, but the truth was, I was engaged with my mother. Now I have to tell you something and I hope you won't be disappointed. I'm afraid I will have to cancel all our dates, owing to a personal nature concerning my mother, and she has asked me to come with her. Of course, I don't really want to go, but you can see she asked me to do her a favour and I can't really refuse her, can I? I didn't want to make you come all the way up here for nothing so I thought I would write. Come and tell me you don't mind some time when you are passing the shop, because I will never be seeing you again.'

'How should I end that? Yours sincerely sounds silly after all that kissing and cuddling, and when he's bought the ring and everything. And Love won't do, because he might think I meant it. You type that out for me nice. I don't want him to think I'm ignorant.'

'You could say, I'm breaking this off because I'm in love with another man,' I said.

'You could say it,' she said. 'I'm not. It's nicer this way, because then his pride's not hurt, see? And I've thought of another sentence. Put in: I know you will understand. That always sounds nice. It doesn't mean anything either. I think you'd better end it just – Rose. No *faithfully*, that'd be silly, wouldn't it?'

'And there's the ring, too.'

She looked guilty and then laughed. 'You can't be nice to two men at once. I'm doing it all for Dickie, aren't I? Well, I'm stark mad. It's not I don't know what Dickie is, and there goes my last chance of a home I can call my own, and I don't even care, and that proves I'm mad.'

She sighed the letter: Rose, Alexandra, Jane, Camellia. 'My mother wanted girls, but all she got was boys, except for me. So I got all the fancy names she liked. A waste, isn't it? Like wearing your fancy panties when there isn't a man about?' She giggled and went to post the letter. She came back singing, 'And so tonight I'm going out with my Dickie again.' Before she could even sit down, Flo came in to say Mrs Skeffington had procured an abortion for herself with an enema syringe. 'I saw the baby,' said Flo dramatically. 'It was as big as this!' She held out her fist. 'Eyes, too. Like a fish it looked. Funny to think it'd grow up to be like us. But there, it's down the drain now.' She laughed. 'Down the drain, that's good. Well, it is. She pulled the plug and said: That's the end of you.'

Rose got up and said: 'You make me sick, Flo.' She went into her room, slamming my door and hers.

'Foolish virgin, that's what Rose is,' said Flo.

In the year I lived in that house Flo believed herself to be pregnant five times. Twice the scare came to nothing; but three times she dressed herself appropriately in her shabbiest clothes, and staggered to a chemist's shop she had marked down for this purpose. There she copiously wept and talked about her family of seven and her drinking husband. She returned with pills, given her good-heartedly by 'the manager himself'. Instead of taking them as prescribed, she swallowed half a bottle at a time. I would find her rolling in agony on the floor of the kitchen exclaiming between groans: 'Well, I've fixed that one, at any rate.' Meanwhile, Aurora wandered about, sucking at her bottle, which she now wore tied around her neck like a St Bernard dog's brandy flask, with bright pink ribbon.

As the doors slammed Flo shrugged and said: 'Oh, well, she'll think different when she's got kids herself and no room to move and she can't ever go out or nothing.'

'How about a doctor for Mrs Skeffington?'

'My Lord, are you crazy, do you want her to go to prison?'

'She might die.'

'She won't die. There's a time for doctors. Mrs Skeffington's managed without, and good luck to her, and I didn't think she had that much fight in her, she's such a lady and all. I'll give her that. But you call a doctor now, sweetheart, and you'll do for her, you will really. I'll go up again and see what I can do for help. You stay here and if I need you I'll call.'

When Flo went, Rose came in. 'I'm going out now,' she said. 'This would happen, just when I want to be happy and not think about anything. Can you hear?'

From above us came the sound of moaning.

'Of course.'

'Yes, I know you can. But I don't want to. I'll see you later.'

Soon afterwards Flo came to say Mrs Skeffington was asleep for the night. And Rosemary had been given a tablespoon of whisky to keep her quiet. We both made trips upstairs to listen outside the door; and Miss Powell made trips down. We couldn't hear anything. Miss Powell said she had arranged to call a friend of hers who was a nurse, if anything went wrong. Flo approved of this: nurses weren't doctors; they were friendly, they were women, they understood.

When Rose came back at midnight, soft-faced and smiling and happy, she seemed a visitor from another country. 'Well,' she said, 'so that's all fixed.' She sat down in my big chair, and began to make herself comfortable. In five minutes she had changed herself from a pretty girl into a plain woman. First, straddled in the chair, she stripped the corset-belt from under her petticoat. Then she undid her brassière, and removed the carefully-bunched cotton-wool with which it was stuffed. She stuck a cigarette in the corner of her mouth – a thing she would rather die than do in public – so that, with her eyes screwed up against the smoke she looked like a wise old sardonic woman. Finally she took a comb from her black packed hair, and reflectively scratched her scalp with it. No man present: she could be herself.

'Have a good time?'

'What do you think?'

'Where did you go?'

'The pictures. I didn't care where we went, so long as I was with him. He wouldn't talk to me at first, not a cheep out of him. I didn't take any notice; I talked nice about whatever came past, so to speak. Then, after the pictures he took my hand and squeezed it ever so hard.' She showed me, with satisfaction, and creased red flesh on her wrist. 'And he said, look if you're going out with me, you're not going out with other men, see? I said: Going out with you, am I? Haven't noticed it recently. He said, As far as I'm concerned, you're coming out with me. So I smiled, secret-like, and played I didn't care either way. Then, when he got mad, I looked at him straight and said: No fooling now. You're not playing me up again, understand? Then I patted his cheek, like that . . .' Rose patted the chair in a brisk maternal way. 'I said: I'm telling you straight. If you don't want me, there are those who do. You can take it or leave it. When we got to the gate, he kissed me proper . . .' She smiled, and immediately her face dimmed to worry. 'He said he wanted to come in. But I wouldn't let him. I don't know what I ought to do. If I let him come in . . .'

'Oh God, oh God!' said a terrible voice from upstairs.

'Serves her right,' said Rose.

'You're a hard-hearted little beast,' I said.

'Yes? You listen to me. My mother had eight children. Well, some of them died early. She's only fifty now. And if she'd done away with one or two before they was born, she didn't start when she'd only one. She liked kids. It wouldn't hurt my lady upstairs to have another kid. What's she complaining about? My mother went out to work, cleaning places for people like you, excuse me saying it, people who didn't know how to keep a place clean, and she brought us up, and she had two no-good men, one after the other, aggravating her all the time. I've no patience.'

'Your mother had a house to put the children in.'

'Is that so? My mother had us in two rooms until she married that bastard my step. She had us all in two rooms. And we were always clean and nice. She only got a house if you can call it a house, I know you wouldn't, when she married and then it was four rooms for ten people.'

'Yes, well I've heard you say you wouldn't have kids until you had a proper house to put them in.'

Anxiety gripped her face. 'Yes. I know. Why do you have to remind me? Dickie's not going to give me Buckingham Palace, if he ever gives me anything. Oh, why did all this happen tonight when I'm trying to be happy?'

'Oh, my God, my God!' came from upstairs.

'Oh, drat her,' said Rose, almost in tears. 'Why does she have to go on. I don't want to think about everything. They're always talking about new houses and new this and new that, I always used to think of myself living in a nice place of my own. But when I left school, all I did was go into a shop, just like my mother did before she had kids. What's new about that? And there was the war. All through the war, they kept saying, everything's going to be different. Who's it different for – Flo and Dan, not me. Half the girls I was at school with are in one room and two rooms with kids. And now they're cooking up another war. I know what that means. I don't care about Russia or Timbuctoo. All I know is, I want to start getting married before they begin again and kill all the men off in their bloody wars while we sing God Save the King.'

'Oh, my God, God, God!' came from upstairs.

Rose got up and said: 'I'll take her up a cup of tea.'

She came down and said: 'She's got a bleeding, all over the sheets. Lucky Rosemary's lost to the world. And that Miss Powell's getting a friend of hers that's a nurse. So she won't die this time. Miss Powell says, will you go upstairs and lend a hand. That's because she doesn't like me, and I don't care, I've no patience. I'll see you in the morning.'

Chapter Five

During the next few days, while Rose was occupied by her worry about whether she should go to bed with Dickie or not, I think she would have been pleased to have some of Flo's crude advice, but the family downstairs was occupied plotting for the court case. She was aggrieved about it. 'My life's hanging on a thread,' she'd say; 'and no one cares except about their dirty money.'

'I do.'

'Yes, but you're different.'

'I don't see why.'

'Yes? Well, if you haven't learned by now my worries about life are different from yours then I haven't taught you much.'

'Then tell me what's going on about the case.'

'What's the use? What I tell you will be different from what Flo and Dan tell you.'

'That's why I want to hear it from you.'

'Yes, but they've made me promise. And, anyway, the whole thing makes me so sick . . . money, money, money; well, I didn't have to tell you that, you know Flo and Dan.'

'You know you're going to tell me sometime.'

'Then I'll be careful what I say, just facts, and not what I think, and then I won't be breaking my promise to Flo.'

The facts were these. Two very old people lived in two rooms on the ground floor. They had been there for years before the war. When the house was bombed, they stayed in it, although the basement was filled with water, and the floors over their heads filled with debris. There was no running water, electricity, no sanitation. They fetched in water from a house down the street; used the backyard as a lavatory at night; burned candles; went to the public bath-house once a week. Flo and Dan had bought the half-ruined house without even knowing the old couple were in it. They paid eighteen shillings a week rent, and could not be got out.

'You don't know about the Rent Act,' said Rose. 'That keeps them safe. Flo and Dan didn't understand it either, at first, and they tried to throw the old people out. Then they barricaded themselves in. That's all I'm going to tell you. What's eating Dan and Flo, I don't have to tell you, is that eighteen shillings. They could get four or five pounds for that flat if it was done up. Don't worry, I heard Flo and Dan talking. They're coming up to tell you, all crocodile tears, about what they suffer, so you'll know.'

'Who's right and who's wrong?'

'Who can say now? I'm sorry for the old people, they're on the old age pension, and when they're kicked out they'll have to go to a Home. But if Dan and Flo go on like a pair of wild beasts, then so does the old lady. The old man's neither here nor there, he's too old for anything but being silly in the head. Now if you keep your eyes open along the streets you'll catch sight of her, lurking and hiding behind her curtains. And that's all I shall say.'

The street was full of old ladies. Sometimes it seemed as if the cliff of grey wall opposite, jutting with balconies and irregularly hung with greenery and flowers, was the haunt of some species of gaunt and spectral bird. As soon as pale sunlight came creeping along the street, each window, each balcony, was settled with its old lady, reading newspapers, knitting, or peering over the barriers of sill and railing down at the pavements where the children played among the screeching wheels and protesting horns of cars and lorries. No child was hurt while I lived there; but every time I looked out of the window I was terrified: the old ladies were considerably tougher than I. They sat immobile, the light glancing from their spectacles and their working needles; and between them and the children was a bond that appeared like pure hatred. From time to time, like a flock of birds propelled into space by some impulse, the old ladies would rise and screech warnings and imprecations into the street. Brakes screamed, horns wailed, and the children set up a chorus of angry Yahs and Boos. Slowly the grey crones settled into their nooks, slowly the traffic flowed on, and the children continued to play, ignoring their guardians above. Sometimes an old lady would descend from her perch and stalk cautiously down the street, laden with shopping bags, baskets, handbags, purses, umbrellas, ration books. She would stop at the edge of a group of children and hold out a bag of sweets. The children, cheeky and affectionate, approached as cautiously as small birds to an apparently harmless old hawk. They darted forward, grabbed the sweets, and ran off laughing; while the old lady grumbled and scolded and smiled: 'You'll get yourself run over, you'll get yourselves killed, you'll be the death of me yet.' Immediately forgetting her, they resumed their play and she her progress to the shops or the market, smiling gently to herself because of the children.

From time to time, the anxiety boiled over into a shower of angry protesting notes carried across from the old ladies to the harassed mothers of the children, by the children themselves. The whole street fomented spite and resentment; fathers, back from work, were pressed into battle; and for a day or two the children, who had acquired a sense which enabled them to evade lorries and cars, had their attention continually distracted by their mothers who would appear in the windows and balconies beside the old ladies, in order to call out: 'Do look out there!' or 'Goodness gracious me!' Futilely wringing their hands, or waving dishcloths, they agitatedly peered into the street where their offspring flirted so lightly with danger, gave the old ladies a glare of frustrated irritation, and finally returned to their housework hoping to be allowed to forget an anxiety which was useless, since irremediable.

For a time I thought of our side of the street, as opposed to the cliff of elderly ladies, as one of ordinary family life; but one sunny day I came up the other pavement and saw that every house, almost every layer of windows, held its vigilant spectator, peering sharply down over the knitting needles. When I came to our house there, sure enough, half-obscured by a dirty lace curtain, was a very old, yellowing, papery lady.

I waited some days for Flo and Dan, but it was Rose again who approached me. She told me what had happened downstairs.

'I really don't know what she'll say about the old people,' Flo had said, with resignation. 'It's not nice for a nice girl, is it, but someone has to tell her.'

'That's right,' said Rose.

'I don't like telling her,' said Flo with a shrinking and fastidious air. 'I don't even like talking about it, it's so horrible.'

'Yes?'

'It's all right for you, but it's me who's unhappy, you are out all day. It's me what has to put up with their noise and their smells and their banging on the floor and all.'

'Yes?'

'Sometimes I think I'll never bear it out, and I'll have to go and live with my grandmother in Italy.'

At this Rose had laughed, in spite of herself, and Dan, who was still black-tempered, said: 'If you do I'll know where to find myself another woman.'

'There,' Flo said. 'You see? Now you just go upstairs and tell her.'

'And so here I am telling you,' said Rose. 'And what do I care? Because last night I let Dickie in.'

'Yes, I know.'

'How? We was ever so quiet.'

'Because you look so happy.'

'Well, I am. Why didn't you tell me how nice it was?'

'But we did.'

'Well, I suppose no one can properly tell in words about it, but if I'd known what I was missing I wouldn't have held out so long. But don't you tell Flo, I can't stand all her winks and nods.'

'She was up this morning to try and find out.'

'No! How does she smell these things, I'd like to know?'

Flo had come toiling up that morning with Aurora and the

158

puppies at her heels, the moment Rose left for work, to remark in an offhand voice: 'Friends should tell their friends the nice things that happen, shouldn't they?'

During the course of the visit, a prolonged one, she said that you could see Rose was learning sense at last, but that if she wanted to hook Dickie, there was only one way to do it, and if I was a friend of Rose I'd tell her to let an accident happen. 'You don't think I'd have got Dan except by being sensible, do you? And Rose doesn't listen to me these days.'

With the puppies and Aurora cavorting around my room, I tried to preserve my belongings from destruction, and Rose's privacy, while from time to time Flo shrieked for effect: 'Drat those dogs. Drat that child!' and kept her anxious eyes fixed on my face. She was suffering torments of curiosity. And I knew it was no use, because it was always useless to lie to Flo. Being a purely instinctual creature she knew what most of us have to learn by experience, if ever, that in order to judge whether people are telling the truth, one doesn't listen to the words they use.

I kept repeating that I slept like a log and never woke at night. I said no, I hadn't seen Rose's face that morning. Flo kept nodding lugubriously; she had sensed the truth. Now she was wondering whether to ask me straight out if Rose had had Dickie in her room. But I said No, I would be committed to the lie, and she might later lose the advantage of my being in a better mood. With Flo, everything was a question of mood.

'Well, dear,' she had remarked, finally departing, 'I like to believe you are a friend of mine, but how can I think it when you're like this?'

'My God,' said Rose, when I told her all this. 'We call Flo stupid and she is, we know she is. But for all that she knows what's true through her skin from what I can see.'

'And now tell me what they said downstairs.'

First she laughed, irrepressibly. 'The trouble is, with Flo and Dan, you always have to laugh, even when they're up to no good . . . Wait, I'll get my face straight.'

She put on a prim and sorrowful face and said: 'Life is hard, things is not easy. It's hard for poor Flo. What she goes through is enough to make a queen cry. Those dirty old people, nothing but criminals.'

'Yes?' I said.

'Don't make me laugh, dear. Wait. No, it's no use. I can't take an interest. They'll come up tomorrow themselves.'

Tomorrow I had Flo and Dan, separately, and together, all through the day. They had decided the time was now ripe for my initiation, and they never did anything by halves, whereas previously I could find out nothing at all, now I couldn't get to speak of anything else.

It seemed that the feud had begun good-naturedly. When Flo first entered the house, she was confronted by an ancient, black-garbed, white-faced crone with burning angry eyes. 'What are you bloody foreigners doing in my house?' she demanded. Flo laughed, and said they had bought the house, and anyway, she had been born and bred not half a mile away. The door slammed in her face when she asked to see the flat. She had to call a policeman to make them open the door. Afterwards the policeman had said: 'Crazy as they come. You'd better get them out before they do damage.' This pronouncement from the Law itself, or so Dan and Flo saw it, had confused them; for a time they had believed all they would have to do was to call a policeman and get the couple turned into the street. Meanwhile, they could not go anywhere near the first floor without shouts and imprecations being hurled at them from behind the locked door. Dan went to a lawyer and was told he could not turn them out so easily. It had been decided between them to go to Court and complain the flat was kept in a disgusting condition. Rose, who had actually been inside it, said this was true. It contained a single bed, with stained bedding; a cupboard made of boxes, and a couple of gas rings. Rose said the filth and the smell was so she was nearly sick. But a week before the Court case, Dan lost his temper and threw a flat-iron at the door with all the strength of his enormous arms and shoulders. The door splintered inwards, the old lady brought a counter-claim, and both parties had been bound over to good behaviour in Court.

From that time, they behaved as if they regarded each

other as a species of wild animal.

When I said to Flo that such and such an action might have killed the old lady, she replied: 'Yes, but she threw a saucepan full of boiling potatoes at me the week before. That might have killed me, mightn't it?' Or: 'Well, dear, if I had, she wouldn't be much loss to the world, would she? She might just as well be dead for all the good it does her.'

But there had been long spells of comparative peace. Flo would make a point of raising her voice in insulting remarks as she passed their door; the old lady inside would retaliate by shrieking like a parrot. And before Dan went to bed every night he had made a point of climbing up to the room I was now in where he stamped up and down for a good ten minutes. The old lady, if she got the chance, emptied her dustpan or shook her duster down Flo's stairs. Or she would summon a policeman to say: 'That bitch is trying to kill me.' The policeman knew her; and would take down her tale in the book, and then drop down for a cup of tea with Flo. This state of affairs might continue for weeks. And then everything flared up into open war.

A few months after the binding over, Dan applied to have the couple removed to a lunatic asylum. The old lady had screamed that her tap was broken and it was the landlord's responsibility. Dan at once went to mend it; he was longing to get his capable hands on to the disorder inside that flat. But he was met with a locked door and silence. Soon there came a lawyer's letter demanding that he should mend the tap at once. Dan attempted to enter the flat in the presence of the police and failed. He pointed out that no one but a crazy woman would behave like that. At once the old lady attempted to prove he was mad because he would not let them use the lavatory or bathroom, but complained because they emptied their slops into the wash-basin in their room.

The rent collecting was a weekly drama. Every Friday at about six, Dan looked meaningfully at the clock, set his teeth and climbed the stairs, followed by Flo, Aurora and Jack. Dan banged on their door and shouted. Silence. He banged again, threatening lawyers, asylums, court cases. Unpredictably, perhaps after five minutes, perhaps after fifty, the door

161

opened an inch, and a handful of silver scattered into the hall, followed by a scream of rage. The door slammed, and continued to shake and vibrate as the old lady hammered on it with both fists and shouted that he must take himself off her premises. Sometimes Dan grinned, shrugged and pointed an ominous forefinger to his head. Sometimes his face swelled purple with anger, and he pounded on the door till he was sobbing with exertion.

Worse than stews and flat-irons was to come. One day Dan was in the yard with Aurora. A heavy ladder rested against the wall near the old couple's back window, where he had been mending a drainpipe. The old lady leaned out and pushed down the ladder, which missed Aurora by a couple of inches. Dan went mad with rage; he replaced the ladder, bounded up it, and in the space of a few seconds was in the flat, shaking the old lady like a pillow and threatening to kill her. He was checked by the realization that the old man, supposed to be a co-villain with his wife, was seated all this time on the bed reading the newspaper. He did not even raise his eyes at the scuffle. Dan was so astounded that he dropped the old lady on the floor, gazed in a hypnotized way at the old man, and withdrew, shrugging and scratching his head. In the basement he said to Flo: 'He's madder than she is. He doesn't even fight. He just sits there.'

The case went to Court, both sides claiming damages for assault, both being bound over for the second time.

Next, the old lady climbed down the ladder in full view of Flo and shook red pepper over a bed of Flo's tulips.

Flo said: 'I told the Judge she put pepper on my tulips once before and he bound us over. It isn't fair. Dan shouted: Is this British Justice? and the Judge got mad. And the old lady said: We'll get our rights in a British Court against the dirty foreigners. She meant me, because of my Italian grandmother. You should have seen her face when the Judge told her she was an old nuisance.'

'He said you were a nuisance, too,' commented Rose.

'That was because he didn't know about the potatoes on the stairs. Do you know – she rolls potatoes down the stairs hoping I'll slip on them and break my neck. Well, I just pick them up and use them. But it's not right, dear, is it? You'll come and be witness for us, won't you, sweetheart?'

'But how can I be? I never see or hear them.'

Ah, my Lord, it's not fair. Dan and me, we've been waiting to quarrel until you're out of the house, and keeping ever so quiet so's you're not disturbed, and now you say you haven't heard them.'

Rose said, speaking loudly as to one deaf: 'Flo, I'm going to explain something to you. And you must listen careful.'

'What, dear, what, darling? Why are you shouting at me, sweetheart?'

'Because I want you to understand. Now there's this oath, this thing they have in the Courts.'

'Ah, my Lord, the whole truth and nothing but the truth, I know about *that*.'

'Yes? But you're supposed to tell the truth in Court. That's what the oath is, just telling the truth.'

'But, Rose, you're my friend.'

'Flo, I've told you, I'm going to answer the questions just what I know. And that's all.'

'Me, too,' I said.

'But there's no use your coming at all, because you didn't see the pepper and the potatoes and the stew that missed me by half an inch.'

'Or that great iron, neither, that Dan threw.'

Flo considered. She said with a sly look: 'And there's that policeman, that Froggy, you know about the police, dear, don't you? And when did they tell the truth in Court?'

'What's that got to do with it?' But Rose was beginning to blush.

Flo was delighted, and pressed on: 'You know as well as everyone else, he was getting fifty, sixty pounds a month along your street, for shutting his mouth about the black market stuff for the restaurants – all that butter? All that eggs and stuff? And I didn't see Rose running to tell anyone, oh no, you was thinking of marrying him.'

Rose was really distressed. She said to me: 'Well, now you'll think bad of me. But you have all those ideas about our police – I've heard you, and I didn't say nothing, because all you foreigners are the same, like my Canadian boy. But the police take this and that on the side, my Froggy wasn't nothing special.'

'That's what I'm saying,' said Flo. 'So why should you be so high and mighty about a little fib for a friend in the Courts?'

'Because I am.'

'Well, I don't hold it against you. But when I think of what the lies were that the police said about your little brother so that he got to go to prison.'

'Flo,' said Rose, desperate.

'What's all this?' I said.

Flo glanced at me, saw Rose in tears, exclaimed 'Ah, my Lord, Dan'll give it to me now,' and rushed out of the room.

'I didn't want you to know, Flo promised not to tell you.'

'What?'

'Because you'd think bad of me. Because my little brother's turned out bad, but he's the only one of the kids that did.'

'I don't see why you should think that.'

'If you don't you've got funny ideas, but you can't help it. But now Flo's told you, I'll tell you proper. My little brother, he got into trouble – he was fourteen, and he was in with a bad lot of kids. He got into trouble over and over, and they put him on probation, and we had those nosey-parkers at us all the time. But the cops had it in for him. And I'm not saying they weren't right, because he was a proper little devil, cheeky all the time. So one night he was with the gang, but he got home early while they did a job. I know he did, because it was me who gave him his supper and saw him to bed. We was sleeping in the same room then, so I know he was asleep when the job was being done. But the coppers said he was with the rest, and so he was sent to Borstal.'

'But how could they when you knew he was with you?'

'It's no good arguing with them, you'd know that if you wasn't a foreigner. They go into Court and tell any lie they fancy, and the magistrate always believes them. Well, the way I looked at it was this: if I spoke up for my little brother, they wouldn't believe me anyway. But if he went to the Reform for a bit, it might settle him down. And, besides, my mother was ill anyway about then, and he was right out of her control. But I've felt bad about it ever since. Because it didn't do him any good. He ran away once, and was took back again. And he's coming out next month and my mother's marrying this man I told you about, and my brother doesn't like him, and there'll be trouble, mark my words. So I want him to come here and live, and Flo's against it because it means the cops'll have their eye on this house. But she thinks, if she lets him come here, then I'll tell lies in Court, and I don't know which way to turn.'

At this point Dan came in. He was scowling at Flo, who was near tears.

'Yes,' he said. 'And has she told you why we need witnesses? Has she told you that?'

'But I didn't mean it,' said Flo, wailing.

'You never mean it. They put her into the witness box. That was the time of the ladder. And they said, did you hear your husband saying he would kill Mrs Black, and Flo here pipes up and says: Oh, yes, and he nearly killed her right then, shaking her so hard.' At the memory, Dan's veins swelled up dark in his forehead; and he clenched his teeth at Flo.

'But it was true,' said Flo, through tears. 'I saw you. I thought her time had come, the old bitch.'

Dan grinned sarcastically. 'You see?' he said to me and Rose. 'You see?' He gave Flo a light slap across the cheek. 'Everybody in the Court laughed. And because my wife can't keep her tongue still I was bound over.'

'She can't help being stupid,' said Rose tolerantly.

'No, I can't,' said Flo eagerly, clutching at Dan's arm. 'I don't understand them Courts. I thought I was to tell the truth, because of what the laywer said, I got mixed up, that's all, next time it'll be different.'

'It'd better be different.' Dan looked at Rose and said: 'You're coming into Court or not?'

Rose hesitated. Dan said: 'If you want that kid brother here for a time you can.'

Rose struggled with herself, and finally said, with a sigh: 'But I'm not telling no lies, Dan.'

'Flo's stupid. Who said lies? The lawyer told me, you just say the things you know, that's all.'

'Yes?' said Rose. 'All of them?'

He ground his teeth again. 'No. The lawyer knows. Will you see the lawyer? The case is the day after tomorrow.'

'My Lord, so soon?' wailed Flo.

'Yes, so soon. And Mrs Skeffington's flat on her back and she'll be there a week yet. Will you see the lawyer?' he said to me.

'Very well.'

'Don't listen to Flo. She's . . .' And he tapped his forehead angrily, glaring at her.

'No, sweetheart, I'm sorry, I didn't mean to say what was wrong.'

'And now you'll come downstairs and get my supper and keep your mouth shut.'

Dan and Flo went out.

'Those lawyers,' said Rose. 'You wait till you see their lawyer. Enough to make God laugh. Well, it looks as if I'll get my Len here for a bit. I'm a good influence on him if no one else is. You won't think bad of me? You'll see him and be a friend?'

'Of course. Why not?'

'Of course, and why not. Well, it's easy for some people. Make me a cup of tea. Thinking about going into that Court scares me, but I suppose I've got to.'

Flo crept back.

'Don't say it,' said Rose. 'Don't.'

'But we've made it up.'

'Let's be thankful for small mercies.'

Flo said to me, 'I know Dan would be pleased at the idea if he'd thought of it, because he did it himself. Just stamp up and down this floor before you go to bed at night so as to get into their dreams a little.'

Rose groaned. 'Flo, it would count against you in Court, don't you ever think of anything?'

'But Dan used to do it every night regular. He'd come up

and me too, and he'd stamp around the floor, he looked ever so funny, going stamp stamp in his shirt, with everything on view going flop-flop.'

'Oh, my God,' said Rose.

'You don't know nothing yet,' said Flo. 'Getting dressed up to go courting is one thing. Men in their underpants is another. One is ro-mance. The other is what we get for cleaning the floors and washing up to keep us quiet. And don't you forget it.'

'Do us a favour and leave us in peace one evening.'

'Yes, well you make the most of Dickie in his courting mood because it won't be like that afterwards.'

'I wasn't born yesterday.'

'You're not cross with your Flo?'

'We're sick and tired. Both of us. Just sick and tired.'

'We could subpoena you, dear, you know that?'

'Yes?'

'All right, dear, I'll go, I'll go.'

The day of the case it was hot, a sunny June day. Flo wore a black astrakhan coat and a muff. Around her black felt hat she had pinned another strip of astrakhan. Both Jack and Dan wore thick striped suits. For the first time, the three seemed commonplace and ugly. As for Aurora, she had on a white rabbitskin coat and hat, and was crying from the heat, but Flo slapped her into silence. As the family walked quietly towards a bus-stop it was the essence of respectability; and I tried to put myself into the position of a Judge, looking down into these lives from his height, and wondered how he would see them. The only sign that this was not in every respect that unit which is the foundation of a sound society was their complete indifference to the sufferings of Aurora. But even this was soon put right by Rose, who was showing her respect for the occasion by wearing her best grey suit, and her independence of it by fixing a look of weary scepticism on her face. She exclaimed: 'Have you all gone nuts today?' and grabbed the child, stripped off the thick fur and set her free. Flo saw Aurora's paper-white face, with the sweat streaming off it, and was suddenly overcome by pity and tenderness. Mother and child sat entwined on the bus seat, presenting a charming picture. As for Rose, she said to me: 'Well, let's get it over with, and then we can start acting sensible again. It all makes me sick and that's a fact.'

We got off the bus and Dan said to Flo: 'Now if you speak out of turn this time I'll wring your blasted neck for you.' Flo was subdued by this until the lawyer came to meet us. Her thoughts at once flowed into their usual channel and she whispered to Rose: 'Now there's a catch for you, sweetheart. A lawyer's something like a husband.'

'Oh, shut up,' said Rose. The lawyer, who had heard this exchange, gave Rose a sympathetic wink and then took Flo's arm. He was a brisk little man with the bloodless London look, a sharp raw face, and shrewd eyes. He handled Flo in an easy authoritative way she did not resent at all. But Dan resented it. He hated the way people responded to Flo, who talked and laughed in her frank, matronly manner with everyone. But they overlooked him, always, because when he was dressed in the ugly suit he was reduced to nothing. He was scowling savagely as we entered the building. It was gloomy, with its surfaces painted shiny brown or tea-coloured or mustard, as if the authorities had been determined to make the processes of justice as grim as possible. Our footsteps had a loud hollow ring.

The old couple were standing with their lawyer near the top of some stairs, and they turned their backs on us with an emphatic scornful movement; and our faces all wore the suspicious wary look people instinctively assume in Law Courts. We looked at each new group as if they might turn out to be enemies. Flo actually drew herself up and shot an angry glance at an astonished old woman before breaking into a ringing laugh – which she at once smothered by clapping a hand over her mouth – and whispered through the cracks in her fingers that 'she thought that was a witness for the prosecution'.

'Not prosecution,' said the lawyer. 'It's not that kind of case.'

'How was I to know? This law is too difficult.'

'You'd better remember that,' said Dan. Flo, protected by

the lawyer, defied him with her eyes for the pleasure of seeing him grow more angry.

Rose whispered: 'Storm warning! Trouble tonight! I'll come and we'll have tea in your room and leave them to kill each other.'

The lawyer was nursing Flo because he remembered how at the last case she had ruined everything by allowing herself to be carried away by the spirit of truth at the wrong moment. Flo, he thought, was the weak point. But Dan did not understand this: he could not understand why Flo, who was so stupid, should get all this attention. He kept his heavy yellow gaze fixed on the lawyer's face, and was looking for an opportunity to impress himself.

We went into the side room to confer with Counsel. It was a dull, yellowish, high-ceilinged room, like a station waiting-room, all the doors standing open, people drifting in and out with the bored yet expectant look of travellers waiting for a train. We had a glimpse, through a momentarily-opened door, into the court-room itself: an old man, the Judge, rested his head on his hand while he listened to black-draped lawyers arguing about some legacy.

As our Counsel entered, Rose dropped her eyes, put on a prim face, and whispered to me: 'Look what's come. Isn't it a sweet little thing?'

Counsel was a willowy stripling, with smooth little-boy cheeks, spaniel eyes, and an assured upper-class manner that caused Flo to gaze at him with incredulous admiration and Rose to whisper again: 'Don't laugh now, but we'll have a good laugh afterwards.'

Counsel's voice was as smooth as milk; he was deferential and beautifully polite as he cross-examined Dan, who began staring suspiciously at him. As for Flo, she looked as if she might cry, and exclaimed: 'I thought you were on our side, sir?'

'But, madam, I am,' purred the youth, who must have been so much older than he looked. He received the potatoes on the stairs, the filth in the basins, and the pepper on the tulips without a smile. Soon tears stood in Flo's eyes, and in order to provoke him into some semblance of sympathy she began repeating herself, raising her voice in the querulous appeal: 'I do my best for the dirty old bastards, sir, and see what they do?' And, as he patiently continued: 'What happened next?' she could only mutter: 'Ask the neighbours, ask my witnesses,' and lifted her handkerchief to her eyes, tears of real disappointment flowing down her cheeks. With a calculated loss of temper Counsel shouted: 'Answer my questions,' and this finished Flo altogether. She had to have a warm response from the people she thought of as friends, and now she sat, clutching at Aurora, both of them gazing with wounded eyes at Counsel.

Counsel, his exasperation checked only by the thought of the fees he was earning out of this ridiculous feud, made a helpless gesture and retired to the window to try and regain his temper. The lawyer tried to explain to Flo, for at least the tenth time, the processes of justice. She kept repeating, 'But he's not on our side, sir,' while the lawyer patted her arm and said: 'There, now, it's all right.'

Then Counsel and lawyer attacked Dan, in an attempt to make him lie consistently. But Dan imagined they objected to the lies themselves, and at every point where his conscience troubled him, he began shouting justification, so that for the second time Counsel retired to the window to smoke and fume.

So far the witnesses had not been questioned; what was the use of satisfactory witnesses if the two main complainants could not be made to sound convincing? At last the lawyer, hot, anxious and amused, came to Rose, and said: 'Perhaps you could explain to them?'

Rose faced Flo and Dan and said: 'Now see here. You're just being plain silly. You don't have to get upset. It's like this – they don't mind your telling lies, see . . .'

'Who's telling lies?' shouted Dan belligerently, while the two legal gentlemen exchanged ambiguous glances.

'Oh, shut up,' said Rose. 'Can't you listen? These two gentlemen here are trying to help you.'

'Are they, dear?' said Flo doubtfully.

'Now listen. What you've got to do is to tell the same lies at the same time, see?' She looked for encouragement to the men, who had turned their backs in order to leave the thing in her far more capable hands.

Meanwhile the old couple, who had finished conferring with their Counsel, sat in the next room through a half-opened door and could hear every word that was being said.

Rose continued: 'What's the use of Flo saying she lets the old people use the bathroom if Dan says he locked the door to keep them out?'

'We didn't do no such thing,' said Flo virtuously, and Rose lost her temper and shook her by the shoulders.

'You said so in your statement.'

'Did I, dear?' said Flo, ready to cry again.

'Now listen. What you've got to do is to say that the dirty old things make such a mess in the bathroom and, anyway, she's got filthy sores all over her legs.'

'But she has,' said Flo sullenly.

There was a parrot-like screech from the next room; Flo and Dan glared; the old people glared back; Counsel and the lawyer still had their backs turned.

'That's what I said, isn't it?' said Rose. 'You was protecting your tenants from disease, see? And every time they went into the bathroom, they made a mess, and you had to clean up after them, they made a mess on purpose, and you thought the old lady's sores might be dangerous to other people.'

The legal gentlemen, standing side by side and gazing out of the window, permitted themselves to nod encouragingly. Point by point, Rose framed their case for them, shaking Dan and Flo into silence whenever they opened their mouths.

'Understand now?' she concluded. By now she felt quite sure of herself. 'What you've got to get into your heads is this,' was her summing up. 'All this law business isn't anything to do with right or wrong, see? You'll just get everybody confused if you start thinking so silly. Nobody cares what really happened. All they want you to do is to tell a good lie and stick to it afterwards.'

The lawyer coughed, in a resigned way. Counsel's left shoulder was observed to twitch. Flo and Dan, released by Rose, sat themselves down, in a heavy worried silence. The lawyer came over, offered Rose a cigarette, and gave her a grateful smile. 'You're a smart girl,' he said. 'You'd do well in law.'

Rose was overcome, and blushed, saying: 'Thanks, dear. But you need an education for the law. It's true I know about it a little, because I had a policeman for a friend once.'

The lawyer and Counsel now tackled Flo and Dan together. At the end of half an hour, they had succeeded in getting Yes and No in reply to certain basic questions. Then they began work on us, the witnesses. After a few minutes, they gave Jack up, for every time they enquired: 'And what happened next?' Jack's admiration for the physical strength of his stepfather, so much deeper than his resentment of him, caused him to break into descriptions of assault and violence which made Dan nod proudly, Flo sigh approvingly, and Rose to groan: 'Lord help us.' They told Jack he could go back to work, but as he had a day off he remained seated in a corner with a bunch of physical culture magazines, oblivious of the furious looks Dan was giving him.

Rose proved admirable but limited. When Flo said: 'But, Rose, you said it was all right to lie,' she replied, with an open contempt for everybody present: 'I was just saying what everybody else thinks. I know what's right and I'm sticking to it.'

As for me, it was decided that since I knew nothing of the old people but what I'd heard, it was no use putting me in the box.

Everything depended on the impression Flo and Dan would make when the time came.

Our case was low on the list. We could hear the Court official calling out names; and as the cases worked themselves through, legal men kept dropping into the room for a cigarette, or to remove their wigs and scratch their hair, or to hold hasty conferences with witnesses. The old couple still sat through an open door, quite silent, staring in front of them.

Dan was restless with suppressed belligerence. He needed to regain his position. He kept shooting glances of resentment at the pink-cheeked boy who had humiliated him, and at Rose, who had treated him like a child. But the discovery that these guardians of morality not merely overlooked but encouraged a good lie had made him feel their equal. We were all relaxed by now out of boredom. Flo had unbuttoned her coat. Aurora was asleep. Dan was leaning his weight on the table in the easy way he would have used in his basement.

'You wouldn't remember the war, sir, would you?' said Dan to Counsel, who flushed angrily. 'I served right through the war. Perhaps you could tell the Judge that. It's more than some can say.'

'My good man, it has nothing to do with the case.'

'I saved a man's life. And now I can't say who's to live in my own house.'

'Mr Bolt, I've already told you, it's irrelevant.'

'He was a Lascar. And what gratitude do I get, nothing!'

Rose hissed resignedly: 'Oh, my God, that tears it, if he's going to start. I hope he doesn't forget to tell how he did six months' hard for nearly killing a man in a bar.' She took out her knitting, which she had brought with her in case of just such an emergency.

Counsel, the lawyer, and various knots of people in doorways or seated on the benches had their eyes fixed on Dan. Every one of them looked slightly irritated. It was the facinated irritation caused by a phenomenon we don't understand. The fact was, Dan was holding their attention simply by sitting there, and they didn't know why. The angry power of his body was not evident, muffled as it was in the commonplace suit. And his face expressed nothing but the desire to express – it was long, flattish, yellowish, and almost contorted with his frustration at not being able to communicate.

'Yes, he was a Lascar,' said Dan, aggrieved, 'a black man if you like, but he was human, and I could have died.'

'Yes, yes, yes,' said Counsel. Dan turned the hot beam of his eyes at him, and the boy became silent.

'There I stood on deck,' said Dan. 'We had docked that day.' He was remembering it so powerfully that although he did not move a muscle, we stood on deck with him. 'It was a black night and dead quiet. I heard a splash.' He closed his eyes a moment. There was a silence. He still had not moved. His great hands lay in loose fists on the table before him, not moving. Yet we heard ripples flow out and break softly against enclosing dock walls. 'I looked over.' Dan stared ahead of him, not blinking. We saw him bent over a rail at a black cold sea. 'There was nothing,' he said. 'But I had my duty. I climbed and jumped.' Even Rose let her knitting lie in her lap, and became part of the story. 'I went down and down, my arms above my head.' Dan clenched his fist and the cloth of his sleeves bulged out. For a terrifying moment we watched him sink through the lightless harbour water under the black hulls of ships. 'I saw him. I grabbed.' Dan's body stiffened slightly. His hand opened and the fingers flexed rigid on the palm. We saw the hand clutch at something slippery. 'I pulled him to the surface by the hair. He was fighting, I hit him.' Dan clenched his fists tight, his head went back, his chin came forward, he half-shut his eyes. 'I shouted. No one heard. No one on deck. Everyone on shore. First night in harbour for six weeks. I held him and I shouted. I held him and I shouted again. Then I dragged him up the side of the ship.' Dan gripped his teeth together and the veins swelled in his neck. We saw him heave the Lascar up the ship's dark side. 'I put him on deck and worked on him till he came round. It was a Lascar. Drunk. Can you blame him, sir? The officers' mess sent for me. Dan, have a drink, they said. Sir, thank you, I said. But I've had enough for one night. Ask me for a drink another night.' Dan half-shut his eyes, and looked woodenly digni-fied. 'The Captain came to me.' Now Dan's deliberate stupid-ity was an insult to all authority. 'I won't forget this my man.' 'Sir,' said Dan, and he suddenly saluted, with a smart quiver. The shock of that movement was like being slapped: it was only when his hand quivered at his temple that we realized he had told the story without gesture, with no more than an occasional tightening of a muscle. It was with a sting of astonishment that we saw the man was still sitting on the bench by the table. He had come to himself, sitting loosely, looking around dazedly, mouth open over prominent white teeth, taking in the bare dusty room filled with the fancy-dress gentlemen in their curly wigs and black robes. 'Yes,' he said. 'Yes.' Then he violently crashed his fist on to the table and shouted: 'But that doesn't help me, does it?' I'll never forget this, my man, the Captain said to me, and that's the last I heard. Justice, they call it. Justice!'

'Dan,' said Flo, warningly, giving ingratiating smiles to everyone.

'I don't care who hears,' shouted Dan, over the drone from the Court, through a door left slightly open because of the heat. Someone from inside the Court tiptoed over and shut the door. Every eye followed the squat figure in folds and tags and pleats of grimy black, who frowned at us so portentously that the young Counsel blushed: he, like the rest of us, had forgotten his surroundings. 'Not so loud, please,' he said.

'Yes, sir,' said Dan automatically.

There was a high titter from the other doorway. The old lady, white-faced and trembling with hatred, glared in at us from among other faces, which were curious or amused or indignant. Our lawyer gave her a puzzled glance and might have asked who she was, but Dan was speaking again. 'When I left the Navy I had four hundred pounds. Do you know how I got that?'

'There are certain traditions of the British Navy,' said Counsel, conveying that he found the word Navy, on Dan's lips, repulsive.

'Oh, I know that,' said Dan, as if delighted to be reminded, sharing them, so to speak, with Counsel. 'For people with the money there's nothing like it. I was personal servant once to the Surgeon Commander. His wife was in England. Ah, he knew how to enjoy himself. There was a girl. She fell for my boss. Five months of it, every night, war or no war, being stuck in harbour on account of a torpedo. I used to let her out, three, four in the morning, five shillings a time. Plenty of money there. Dan, she used to say, I know you are my friend. Yes, miss, I used to say. She was a lovely girl. Black hair. Black eyes. Lovely figure.' Dan let his fingers curve together on the table, with such appreciation that various eminent legal gentlemen winced and looked away. 'I used to sit down below and envy him. Then his wife came. She went sniffing about in his pyjamas and all over.' Dan imitated a cold shrewish drawl: '"Really, darling, I cannot *think* what you've been doing." She thought all right. She used to come to me, smiling sweet as cherries in syrup. "Dan, I do hope my husband has been comfortable?" And she'd give me a look to kill.' Dan, without moving his head, let his eyes move in a cold curious stare from Counsel's face, to the lawyer's. 'But sixpence, that's all.' He bared his teeth in a silent, contemptuous laugh. 'And all the time, my boss was hanging around trying to hear. He'd come in, casual. "Women are curious," he'd say. "They're as curious as monkeys." I'd say: "That's right, sir. Wear the life out of a man, a curious woman. They go on and go on until you think what's the use, might as well tell and be done with it."' Dan stuck his fist into his left pocket and brought out an imaginary note. His right hand accepted his note with offhand gratitude, stuffing it carelessly into the other pocket. '"That's right," he'd say. "But it's worth keeping your mouth shut in the long run."' Dan heaved out more soundless laughter. 'In one way and another I did well out of that couple.'

'Tell them about the nylons,' shouted Flo, 'go on, tell them.'
Dan froze. 'What nylons?'

'You know, the nylons ...' Flo saw she had made a mistake, and sat smiling pathetically, while Dan glared at her.

Rose whispered to me: 'Dan brought in nylons all through the war, he wound them round and round his body under the uniform. A smuggler, that's what he was.'

Dan said hastily, 'And so that's how I bought my house, fair and square, with four hundred pounds I had after the war.'

'My house. My house!' came a shrill voice from the door.
'Who is that?' asked Counsel sharply.
'That's those dirty old beasts, dear,' said Flo. 'Them what we're here for.'

'Good God,' said the lawyer. He dropped his voice: 'How long have they been listening?' He rose and slammed the door.

'But I didn't know you'd mind,' said Flo. 'They always listen, dear. That's what they're like.'

'Well, I really don't know!' said the Counsel. He looked at his watch. It was nearly lunchtime.

'So if the Judge could take my war service and the Lascar into account,' said Dan, remembering why he had begun his confidences.

'I'm going to lunch,' said Counsel, and went, deeply offended. The lawyer went with us to lunch, to make sure nothing worse could happen. It was a difficult meal. Dan's bad temper had focused itself on Jack. 'Yes,' he kept saying, belligerently. 'Yes. And if we lose the case I'll know who to thank.'

'Now, now,' the lawyer said. 'Now, now. It's not everyone who can make a good witness.'

'That's right, sweetheart,' said Flo, trying to shield her son. 'And he took a day off from work and all to help you.'

'Work,' said Dan. 'Work. It's not everyone who can work, either.'

'Jack, why don't you run along off to the pictures,' said Rose.

'But I want to see what happens in Court,' said Jack.

Rose signalled to him with her eyes that Dan should be avoided; but Jack said: 'The Court's for nothing, and I'd have to pay for the pictures.'

'That's right,' said Flo, trying to smile her man into good temper. 'And so it won't cost nothing if he stays.'

'You can say cost,' said Dan. 'You can say it, you're always saying you're short of money, and I know where it goes.'

'Now, now,' said the lawyer. 'There's our case to consider. Let's all keep calm and cool.'

Our case was on first after lunch. We went into the Court with Counsel's anxious voice in our ears: 'Do be careful what you say, please, please.'

They put Dan into the witness-box first. As soon as he was asked a question he replied: 'I served my King and my

Country, sir.' 'Yes, yes, yes,' said our Counsel, in a coldly disapproving voice. 'But I did. All through the war.' 'What's that?' said the Judge. Counsel, very irritated, said that this man had served in the Navy. 'So I see from his papers,' said the Judge, indifferently. Dan's face darkened. His mouth had already opened in a shout of 'Justice!' when Counsel hastily dismissed him, and before they had time to establish even one of the rehearsed points.

Counsel now made a long and efficient statement, from which it appeared the old people were a variety of maniacal criminal. Everyone listened in a matter-of-fact way, like actors at a play. 'How well he does it,' the Court officials seemed to be thinking, as they listened to the earnest and accomplished young man practising a sober rhetoric which would one day take him to far more impressive surroundings than these, to argue big cases, important cases, involving large sums of money and large reputations. They were watching him as if he were a promising schoolboy in his last year, overripe to show what he could do in the great world; and when he concluded, elaborately grave, his voice sinking to a well-sustained note of quiet confidence, the Judge nodded, as if to say, 'Yes, yes, you'll go far.' Then he returned to his notes.

In a few moments the opposing Counsel called Dan back again. This was a poor sort of man, who had long ago lost all hope of taking flight away from this dreary and unimportant Court. He was thin, worried-looking, and his voice was edged with a persistent sarcasm. He kept saying: 'I put it to you . . .' at Dan; and with every repetition of the phrase, Dan's face clenched with uncertainty, tasting each separate word for a hidden trap. He was quite confused, and waiting for a familiar landmark. He did not understand that this Counsel was trying to establish the fact that he was a liar. He had been counting on Dan to deny he locked the bathroom against his clients. After a long preamble, designed to trip Dan up, which luckily he understood not one word of, Counsel arrived at the bathroom and was confounded by the way Dan, finding himself on prepared ground, drew himself up and entered into the part of a landlord concerned only to protect his tenants from the dirt and disease of the old couple. 'And there are children in the house, too!' Dan ended on a note of real sincerity. Thrown off balance, the opposing Counsel dismissed Dan, in order to find a fresh approach.

All this time the old people were sitting by themselves in a corner. The old man was slumped defeatedly against the back of a bench, suffering the continual jogs and jerks of his wife's indignant elbow so slackly that each time she pushed that sharp bone into his side, his whole body slid a little way along the seat, till he righted himself with a straining pull of his shoulder muscles, pulling at the back of the high polished bench with a trembling hand. They were even older than I had thought, incredibly old, with the trembling fragility which comes to people so near their end that they have to conserve every movement in order that their strength may last through what they have to do. The old woman was trembling. A tiny parchment bag of bones, with a small white violent face on top; that was all she was, this terrible old woman of whom I'd heard so much and not really seen before. As the shameful disclosures about her way of living were made aloud for everyone to hear, she twisted her head about in a grimacing parody of scornful laughter, and cried in small gasps: 'No, no, a lie,' until the Judge looked gravely at her over his throne's edge, and told her to be quiet. She put a handkerchief to her stretched and agonized mouth and remained still, but her trembling made the flowers on her soiled white hat rattle together, with a tiny dry sound; and the persistent dry rattling went on till people turned around to look, but the evidence of such misery in the midst of this official scene made them uncomfortable, and they turned away again.

By the time Dan had been dismissed for the second time, the Judge was in a bad temper. Details of emptied slop bowls, dirty lavatories, filth thrown downstairs, it was an offence to have to listen to them.

At first sight, Flo was a welcome change in the witness-box; a starched black Britannia, the embodiment of wrathful virtue. But as soon as she began to answer questions, it was a different matter, for the blood of her Italian grandmother responded at once to the drama of the situation; and our Counsel, with the expression of a man hurrying over the last few yards to safety, kept cutting her short, for fear of what might emerge.

Then the other Counsel took over. As he stood there in his dull black, the knobbly wig kept slipping backwards, exposing a large sweating expanse of red scalp, and he glanced continually at the notes in his hand, like a dull pupil in class. It was not that he had a bad case, in fact I think both our Counsel and lawyer expected him to win it; but he looked as if he hadn't had a good one for years, and had forgotten the habit of confidence. And his manner was even more ponderously sarcastic than with Dan. With each supercilious phrase, Flo got more upset; she was already off balance because our own Counsel had shown no friendly emotion; and this man's display of thin and peevish hostility caused her voice to rise and her gestures to enlarge.

'Surely,' grated Counsel, '*no* reasonable person would put *pepper* on tulips?'

Flo shrugged. 'That's what I keep saying all the time, dear.'

'You say . . .' and Counsel consulted his notes, for the effectiveness of the gesture, 'that she had a dish of pepper. Now what do you mean by that?' Flo stared at him. 'A *dish* of pepper,' he creaked; and stood smiling with prepared amusement.

'Well, if you don't know what I mean I can't help you.' Flo held an imaginary pepper-pot over the edge of the witness-box, and shook it hard.

'You mean a pepper-pot perhaps?' smiled the Counsel.

'I don't mind what you call it, dear, it's all the same to me.'

'Mrs Bolt,' said the Judge severely, 'you really must not call Learned Counsel dear.'

'Sorry, sir.'

'Proceed.'

After a pause Counsel said: 'You will admit that pepper is very expensive.'

Flo raised her hands. 'God knows,' she exclaimed, 'the way prices are going up it's a wonder we are alive to tell the tale.'

'I asked you if *pepper* was not very expensive.'

Flo stared again. 'That's what I said.'

'Just exactly how much does pepper cost?'

'I don't rightly know, because I'm still using the pepper my friend from Edgware gave me when she had the blitz on her shop.'

'Mrs Bolt,' drawled the Judge, peering over the edge of his table like an irritated tortoise, 'do please answer the questions put to you.'

Flo blushed at the injustice of it. 'But I did answer. He said, how much does pepper cost, and I said I don't know because . . .'

The Judge said reprovingly to Counsel: 'I really do think the price of pepper is irrelevant to the point at issue.'

'I was trying to establish a point, my lord.'

'I think I can see the point you were trying to establish.'

At this evidence of the Judge's short temper, our Counsel visibly brightened; but Flo was still miserable. 'I was only trying to tell him because he . . .'

'Yes, yes, yes, yes, yes, yes,' said the Judge.

After a long pause, Counsel pulled himself together for another onslaught. 'What time of the year was this?' he demanded cunningly.

'Time of year? Tulip time.'

'You don't know the exact month?'

'The time tulips bloom,' said Flo, with irritation. 'Spring. Don't you know the time tulips flower?'

'And when you saw pepper on the tulips, what did you do?'

'Well, dear, I went out to have a look at it.'

'Mrs Bolt, will you kindly not refer to Counsel as dear, I've told you already.'

'Ah, my lord, it slipped out, and I'm sorry, sir.'

'How do you know it was pepper?'

'How did I know? It was red, like pepper.'

'Red? *Red* pepper?'

'Paprika,' said Flo, patient but exasperated.

'Oh!' He consulted his notes. 'I took you to mean white pepper.'

The Judge said: 'I really do feel that the colour of the pepper was immaterial.'

'My lord, is it likely that two old people on the old age pension should use red pepper. A rather exotic commodity, I should say.'

'Y e e e e s,' mumured the Judge.

'Mrs Bolt, is it likely that your tenants should use expensive red pepper?'

'Why not? The old witch crawled downstairs and stole it from me, you don't catch her buying anything she can nip out of my cupboard if I forget to lock it.'

'Mrs Bolt,' said the Judge, 'I see nothing about theft in your statement.'

'Did I forget to put it in, dear? Well, it slipped my mind what with all the other things.'

'Mrs Bolt, if you don't show some respect for this Court, then I really am afraid I must fine you for Contempt.'

'Contempt?' cried Flo, on the verge of tears. 'What's that? But, sir, it gets me all flustered, with this talk about the price of this and the price of that.'

The Judge said to Counsel: 'Do you intend to take this matter of theft up?'

Counsel gave a dubious look at the old lady, shook his head hurriedly, and went straight on at Flo: 'How did you know it was pepper? It might have been dust.'

'Know? I saw the old witch sprinkle it on.'

'Mrs Bolt, you really must not use this language in Court.'

Flo burst into tears, saw Dan grinding his teeth at her, and dried her eyes, dolefully.

'Did you smell the pepper to make sure?' asked Counsel.

'No.'

'Why not?'

'Because if you smell pepper you sneeze.'

'Yes, yes, yes, yes, yes, yes,' said the Judge. He looked at the clock and sighed.

Defence Counsel in order to gain time, asked: 'Let me put it to you that you sprinkled the pepper on the tulips yourself.'

The Judge sighed again.

Flo shouted: 'Now is it likely I'd put pepper on the tulips I'd planted and watered with my own hands?'

'Don't shout,' said the Judge.

'But he doesn't believe me,' said Flo, in genuine distress, pointing at the Counsel.

'My good woman, it's his job not to believe you.'

'Well, it seems silly to me.'

'It's not for you to say what's silly and what isn't.'

'Well, who's paying for it? It's cost us over a hundred pounds already, and more to come for today's foolery,' said Flo bitterly. 'Why can't we decide who we want to have in our own house, that we bought and paid for?'

'Mrs Bolt, for the last time, will you restrain your language?'

Flo shrugged, as if to say: 'Well, let's have done with it, and I want my tea.' It was clear she had lost all hope of gaining anything by the case. But she had worn out the Counsel, who dismissed her.

They now called Rose, who had been sitting next to me. I had felt her trembling at the idea of standing up, thus exposed in public. She was very white, and her voice was faint.

Our Counsel got his witnesses mixed, and asked Rose about the noise the old people made; which was what he was to have asked Jack, had he been called. Rose had refused to give evidence on this point, since she had not heard any noise.

'What did you say, do speak up,' said the Judge rudely.

Rose's lips moved, without sound. She was on the point of fainting. 'I don't hear it,' she brought out at last.

'Why not?'

'I don't know about the noise. What I know about is the mess in the bathroom.'

'That was not what you were asked,' said the Judge.

Rose looked at him in appeal, her tongue moving over her lips. Our Counsel hastily dismissed her, and Defence took her over.

'You say you never hear any noise?' he said.

Rose said: 'Either I'm in or I'm out, so I don't hear it.'

'I fail to see the logic of that,' said the Judge.

'Kindly answer my question,' said Counsel, with extreme sarcasm, delighted to find someone he could bully.

'I'm out at the times they make their noise,' she said.

'Then how do you know they make it?'

'Because Mrs Bolt tells me so.'

'Then why did you claim to have heard it yourself?'

'I never did,' said Rose. She had got her colour back. Now she grasped the edge of the witness-box with both hands, took a breath and said with dignity: 'You're trying to make what I say sound how you want. But I said, I said all along, I'd only say what I know is the truth.'

'It is correct,' said the Judge, 'that the witness did not claim to have heard the noise herself.'

Counsel fussed a little, and dismissed Rose, who slid into the bench beside me, clutched at my hand, and sat breathing deeply, trembling all over, her eyes shut.

There was a feeling of inconclusiveness in the air as the old lady went to the witness-box. The Judge leafed through his papers, and it seemed as if he might say, 'People living together should use tolerance,' as the last Judge had; and bind everyone over for a further period.

The old lady entered the witness-box as if the act of doing so was a protest of innocence. She took the oath with trembling fervour. She said she had never insulted Flo because she was a foreigner; and in the next breath that she would not have foreigners turning her out of her house. She said that as a decent British woman she never swore; and then delivered a fluent imitation of Dan at his best.

'That will do,' said the Judge frowning, so that the people in the Court who were smiling composed their faces.

He went on leafing over his notes, in a worried way, looking for some final conclusive point on which to deliver judgment. Besides, what could be done with the old people?

But then, if they were undesirable, so, clearly, were Dan and Flo. The silence continued. Then the Judge made a gesture and the two Counsels both gave short summing-up speeches, for form's sake, for it was clear that the Judge was not listening. He was peering at the old people and at Flo and Dan as if to say: '*Must* you behave like this?'

Suddenly the old lady shot to her feet and announced loudly: 'They are all in conspiracy against me.'

The old man painfully stretched up to pull her to her seat, but she shook him off, so violently he slid along the bench in a heap, and pointed to our lawyer and our Counsel, shouting: 'They were telling the landlord to tell lies, I heard them.'

'Please sit down,' said the Judge.

'In that room,' shrieked the old lady, pointing a trembling finger across the Court. 'They were there, I heard them, they were saying they must tell lies, the truth doesn't matter, that's what they said.'

Now the Judge looked really angry. 'You can't say things like that,' he said.

The old lady burst into shrieks and oaths, dancing up and down between the wooden benches, and pointing at various legal gentlemen around her. 'He – that one – look! Lies! Lies! Lies! Justice, British justice, it's all Jews and foreigners, it's a plot, it's a conspiracy . . .'

An official pushed the old lady down in her seat. In a minute, the whole thing was over. The Judge, at express speed, gave the old people a month to find somewhere to live. Then, feeling perhaps that his manner was not in the highest traditions of legal solemnity, he pulled himself together and made a short but admirable summing-up, which was understood by neither of the parties, because the words he used were out of their experience.

In fact, Dan and Flo believed that the case had gone against them, because of the gravity of the Judge's manner. And it was certainly impressive to think that if the old lady had not suddenly gone crazy, the Judge would, at that moment, and with equal ease, be summing up in the opposite way.

When he said: 'We recommend both sides, for the limited amount of time left, to use their best efforts in the interests of mutual harmony.' Flo said crossly, 'Harmony yourself,' in a voice which reached him. He looked puzzled, since he had just put their point of view: ' – people who have behaved, perhaps not quite as they normally would have done, if not under severe provocation by a couple who clearly need asylum in a place run by sympathetic people.' Dan nodded emphatically at the word asylum, and tapped his forehead, muttering: He says they're nuts, so why is he against us?

Outside Rose pointed out that the case was theirs.

'Oh, no,' said Flo sorrowfully, 'he was awfully cross.'

We had to call over the lawyer, in order to assure Flo and Dan that they had won the case.

Back in the basement Dan unloaded bottles of beer all over the table. Flo shed bits of thick black off her in all directions until she arrived at the comfort of an apron. Dan ripped off jacket and shirt, loosened his trousers, and let his singlet hang loose.

'I can't really believe it,' said Flo. 'Getting our own house to ourselves at last.'

Dan gave his bared-teeth smile; the heavy forearms resting on the table before him were taut with muscle; Rose nodded towards him and whispered to me, 'Look, Dan's already imagining how he'll get his hands on to that flat and do it up.' Dan heard her; looked up, and nodded at us. At that moment he was not even thinking of the money. 'It's like this,' he said, frowning because of his deep disbelief in his power to communicate: 'I go into a dirty room, it's all dirty . . .' His eyes moved from side to side, disliking what they saw. 'And then . . .' his hands clenched and opened out again, waiting: 'I can make it all like new. See?'

Flo laughed, and said to us, full of pride: 'It's nice to watch him, I like that, you'd never believe a place could be nice when he starts, and then it is.' She drank gulps of beer and said: 'I feel so happy, I don't know what to do.' She nodded towards Jack and said: 'Look at Jack, he's happy, too.' Jack, already back in his singlet and running shorts, was trip-stepping about the kitchen, humming, with a puppy in his arms.

Dan turned his head sharply to look, his fists clenched up again, this time in irritation, but he said nothing for the time.

'Yes,' went on Flo, not noticing Rose's steadily critical look at her: 'And just think, two years ago, we had six hundred pounds between us from the war, and this old house, just ruins it was, and now the old people are going we could sell it any time, for three thousand, four thousand, it makes you think.'

Jack let out a little yelp of delight, did some fancy kicks, and began to sing 'The best things in life are free.'

'Yes,' said Dan. 'And no thanks to some people who are going to benefit.'

Jack gave him a dubious, scared glance, smiled in appeal at him, and danced the faster.

'Ah, the poor old things,' said Flo. 'I wonder where they'll go now.'

'For crying out aloud,' said Rose in disgust.

'Funny, isn't it?' said Flo. 'I never really saw them before, not like that, to look at steady. When I saw them in that Court I felt sorry for them, I did really.'

Rose grimaced at me, and raised her eyes.

'They've got four kids,' said Dan. 'She let it out once. Three grown-up sons and a daughter.'

'Well, it's all right, then,' said Flo, 'they'll have a home.'

'Except that they haven't seen their kids since before the war,' commented Rose.

'No sense depending on your kids,' said Dan, looking at Jack.

Jack was scared now, and he stopped dancing, and sat quietly by himself on a chair by the sink.

The bell rang, and Flo went up to answer it. While she was away, Dan stared steadily at his stepson, trying to force him to raise his eyes and face him. But Jack pretended to be unaware; he played with a puppy at his feet, keeping his head down.

Flo came back, and stood in the door, wiping her hands

unconsciously, over and over, on her apron, and her mouth was open.

'What's up?' said Rose.

'It's the Welfare. From the Court. There's a lady and a man and they've got a sort of ambulance. They're taking away the old people to a Home. They say they're not fit to look after themselves. Well, why couldn't they have said it before, that's what I want to know, instead of making us miserable and costing us all that money.'

'What sort of a Home?' asked Rose.

'How should I know, dear?' She was looking up at the ceiling, to avoid Rose's challenge. 'Well, it won't take them long to pack – nothing but a fistful of rags between the two of them.' Over our heads were heavy and purposeful footsteps, and the sound of a high steady whimpering.

'It wouldn't be a lunatic asylum,' enquired Rose steadily. 'We know what them places are like, don't we?'

'But better off there,' said Flo hastily, smiling in terrified appeal at her, 'much better off there than here.'

'Better there than being killed by you and Dan one dark night,' said Rose.

Dan was now moving about in his chair with heavy restless movements. He was grinding his teeth – at Rose, at me, at Jack.

Rose stood up. She was still buttoned up in her suit, and she had drunk no more than a mouthful of beer.

'Where's you going, sweetheart?' said Flo. 'Out with Dickie? That's nice, and I hope you'll have a nice time.'

Rose did not answer. She gave me a meaning glance – Come with me, and avoid trouble. I got up, too.

Jack suddenly cried out: 'Why are you cross with me? Just because I didn't know how to talk right in the box? You're not cross with Rose, and she didn't say nothing in the box.'

'Oh, but Rose was clever,' said Flo hastily, sacrificing her son to her husband. 'She told us better than the lawyers did, they said so themselves.'

'But she didn't say nothing in the box,' said Jack, helplessly, in terror of his stepfather.

'You didn't even try,' said Dan.

'Well, don't take it out on Jack, just because your consciences are hurting you,' said Rose crisply.

'I don't know what you mean, darling,' cried Flo.

Upstairs the noise had ceased and we heard a car drive off.

'Well, they've gone,' said Flo. 'And now let's sit down and have a nice little drink and be happy.'

Dan said, looking steadily at Jack: 'And now I'm going right upstairs, to start work. It'll take a month or more. And you're going to do something for your keep for once.'

'Oh, not tonight,' cried Flo, 'not tonight, sweetheart. It'll do tomorrow.'

He shouted at her: 'You get me my supper. And then I'm to start.' And at Jack: 'Well, are you coming?'

Jack shrilled up; 'Why should I? When I work for you it's for nothing. I can work every night till one or two in the morning, and I don't get a penny for it.'

Flo said: 'Jack, don't talk back to Dan.'

Dan said: 'So you don't? And who feeds you? Do you think you'd get the food you get from your mother on thirty bob a week?'

Flo said: 'Oh, Dan, oh, Jack – but the food's nothing, I just make it up as I go along . . .'

Dan said: 'You know the restaurant business. Tell me what it'd cost for Jack to get fed as he gets fed here.'

'Oh, sweetheart . . .' began Flo, and burst into tears.

Rose took my elbow, and we went quietly to the door. 'Quick,' she whispered, 'or the Lord knows what we'll have to be witness to.'

Jack backed against the wall. Dan was on his feet. Jack shouted out to his mother, who had her hands over her face: 'And you're not my mother since you married him, you've not treated me right since . . .' Dan slapped him across the face. Jack fell over and picked himself up, crouching under the powerful figure of the man towering over him. He was cut off from help in the corner. He shrieked: 'Mum, mum, don't let him hit me.'

189

'Are you going to help me get that place straight or not?'

'No, no, I won't. Why should I? You don't pay me for my work.'

Rose and I had reached the bottom of the stairs. She was clinging on to me. I could feel her trembling again, as she had earlier in Court. 'Wait,' she said. 'I feel sick. People shouting, people fighting, it makes me feel all sick.'

There was a silence in the room we had left. 'Thank the Lord,' whispered Rose. 'They've stopped.'

There was a yell of pain from Dan. 'He's bitten me,' he shouted. 'Your precious son has bitten my thumb right through.' Flo sobbed out: 'Dan, Jack, Dan, Jack . . .'

Jack had rushed out and was in the dark passage with us. In a second Dan was after him. He picked up the boy in his arms and with one hand opened the outer door and flung him outside on to the cement of the passage. Jack got to his hands and knees, Dan was over him, and kicked him. Jack crawled up the steps out of sight, groaning, as Dan kicked at him, in a heavily-breathing silence.

There was a screech of brakes as a lorry swerved. Dan shouted: 'And you needn't come back, this isn't your home any longer.'

'For God's sake,' said Rose, 'help me, dear. Help me out of here.' I got her up into the hallway, where she leaned against a wall, eyes shut, her hand at her stomach.

In a moment she opened her eyes, smiled and said grimly: 'Well, Dan's done it at last. He's been trying to pick a fight long enough.' Beside Rose a door stood open that I had always seen shut. 'Go in and have a look,' she said. 'You'll never see nothing like that again in your life.'

There were two rather large rooms, and a small glassed-in space that had once been a conservatory in a middle-class house. The rooms were high-ceilinged, well-proportioned. But it was not possible to see this at first glance, because the walls were not surfaced, but had a shaggy protuberant look, and the ceilings appeared as if they were growing fungus, or mosses. The window into the street was open, and all the surfaces were in movement. Damp paper hung in strips and shreds from above, stirring and writhing. All around the walls it looked as if soiled stuffing burst from cushions, and wriggled and coiled as it forced its way out through a dingy, yellowing-grey substance. The floors were so thick in dirt that pieces of string and paper and plaster were embedded in a hard gluelike lumpy surface. Shreds of dirty lace hung at the lower half of the windows. Everywhere were bits of newspaper, bits of rag, smelly scraps of food. The smell was a sour thick reek. There was a small iron bed, with a thin stained mattress, and some cardboard cartons, balanced on top of each other. A wash-basin was yellow with grease.

And that was all. I came out, shutting the door on the smell. Rose had recovered. Flo had come up the stairs. She said: 'Why does everything have to happen together, can you tell me that?'

'Because people make them happen together, that's why,' said Rose.

Chapter Six

Winning the case was the beginning of a revolution in that house; in a few weeks everything had changed, and I was looking for somewhere else to live. First: Dan and Flo bought themselves a television set on the hire-purchase to celebrate their victory. At the time this didn't seem nearly as important as the second event -- Dan went up to the War Damage people and made a successful scene; the workmen moved in next week.

'It'll be ever so nice to have a telly,' said Flo. 'We can all sit and watch in the evenings and have a good time.'

This did not happen; at least, not at first. We had a great inaugural party on the evening the set was installed, with Flo's best spaghetti and a rich almond cake and beer. It wasn't a success. Rose had given up a date with Dickie; I wanted to work; and Dan resented every minute he was taken away from his labours on the empty rooms on the first floor. 'Besides,' Flo kept saying, with defiant glances at Dan, who scowled every time the boy's name was mentioned: 'It's not the same without Jack, is it?'

From one day to the next, the basement fell silent. The age of the radio was over, no longer was the house filled with the roar of sound – music and voices. The yapping and playing of the half-dozen puppies distracted Flo from her magic box, and she disposed of them. Soon the basement was inhabited by Flo, Aurora, a single sleep-drugged cat, and the television screen. Flo kept coming upstairs to say pathetically to Rose and myself: 'Why don't you like it, darling, why don't you like our lovely telly?'

Rose said: 'I do like it, but I've got better things to think of.' Rose at that time was oblivious of everything but Dickie.

I hardly saw her, save in the mornings before she went to work, when she came into my room, to run a wetted finger over her eyebrows, smiling at herself contentedly in the mirror, and to say: 'That Dickie, he makes me laugh. Do you know what he said last night? He said I'm like eating ice-cream. That's when we was in bed. He made me have no clothes on. I could have died blushing, but he just laughed. Well, to think what I was missing so long, I could kick myself. But don't hold it against me, because I don't come and talk to you the way we used to have our nice times. I'm still your friend. You wait, when I and Dickie get married, you can come and see me when he's out and we'll have a good laugh.'

Flo said to me: 'Married, she says? Is that what she says? Well, have you told her to get in the family way? And you call yourself her friend? You think men care about lipstick and hair this way and that way – well, she'll find out.'

This was a reference to the revolution in Rose's appearance. She had seen a fashion programme on Flo's television; she brooded about it for some days; then suddenly went off and had her hair cut short and soft, and was wearing light make-up. Her eyebrows were no longer black half-circles; her mouth was its own shape. All this went well with her happiness, and she looked like a girl.

But Flo merely shrugged, and said: 'We'll see, you mark my words.'

Meanwhile the house was in chaos. What Flo referred to as 'The War Damage' were beginning at the top of the house and working downwards. The roof of the attic had collapsed under a weight of stagnant water, bringing down part of the walls.

'Lucky I wasn't in it,' I said to Dan, but he was in too bad a mood to laugh. His quarrel with Jack was a disaster for him.

The War Damage people were responsible for structural damage, but not for repainting. Soon, they would have rebuilt the attic, and before it could be let, it must be decorated. The work on the old people's flat was slow. Dan was still scraping the layer of filth off the floor, with long steel scrapers. He had poured gallons of boiling water on it; used all kinds of chemical, but the residue had to be taken off by hand. He had not begun on the walls and ceilings, which would have to be stripped right down and resurfaced. The rooms were still crawling with lice.

When the attic was done, the workmen needed to get into Miss Powell's rooms; and she was angry because Flo had said to her: 'But it won't matter, sweetheart; they're just going to pull down that wall that's cracked a little, you can stay quite comfortable, if you go out in the days to see friends, the workmen won't be there at night, and you'll be ever so happy.'

Bobby Brent had said that if space had not been found for Miss Powell inside a week she would leave. This terrified both Flo and Dan, because relations were bad with Mr Brent for another reason. It had been agreed that Dan would do all the decorations for the night-club; it was now waiting for him.

'Well,' said Bobby Brent, when Dan made excuses: 'If you're no longer interested in our proposition, then I know what to do.'

Flo wanted to get rid of Mrs Skeffington so as to move Miss Powell down to her rooms. But Rose, who had never had one good word for Mrs Skeffington, told her she should be ashamed even to think of it: 'You kick her out, Flo, and you can go looking for someone for my room, too.'

'Ah, my Lord,' said Flo, 'what's come over Rose? Little miss never-say-boo-to-a-goose, and now look at her – she gets herself a man in her bed and she says Do this and Do that.'

'Besides,' said Rose to me, winking: 'Flo doesn't know it but Mrs Skeffington'll be going of her own accord any minute.'

'How do you know.'

'It stands to reason. Have you heard Rosemary crying at nights?'

'No, I haven't, come to think of it.'

'The way I look at it is this. My lady upstairs knows she's had that precious husband of hers for good. She's stopped fretting. Or at least she's stopped working herself up, and she doesn't have to fetch and carry for the lazy beast. So she's not taking it out on Rosemary.'

Rose was right. Mrs Skeffington said that she was going to live with her married sister, because 'My husband has got a nice engineering job in Canada.' She said good-bye to us all with pretty formality, shaking us by the hands and saying: 'It was nice knowing you.'

'Can you beat it?' said Rose. 'There she was, and we holding her hands while she was rolling and screaming with half her inside gone, and now she says: Good-bye, good gracious me, but it was nice knowing you. Some people.'

Dan perfunctorily cleared the Skeffington rooms and invited Miss Powell to move her things down. She said she must ask Mr Ponsonby. That evening there was a terrible row just over my head; with Dan and Bobby Brent shouting each other down, and Flo and Miss Powell sighing and complaining in counterpoint. Dan stamped, swearing, downstairs, Flo waddling after him.

'Ah, my Lord,' she was saying, 'all we ask is, she should move into those lovely big rooms till the Damage has finished in hers. Then she can move back up, and the rent the same.'

'Rent,' shouted Dan, 'rent you say? We're not going to have money to put food into our mouths, all our tenants leaving because you're too stupid to live.'

Dan had given up his job with the Gas Board, on grounds of urgent family illness. He spent his days over in the night-club, and his evenings on his house. The hundreds of pounds he had made on the side during the past two years were already re-invested. He was joint owner, with Bobby Brent, of two slum houses in Notting Hill Gate. But there was little cash coming in. Flo was serving fish and chips and corned beef hash at every meal.

Over my head Bobby Brent was now quarrelling with Miss Powell. I had never heard them quarrel in all the months I had been there. Soon, she came downstairs, tear-stained but soignée in a slim black suit and furs. At the turn of the stairs she hesitated. Then she called up the well of the staircase in her refined voice, now plaintive: 'Raymond – Raymond?' No reply from Mr Brent. 'I shall be staying at the X Hotel, if you want me.' No reply. She waited a little, then went on down. In a moment I saw her driving away in a taxi. Bobby Brent now entered my room, with dignity. Our relations had formalized themselves into mutual insult. Yet he was always a little wary of me; and I was unable to prevent myself being frightened of him. He knew it.

'And good riddance,' he said.

'It would seem short-sighted to quarrel with Dan, so much satisfactory bread and butter, just because you want to get rid of Miss Powell.'

'Dan Bolt,' said he with a heavy sneer. 'He's not my class.'

'But with such a talent for making money!'

'People never understand a man has to better himself. Women never understand that.'

'Now you can marry the daughter of the Member of Parliament who is a lady.'

'I could, if I wanted to, but as it happens I can do better.'

'That's nice.'

'Marry, marry, marry. That's all women ever think of. And why should I get married?'

'Why indeed?'

'Raymond Ponsonby,' he said, 'has no need of any blasted women.'

'But how about Bobby Brent?' I said.

'I say! You'd better be careful what you say. Just because I have a friend, and come to see her, it needn't mean more than that. Miss Powell's a friend of mine, and she needn't go preventing any banns being called.'

'Good Lord,' I said, 'are you married to her all this time?'

He made an involuntary startled movement, as if to go. He looked at me some time, frowning. Then the impulse to boast bettered him.

'With a lawyer who knows his way about, you'd be surprised.'

'No I wouldn't.'

'Yes you would if I told you. And I will. I put it this way. You hit the thing on the head, as it happens. Raymond

Ponsonby is married, but Robert Brent isn't.'

'And Miss Powell?'

He laughed triumphantly. 'How can she be married to a name that's not on any registers the law would recognize?'

'I see.'

Suddenly he went black with anger at the thought of how he'd given himself away. He poked his chin out at me, half-shut his eyes, and said: 'Blackmail's a game two could play.'

'As a matter of interest, how would you blackmail me if you set about it?'

He smiled, considering the thing on its merits. 'Ah,' he breathed. 'Ah!' He began stalking back and forth across my room, vibrant because of some scheme he had just thought of; or perhaps had had up his sleeve for some time – or perhaps because he was waiting for inspiration.

Looking back, I think I gave it to him, by what I said next.

'I've often wondered,' he remarked, 'what you think of me. We could be friends, but you don't give yourself away. I like that. Yes, I like you for it.'

'I'll tell you,' I said. 'I think you're a psychopath and a sadist, but luckily for you, in this society it won't even be noticed. The sky's your limit as far as I can see.'

'I say!' he exclaimed. 'That's libel. That's slander . . .' He took a few more turns up and down, his eyes narrowed on some increasingly delightful thought.

'I *say*!' he exclaimed, finally, sitting on the arm of a chair. He offered me a classy cigarette out of a gold cigarette case and said: 'Have you ever been to the 400 Club?'

'No, but I'd love to go there with you.'

'I'll take you now.'

'Give me five minutes to change.' I was wearing a skirt and a sweater.

'No need. They know me there. And when we're there I'll introduce you to a friend of mine. He'll interest you. There's a lot of money to be made out of writing best-sellers.'

'So you keep telling me.'

'On the other hand, there's no sense in living in a room like this if you've a best-seller in your pocket?'

We looked around my room together. War Damage would
have a good deal to do in it. There was a great crack up one
wall which widened blackly across the ceiling to end in a
great hole through which dust fell lightly day and night. The
floorboards were at varying levels. Two big brown rexine
chairs, bought by Flo at five bob each at a sale, had strips of
pink sticking plaster across the backs where they had split.
The suite of fine new utility furniture, wardrobe and dressing-table, for which Flo and Dan would be paying weekly
for a year yet, already lacked handles: they had been stuck
on originally with glue. The door of the wardrobe had
warped and would not shut. The glass in the big french
windows which must once, years ago, have opened into a
fine tall, cheerful room kept clean by the labours of heaven
knows how many housemaids, had cracked and were pasted
over with paper.

'Yes,' said Bobby Brent thoughtfully. 'Yes. Well, are you
coming? Aren't you even going to put some lipstick on?'

'I very likely would, if we were going to the 400 Club.'

'The trouble with you is, you can't take a joke.'

On the pavement he hesitated, and said: 'I tell you what,
I'll take you to the 400 by taxi. I'll do that for you.'

'I don't see why not. You've still got the two pounds I
gave you.'

'I say! You've had far more than two pounds' worth of
service out of me.'

'Yes. Tell me, how are you and Colonel Bartowers getting
on these days?'

We were now heading West fast in a taxi. Bobby Brent
straightened himself, looking every inch an honest soldier.

'The Colonel and I have a sound working agreement.'

'Good.'

'He trusted me. Unlike some I might mention. I made a
cool hundred for him only last week. Yes. And would Dan
Bolt own two properties, two gold mines at Notting Hill
without me? You've got to trust people. That's your trouble.
You don't.'

We got out half a mile beyond Notting Hill, ouside a
corner building whose street windows were still boarded up

from war damage. But there were lights in the upper windows.

Bobby Brent let me in to a long low room, badly lit, that had Dan's trestles and working tools standing neatly stacked in one corner. A half-circle bar had been installed. I saw the dim lighting was designed. A dozen wall-lights shed a reddish glow. Bobby Brent turned on a white working light, and the wall-lights became regularly-spaced red spots on arsenic-green surfaces.

'Is the décor your idea?'

'Décor! That's not how it will be. Think I don't know how to do things?'

He took out a sheaf of poster-sized papers and spread them on the counter. They were all erotic semi-nudes, of an exotic nature.

'We're going to have these stencilled on the walls. What do you think?'

'What sort of clientele do you have in mind?'

'Take a look out of the door and see for yourself. This'll be a place people can come at evenings, not too expensive, and plenty of class for their money.' He pulled a clean sheet of drawing-paper to him and began sketching another nude. 'See the idea? It'll be the same as a night-club I saw in Cairo in the war. Now that was a place.'

'It seems a bit old-fashioned to me.'

'That's what you think. Your ideas might be all right for the West End. People who can buy what they like don't like to have their dirty ideas pushed down their throats. But in a neighbourhood like this, they need to know what they're getting.'

'Why, is it going to be a brothel as well?'

'I say! You'd better be careful you know. That reminds me. You stay here. I'll telephone my friend. He'll have an idea or two that'll interest you, you'll see.'

I waited for about half an hour. Then Bobby Brent came back with a small ratlike man who introduced himself as Mr Ponsonby's lawyer, Mr Haigh.

Bobby Brent could not prevent himself from smiling with premonitory triumph.

'And now,' I said, 'let's have it.'

They exchanged glances. Bobby Brent nodded.

Mr Haigh said: 'You're a writer, is that correct?'

'That is correct.'

'And you'd like to make some money on the side.'

'Mr Ponsonby thinks so.'

'Mr Ponsonby knows his way about. Now. You know about the libel laws?'

'You tell me.'

'That's right, we like someone who's careful about what they're getting. But I know my trade. Now. You write a story. You get it printed. Doesn't matter where. Anywhere will do. And then – bob's your uncle if you go about it right.'

'I don't follow.'

'All right, all right. We'll start from another angle. Have you had a story published in a magazine lately?'

'As it happens, yes.'

'Good. Right. Take a look at Raymond here.'

'I'm looking.'

'He's in your story. How would you describe him?'

'Tall, dark, handsome.'

'Not enough.'

'Sinister.'

'No, no. It's the distinguishing marks you have to go for. Take another look – right? He's got a scar under his jaw.'

'Bayonet,' said Bobby Brent, modestly. 'Commandos. The man next to me – should have stuck the dummy, stuck me instead.'

'Right. Now. A tall dark handsome man – sinister is not the right note, it's the wrong touch. With a scar down under his jaw. Now, what does this man do in your story? Right, I'll tell you. He breaks the law. Doesn't matter how. Bob's your uncle. Right?'

'Not yet.'

'Raymond here comes to me. A lawyer. Right? I write to the publishers. My client's been libelled. Easily identifiable. Damages. Settled out of Court. One hundred nicker, just like that – split.'

'Nice for you,' I said. 'But what about me?'

'Insurance pays. You don't. The publishers don't. I've made hundreds that way. Hundreds. Always settle out of Court, they do – frightened of Court. The libel laws work against them. Only once went to Court. We lost. Mistake. But what's one mistake with so much to gain? How about it?'

'I'm not entirely clear in my mind.'

'Right. Try again. Take me. How would you describe me – as a writer, mind.'

'Small, furtive, rodentlike.'

'Nah, not those fancy words. Look at my face. What do you see? I've got a mole. Look. Now, there's your character for you – a lawyer with a good practice, his office situated so and so, and the name's important, not Haigh, too close, something like Hay, or Hag – enough to establish malice. And with a mole on his upper cheek, he does something he shouldn't. It's in the bag. Not that I want you to use me – it's too close the knuckle in a manner of speaking. But Raymond here. Or I can find someone. I got three hundred once, split three ways, it's a hundred nicker each – what's it cost you – spend an evening scribbling something, good enough to sell. I know three writers – they've lived off the libel laws these five years. Right. Now, what do you say?'

'What immediately strikes me is, I'm surprised you're interested in such small stakes. Knowing the way Mr Ponsonby operates, what's even a hundred to him?'

They exchanged another glance.

'Raymond Ponsonby's in a class by himself,' said Mr Haigh. 'That I grant you. And I'm not saying it would be Mr Ponsonby who'd oblige. I'm not saying that. I was using him and myself as examples. Right?'

'I'll think it over,' I said.

Bobby Brent controlled, with difficulty, a look of pure vicious triumph.

We all shook hands. Mr Haigh departed, hoping he would have the pleasure of my further acquaintance.

We locked up. 'And now, a taxi,' I said.

'You want your pound of flesh, don't you?'

'I'm learning.'

I saw him laugh silently.

In the taxi he pulled out a piece of paper. 'Here's the contract,' he said. On it was typed: 'In pursuance of an arrangement come to this day the .... 1950, ... contracts to pay Raymond Ponsonby the sum of £50 or half the proceeds of the damages gained from .... Publishing Company, as a result of the story written by the said .... libelling the said Raymond Ponsonby, in terms to be agreed in private treaty between the said .... and the said Raymond Ponsonby before the story is written by the said .... such payment to be made within a week of settlement being received from the said publishing company.'

'You just fill in your name,' he said casually. 'Of course it's a draft. To give you the idea. We knocked it out in Mr Haigh's office while you were waiting.'

'The only thing is,' I remarked, 'I used to work in a lawyer's office.'

I heard his breathing change. In the dark of the taxi he laboured to hide the murder on his face.

'I say!' he said at last. 'You should have told me. It's not fair. That's taking advantage. You can't call it anything else.'

'Well, it's not bad,' I conceded. 'Take quite a lot of people in, that document, I should think.'

'Now, if you'd done the decent thing and told me you worked for a lawyer, you'd have saved me a lot of trouble, wouldn't you?'

'Collusion, wouldn't it be? Of course, the Law's different here, but it's probably collusion for the purposes of fraud. And you could have blackmailed me for years and years.'

'Well, how was I to know you knew about the Law, if you didn't tell me?'

'Your trouble is, you haven't yet learned what people you can double-cross and who you can't.'

'Nobody's using words like that to Andrew MacNamara. You'd better be careful.' He thought a while. 'Besides, look at it one way – I was doing you a good turn. After all, there is a lot of money to be made out of the libel law. That's a fact. Of course that stuff's not really in my class any longer, but a couple of years back I made a few hundred nicker out of writers.'

'It all helps.'

'You're coming on,' he said at last, after a long silence. 'I must say that you – you're coming along fast. Well, I like that. You might turn out to have a real head for business. We could work together yet, if you just learned to trust me.'

'It's a terrible thing, lack of trust between friends.'

'Yes. And loses money in the long run. Well, Mr Haigh will be disappointed. He's not been doing too well recently, and he could do with a hand-up. I tell you what. I've a proposition. We'll sign a real document, fair and above board, I don't want any money for myself, but you and Mr Haigh split between you. I'd like to do him a good turn, and you, too. And that would show you I'm on your side.'

'I don't think my head for business is highly enough developed yet.'

'Not yet, I grant you. But it comes with practice. Mind you, I'll tell you this, when I first met you, I'd never have believed you'd come on like this, but you just let me know when you're ready, and I'm your man.' He left me at the door and took the taxi on, saying: 'No hard feelings, mind you!'

'None at all, I assure you.'

'That's right.'

I did not see him again: he left the Bolts' house that night. Dan and Flo were worried about the loss of rent but not, as I thought they should be, about their capital.

Dan said it had all been done through a lawyer. Who chose the lawyer? Bobby Brent, said Dan, but a lawyer is a lawyer, when all is said and done.

Two years later their partnership broke up, in violence. They had filled their two houses with West Indians; but Bobby Brent was making off with more than his share of the rents. Dan got to hear of this, and challenged him. Bobby Brent denied it. Dan lost his temper and assaulted him. Within a few seconds he found himself lying on his back, under the ex-Commando, the ju-jitsu expert; helpless, the knife that he had in his hand pointing at his own throat.

They made a deal, in that position. They would each take one of the houses. Dan would sell out his share in the night-club, now doing nicely, to Bobby Brent. He would say nothing more about the fact he had never been paid for the work he did decorating the place.

Dan lost a good deal of money in this settlement, but not so much that he could not immediately afford to buy a third house for himself.

But this glory was still well in the future; they were occupied now with getting in enough money to keep up the hire-purchase instalments and pay for food.

The campaign against me began when Dan came up to demand a month's rent in advance. I paid in advance weekly. There was no proof, because we had agreed that rent-books were not necessary between friends. I refused; and Dan stamped out, saying that there were marks on the table that had not been there before, and I was going to have to pay him for the damage.

I told Rose, and she said: 'They're cross. They want you to take the rooms on the ground-floor when they're ready, and I said you wouldn't want to. They're charging five pounds a week. You wouldn't want to pay that, would you? And I said that no one who'd seen that place so filthy and smelly would live in it, no matter how nice Dan does it up.'

'I wouldn't be able to.'

'No. Nor me. They might see that for themselves, but they don't, Just hang on tight, their tempers'll improve. Flo's got a scheme on to get Jack back. He came into my shop yesterday and sent a message. I told Flo, but she daren't tell Dan. She's written out an advertisement to lie on the table for Dan to see: Come back, Jack. All is forgiven. But Dan pretends not to see it. Well, they'd better be quick, because Jack's thinking of going to Australia. He says there's no room in this country for a lad of enterprise. He can say that, looking at Dan. He makes me laugh, he does really.'

She said 'he makes me laugh' in a sad heavy voice I had not heard for some weeks. Three evenings she spent in my room, one after another, saying that she wasn't going to let Dickie take her for granted. In other words, he was standing her up again. Also she was troubled about her brother, now due out of Borstal. War Damage had finished with the attic, and she wanted him to live there. Flo and Dan refused; they were prepared to let Len sleep where Jack had, in the kitchen, rent-free, provided he helped Dan with the decorating.

'But it's not nice,' said Rose. 'He'll want a little comforting and petting after that place, and all he'll get will be work, work. And no money for it. So what can I do? My mother's married that fancy man and he's already started to treat her bad. I could have told her. But she's got a real weakness for bad ones, the way I told you.'

'Like someone else I know,' I said.

She was distressed. 'Don't say that,' she pleaded. 'Don't say it. Not yet, any rate. Perhaps things'll come right. I mean, I know he loves me and that's what counts, isn't it?'

'Perhaps Flo's right,' I said.

'But I couldn't be happy, knowing I'd got a man that way. It stands to reason, you'd always be thinking – you'd remember you tricked him and you wouldn't feel good. Mind you, it doesn't trouble Flo, she's happy enough.'

'Not at the moment.'

'No. But they'll make it up.'

Downstairs, Flo had been reduced by Dan's persistent bad temper into a state of permanent near-tears. When he entered the basement he was confronted by Flo and Aurora, sitting in each other's arms, staring at him in helpless pathos.

He swore and blustered, but Flo replied through Aurora, thus: 'Ah, my Lord, your daddy's cross with us, Oar, he doesn't love us no more, he just wishes we were both dead.' At which Aurora wept, and Flo with her, genuinely and copiously.

Soon he counter-attacked. He was waking very early these days. He sneaked Aurora out of her bed while Flo slept, and took her into the kitchen. There he built up a great fire, and ate his breakfast with the child on his knee, feeding her bits of fried bread and egg. One morning the builders had blocked the front door with their gear and I had to go out through the basement. Dan forgot his ill-humour with me, and gave me a smile, pushing forward a chair, and setting a cup of tea. There was a great red fire. Aurora sat sleepy and smiling in her white nightgown with her arm round her father's neck. 'Look,' said Dan, 'she's eating. She eats for me, if she won't for her mother.' He was cheerful and at ease there in his hot kitchen. He cooked more bacon, more egg, for me and for my son, and Aurora ate everything put in front of her.

'You see?' he kept saying, awed by this miracle. 'It's just that stupid cow her mother that stops her eating.'

Dan kept this up every day, and when we went up to work in the flat, took the child with him. But it was all too much for Aurora, who spent half the day as Dan's ally, and the other half as Flo's. She became silent; all the obedient clown went out of her nature, and she sucked at her bottle hour after hour.

'No, I don't love you, I don't love you, I don't love,' she murmured automatically whenever either parent came near her. If she was picked up she went rigid and shrieked.

At this juncture Welfare came again, and insisted on seeing both parents. Dan, who resented Welfare as much as Flo, was prepared to use her in his battle against his wife. He took Aurora to the doctor himself, allowing Flo to go with him.

What they heard subdued the parents into friendship for each other. They were inarticulately miserable. They both deeply loved the child. Yet the doctor said they had ill-treated her to the point where she had a patch on one lung; her teeth were rotten; her bones were rickety. She had to have regular food, fresh air, and the company of other children. If her condition had not improved by the next visit, she would have to be sent to a sanatorium.

Rose discussed all this with me; and went down to the basement to say Aurora should go to a nursery school.

She came back to say: 'Would you believe it? They say they have no money for nursery schools. I said, it's your kid, isn't it? And all that money with Bobby Brent? If it comes to the worst, sell out your share in one of the houses. But, oh no, perish the thought, money before Aurora every time.'

'But they love that kid,' I said.

'Love?' said Rose. 'Don't use that word to me. I've heard

all I want for the time being.' She was going out with Dickie again; but all the joy had gone out of it. She had told him he must marry her; and he was replying: 'What for?'

'What for? he says. What for? Well I'm not getting any younger. I say to him, Don't you want your own home? Don't you want children? But, oh no, not Dickie Bolt, he just laughs and twists my arm and says Let's go to bed.' She leaned forward in her chair, staring into my fire, her hands trembling together in her lap. 'And what's sad is, making love isn't what it was, the way I feel. I've gone all cold on him and I can't help it. And he says: What's biting you, Rose? Funny, aren't they – what's biting you, he says, enjoying himself, and me scared even to think of what's going to happen. Suppose I don't never have a kid? I want to have kids bad.'

'Give him up,' I said. 'He's no good to you.'

'Oh, don't say it. I know he isn't. But I love him and I can't help myself.' She sat, staring, silent. Then she said fiercely: 'And downstairs, that Flo and that Dan – if I had a kid I'd know how to look after it. I know. I'd treat it right and have some sense, not all that shouting and slapping and kissing.' She wept hopelessly, and would not be comforted.

Downstairs, now that her parents were no longer quarrelling, Aurora began to improve. Flo took her to the Park every afternoon and pushed her on the swings. She was made to go to bed early. She ate badly but better than before.

Meanwhile Jack, against Rose's advice, chose this moment to present himself truculently one evening, demanding to come home. The parents were concentrated on Aurora and their fright over her. He was told he could come back if he helped Dan. Jack had heard of Dan's need for him, and demanded union rates for whatever work he did. Dan lost his temper again. Jack went off, and soon we heard he had gone to Australia. It was much later that Flo discovered the fifty pounds nest-egg she kept rolled in an old corset at the back of her cupboard was missing. He had used it to pay his passage.

War Damage had now finished the two top floors. Dan left his work on the ground-floor flat and was painting them.

The workmen wanted to come into my room and Rose's.

The following conversation took place between me and Flo.

'Well, dear, isn't it nice, they're going to pull down one wall of your room and make it all nice, I don't know what you're going to do, I'm sure.'

'What do you suggest?'

'Pardon, dear?'

'Am I going to sleep with a wall down?'

'You can't sleep in Rose's room, because she's moving downstairs to us, it's no trouble to her, now she and Dickie's cooled off, she doesn't need a room to herself. They're pulling down her wall, too.'

'Well, and where am I going to work?'

'You could take your typewriter to the bathroom, couldn't you, sweetheart?'

'I could, but I won't.'

'Ah, my Lord, I knew you'd say that.'

'Tell me, Flo, do you think it's fair for me to pay you full rent when I can't even use my room to work in?'

'Pardon?'

'Why should I pay you for something I don't get?'

'But the blitz wasn't my fault, dear. Tell me now, is it true you're looking out for somewhere to live?'

'Yes, it is.'

'There's that flat downstairs, it's going to be ever so nice.'

'But not for me.'

'Because you don't want to pay what we'll have to ask when this room is all done up and nice, do you?'

'No.'

'I'll talk to Dan,' she said, distressed.

Eventually the builders decided not to rebuild the wall but only to patch it up a little.

'It'll be ever so nice for you,' said Flo. 'They're nice men and you won't be so lonely working away by yourself all day.'

This turned out to be true.

At nine o'clock every morning the men knocked on my

door and enquired: 'Ready, miss? Any dirty work before we start?'

They would then descend to the cellar and carry up coal for me. During that time I had my fire roaring all day and night; I hated so much the thought of going down into the black damp cellar down half a dozen flights of stairs that often I would let it go out and get into bed to read instead.

I had them in my room, three of them, for a month. Two were small, pale, underfed little men who should by rights have been plump and applefaced and amiable, but who were too cautious to do anything but smile, tentatively, and then instantly restore their defensive masks; and their foreman, an offhand, good-humouredly arrogant young man who talked for them all. His name was Wally James, and after he had fetched my coal, we all had a cigarette and many cups of tea. About nine-thirty, he would stretch and say: 'Well, this won't keep the home fires burning,' and in the most leisurely way in the world he set out his tools and began to work.

I gave up all attempts at working, for he would say: 'That's right, miss, don't take any notice of me,' and start to chat about his wife, his children, the state of the world, and the Government; but most particularly the last two, for he had them on his mind. Eventually I pushed my typewriter away, and we brewed tea and talked.

When this foreman was not there, even if he were out of the room for a few minutes, I would find myself thinking of him as a tall and well-built man, even handsome, for this was how nature had intended him to be. The frame of his body, the cage of his skull, were large, generously defined; but at some time in his life he must have been underfed; for the flesh was too light on gaunt bones, his face was haggard, the eyes deep and dark in their sockets. He had a mop of black hair, rough with bits of dust and plaster; his hands were fine and nervous, but calloused; and the great head was supported on a thin, corded neck.

It took him and his mates four days to remove two panes of glass from my french windows and insert new ones. He assessed the work to last that long; it was what he thought he could get away with. I used to watch him and feel homesick; for I come from a country of accomplished idling.

The memory, perhaps, of a black labourer, hoe in hand, commanded to dig over a flower bed ... He saunters out, hoe over his shoulder. He lets the hoe fall of its own weight into the soil and rest there, till, with a lazy lift of the shoulders, the hoe rises again, falls ... the man stands, thinking. He straightens himself, spits on his hand and fits it lovingly around the sweat-smoothed wood handle. He gazes around him for a long while. A shout of rage comes from the house. He does not shrug, move, make any sign; he is attacked by deafness. Slowly, the hoe rises, falls, rises, falls. No sign from the house. Leaning on the handle he gazes into the distance, thinking of that lost paradise, the tribal village where he might be lounging at that moment, under a tree, watching his women work in the vegetable garden while he drinks beer. Another shout of rage from the house. Again he stiffens, without actually hearing. The hoe seems to rise of its own accord, and lazily falls, rises and falls, so slowly it seems that some invisible force fights against gravity itself, restraining the hoe in its incredibly lazy down-curve to the soil. 'Can't you go any faster than that?' demands the white mistress from the verandah of the house. 'What do you think I pay your wages for?' Why? Well, of course, so that I can pay that stupid tax and get back home to my family ... this thought is expressed in the sullen set of the shoulders. By the end of the day he has achieved the minimum amount of work.

Wally James, lazily allowing his chisel to slide over the cracked putty that held the cracked glass in place, remarked: 'When we put the Labour Government in, we thought things would be better for the working people. But the way things would out, what's the difference?'

'According to the newspapers ...'

'Now, miss, you won't hold it against me, but you don't want to go reading those newspapers now.' Scrape, scrape, scrape, scrape. 'This is a real nice window, say what you like.'

'It will be, when it's mended. Been cracked ever since I came in.'

'You don't say. Well, next time you just let me know. You don't want to go wasting time with those forms. Takes it out of a person, those forms do.' He stood back and looked musingly down into the street. 'Who'd have thought a working man's Government would get itself all messed up with forms and such.'

'I don't see it's much worse than the last, do you?'

'I didn't say worse, couldn't be worse, could it? But when we put them in, we meant them to be better.'

'Surely it's better.'

'We-ll,' he grudgingly admitted, 'you could say it's better. But take me. I've got a wife and two kids. Two kids isn't a big family. *And* my wife works mornings. *And* I earn eight quid a week. We earn eleven quid between us. Sounds a lot, don't it? And I can't afford to take the kids for a holiday, not a proper one. What do you think of that now?' He scraped a little more, and stood back. 'Working since I was fourteen. I'm thirty-four. And all the real holiday I ever got was the Army. Join the Army and have a nice rest. My old woman gets mad with me when I say that.' He lit a cigarette and said: 'How about a nice cup of char? Can you spare it? If not, I'll bring you a bit of my ration tomorrow.'

Drinking tea, he remarked: 'We could do that job in half a morning.'

'Yes?'

'Easy.' He smoked peaceably. 'Don't see any point in slaving my guts out and getting nothing back. I'm fed up. What's the sense in everything?'

'Don't ask me.'

'I'm not asking, I'm telling. When I think of what those boys said before we put them in and what they do now. All the same, once they get in, that's right, isn't it, mate?'

'That's right,' assented the other two. They listened to their foreman speaking with detached interest. I got the feeling that if he had made a passionate speech about raising production, they would have assented, with equal indifference: 'That's right.'

'Listen to them,' he said scornfully. 'That's right, they say, that's right. Not an idea in their bloody heads. Do you know what they are? Slaves, that's what. *And* like it. Let me tell you. Last week all the men were complaining about the tea in the canteen. It came cold every time, and the food was muck. There they were, grumbling their heads off. I said, All right then, who's coming with me to complain to the boss. Oh, yes, they were all coming. The whole bleeding lot. So I walked out of the canteen and went to the office, and when I turned around, where were they? Yes, where were you?' The two men continued to strip paper off the walls, without turning around. 'Scared. Can't talk up for themselves. I said to the boss, We're sick of the food and the tea isn't fit to drink. He said: Where's the men, then? Why don't they complain. Well, the tea's better, but no thanks to them. No thanks to you two either.'

At five o'clock, they knocked off. Wally refilled my coal-box, swept out my room, dusted it, asked for another cup of tea. We talked until it was time for me to go to the nursery to fetch my son.

'You might not know it,' I said, 'but outside this country I know newspapers which say the working people here are getting big wages and are better off than the middle-class.'

'Is that so? Well you know better now, don't you? Yes, I know your sort – no harm meant. I've seen the books on your shelves. You're an intellectual, you are. You mean well. But what this country needs is a strong-man government. Oh, not that Hitler stuff and all that about the Jews. I don't hold with it. But we've got all these blacks coming in, taking the bread out of our mouths. And what the Government gives with one hand and it takes back with the other. Before we know it, we'll have unemployment again. Oh, I know. Well, I've enjoyed our little talk. See you tomorrow, miss, and if you greet us with a cuppa we'll not say no. And none of your lugging coal up behind my back. Don't hold with women on that kind of caper. Wouldn't let my wife carry coal and lug furniture about. No, any dirty work about, you let me know, and I'll fix it.'

When the paper was stripped off, if could be seen that

bombing had loosened the walls so that they stood apart at the angles from half-way up to the ceiling, between a quarter and a half inch. They pasted strips of paper over the cracks, and wallpapered over the whole. The great crack across the ceiling was filled in with putty and papered over. 'It's a crying shame,' said Wally. 'Such a nice house it must have been once. Well, these swine I'm working for, if they could use old newspapers for building materials and get away with it, they would. Don't you hold it against me, miss. I know what's good work and what's not. Well, it'll hold together. Hundreds of these houses, you'd be surprised – you'd think they'd fall down if someone gave a shout in the street. But they keep on standing out of sheer force of habit, as far as I can see.'

Chapter Seven

Soon the rooms on the ground floor were done. Because Dan was pressed for time and money, none of Flo's ideas for decorating were put into effect: she had wanted dadoes, friezes and tinted mouldings. The walls and ceilings were white; and the floors black. The conservatory end, now a place of shining glass and polished stone, had potted plants from Flo's backyard. No money for fine curtains: they had to use the cheapest thing they could find, government silk, in dull white. No money for the heavy varnished furniture Flo had planned. Neither Rose nor I would give up our furniture, as of course Dan expected us to do; they had to take down stuff from Miss Powell's and the Skeffingtons' flats, which they had picked up at sales and which was mostly unobtrusive and even at times pleasant. Flo mourned over the flat, which was large, light, and pretty. 'We'll never be able to let it for what we wanted,' she said. Rose had a student in her shop asking for a place, and brought her home; she was so enthusiastic over the rooms that Flo raised the rent from five pounds to eight pounds a week and got it. Four Australian drama students moved in, and at once the ground floor, which had been the unspeakable hidden sore of the house, became its pride. The girls were pretty and self-possessed; had insisted on a proper lease; paid their rent; and merely looked impatient when Flo and Dan tried to play them up.

'You'll have to behave yourselves now,' Rose commented, when Flo complained the girls had no sense of humour: they had not been amused at her heavy hints about their boy-friends. 'You can't carry on the way you do, not with decent people, or they'll leave.'

Flo and Dan realized at last that this was true; and left all negotiations with the girls to Rose, who, when approaching them, used a manner of ingratiating propriety. She copied it, as she explained to me, from her favourite television announcer. 'After all,' she said, 'it stands to reason it must be the right way the upper-class people carry on, or he wouldn't be paid all that money for smirking and smiling and minding his manners, would he now?'

On the strength of the eight pounds a week, Dan hired labour. Mick, a building apprentice, and Len, Rose's brother, moved into the Skeffingtons' flat, for their food, a bed, and pocket money. They soon finished the top flat; Rose was negotiating to let it to a woman who had come into her shop; when Flo announced, with a mixture of guilt and furtive delight – that she had let it to 'an ever so nice lady who's French.' Rose noted Flo's expression, made her own enquiries, and told Flo she should be ashamed. 'And who's talking? Little miss prim-and-proper? And what was you doing with Dickie not a month back, may I ask you?' This shaft hit Rose so hard that even Flo was ashamed. 'I didn't mean it, sweetheart, I didn't really,' she kept shouting, as Rose stood silent, trembling; and finally crept upstairs to cry in her room.

Rose said to me: 'Do you know what? Flo's let the top flat to one of them dirty beasts. And why? Because she gets twice the rent from her. And just now when I've got my little brother here who needs a good example set.'

'How do you know?'

'How can you ask? Through my old boy-friend who's a policeman. He came into my shop to pass the time of day and he knew about her. And now there'll be men in and out day and night, and what about my Len?'

Flo said, licking her lips: 'I've put a nice chair beside her bed, and she can entertain her friends ever so nice when they come.'

In the event, when Miss Privet – pronounced by Flo as Preevay – arrived, she was just out of hospital after a bout of pneumonia and she went straight to bed and stayed there. Once or twice she called the lads working in the rooms below to go out and buy her food; but Rose went straight up to her and said that if she ever so much as looked at Len she, Rose, would call the police.

'My God, Rose,' I said, 'the poor woman's hungry.'

'Poor woman, you say? With all the money them beasts earn she could pay for a restaurant to send it in.' She gave me a shrewd, hard, sorrowful look, nodded and said: 'Yes. I know. So you're going up. Curiosity killed the cat.'

Miss Privet's brief stay in the house was to cost me Rose's friendship; I did not understand how deep her feeling was.

I went upstairs, knocked, and saw a plain middle-aged woman sitting up in bed reading. I asked if she needed anything. She replied coldly: 'I have no need of anything, thank you,' and returned to her book.

For a week she stayed in bed, brought food and drink by Mick. Then I passed her on the stairs on her way out. She wore a fur coat, a small black hat with a veil, and a hard make-up. Her handbag was enormous, of shiny black. I could not keep my eyes off her shoes. They were black patent, with wide black ankle-straps. The soles were platforms two inches deep, the toes were thick and square; but the instep was displayed in a deep curve, giving an effect of brutal intimacy. She saw me looking, remarked coolly: 'Interesting, aren't I?' and walked out, pulling on her gloves.

She came back an hour later with flowers, food, and some library books.

I wrote her a letter as follows, drawing upon past experience: 'Dear Miss Privet, I shall be very happy to have the pleasure of your company to coffee this evening at nine o'clock,' and pushed it under her door.

Rose saw me. 'You're not going to have her down in your room?'

'I've invited her to coffee.'

'Then you'll never have me in your room again.'

'Oh, Rose, don't be silly. Why not?'

'She's filthy, a filthy beast.'

'But what she does doesn't affect you or me.'

'I'll tell you something, if she drinks out of your cups, you'll have to sterilize them before I use them.'

A note came down by Micky, saying: 'I shall be very

happy to join you. Yours sincerely, Emily Privet.'

At five to nine Rose came in to say she was going out to the pictures by herself. She went, with a look of sorrowful reproach.

At nine Miss Privet arrived, wearing slacks and a sweater and without make-up. The first thing she said was: 'I see your friend has gone out to avoid the contagion.'

'She's just gone to the pictures.'

'Yes?' she said, in exactly the way Rose did. Then she shrugged and said: 'But I'm glad of a bit of company, I'm getting the pip up there in that box.'

'I was there for a bit myself.'

'Your kid, too? How much?'

I told her, and she put her head back and laughed. 'Yes, we have to pay for our sins,' she said. 'I'm paying that old tart downstairs four quid a week.'

'You're mad,' I said.

'Is that so?' she said. 'And why did you pay? If you've got a kid, or you're on the wrong side of the Law you've got to pay. But I'm not staying. That old floozie downstairs'll see my back before the week's out.'

'You don't seem to like Flo.'

'She's sex-mad,' said Miss Privet. 'Makes me sick.'

'She told me you were French.'

Miss Privet got out of the big chair, and hippily walked about the room, saying in a throaty voice: 'Cheri, I love you. Je t'aime. Ça va? Ah, cheri, cheri, come – for – a little – walk avec moi . . .'

She sat down again and said briskly, in her normal voice, which was Midland-bred, as far as I could judge: 'I know enough catch-phrases and put on an accent to spice it up for those who haven't met any French. I knew a French girl once. But she had to pretend to be English when she went back to Lyons. Give the poor fools what they want, that's my motto.'

She never spoke of men in anything but tones of amiable contempt.

That evening we discussed literature. Her tastes were decided. She liked Priestley, Dickens, and Defoe, particularly the *Journal of the Plague Year*, which she knew practically by heart. 'And do you know that man called Pepys? He knew his London. I often read a bit of his *Diary* and then walk over the streets he walked and think about things. Nothing's changed much, has it?'

At that time I still had not learned to like London. I said so and she nodded and said it took time. But if I liked, she would show me things. Later she ran upstairs and fetched down a print of Monet's 'Charing Cross Bridge'. 'That's London,' she said. 'But you have to learn to look.'

Before she went to bed, she said that if the light was right tomorrow she'd take me to her favourite place in London.

Rose did not come to say good night to me that evening.

Next evening, about five, Miss Privet came down to say: 'Quick, get a coat on. I'll take you now.' She had already turned to go and get her things, when she gave me a shrewd glance and said: 'What's the matter, afraid I'll be in my warpaint?'

She came down wearing a straight cloth coat, flat shoes, and a scarf over her head. She saw me examining her, and smiled. Then she posed; and let her face assume a look of heavy-lided, sceptical, good-natured sensuality. This she held a few seconds; then switched it off, saying with contempt: 'Easy, isn't it? That and the shoes.'

We took a bus to Trafalgar Square, and at six, with the bells rolling from St Martin's, she grabbed my arm and raced me up the steps of the National Gallery.

'Now,' she said.

It was a wet evening, with a soft glistening light falling through a low golden sky. Dusk was gathering along walls, behind pillars and balustrades. The starlings squealed overhead. The buildings along Pall Mall seemed to float, reflecting soft blues and greens on to a wet and shining pavement. The fat buses, their scarlet softened, their hardness dissolved in mist, came rolling gently along beneath us, disembarking a race of creatures clad in light, with burnished hair and glittering clothes. It was a city of light I stood in, a city of bright phantoms. But Miss Privet was not one to harbour her pleasures beyond reasonable expectation. For ten minutes I was allowed to stand there, while the light changed and the thin clouds overhead sifted a soft, drenching golden atmosphere.

Then she said, 'Now we should go. It'll be dead in a minute, just streets.'

Unfortunately I did not go out again with her, for she left.

Her history, or rather, what she told me, was this: She was the daughter of a lawyer's clerk from the Midlands. She worked as a shorthand-typist until the war began, when she married a pilot who was killed over Germany. Then she was lonely and had a number of affairs. She was sharing a flat with a girl-friend. This friend married and Miss Privet found herself alone with three months' instalments due on the furniture. Coming home one evening from work, thinking about the money she owed, she was accosted by a GI, and took him home on an impulse. He gave her the equivalent of ten pounds. For a few weeks she worked in her office as usual, and walked home afterwards, slowly – 'practising the walk and the look'. Then she gave up her work in the office.

She became friends with one of her clients who was a businessman, married. For a while she was his mistress. But he had other friends. For three years, she had been kept by four of them. They all liked racing, drinking and gambling. They used to go to the races together, all five of them.

One evening, she was walking home by herself, thinking as she put it, 'of my own affairs, but I must have been sending out the allure out of sheer force of habit' when she was accosted by an American. She took him home and was discovered by one of her regulars, who told the others. The four of them made a mass scene, in her flat, where they had complained she was nothing but a common whore and a tart. 'Which they might have thought of before, mightn't they? Bloody hypocrites they are,' she said. So she told them to go to hell and went back to the streets.

Then she got sick, neglected it, and found herself in hospital with pneumonia. Out of hospital, she went back to her flat and discovered someone had informed on her, and she had been dispossessed. She managed to rescue some of her furniture which was in store. Now she was looking for another flat. She had had a letter from one of the four businessmen whose wife had died. 'He's offering me holy matrimony,' she said, with a wink.

'Are you going to marry him?'

'We-ell, I don't think he should marry a common tart and prostitute, do you?' she drawled.

'Do you want to be married?'

'The way I look at it is this. You get bored with one man, don't you? You get just as bored with four. So you might as well settle for one. The trouble is, he's not the one I like the best. That's life, isn't it? If the one I liked ditched his wife, I'd think about it. As it is, I think I'll just get myself a flat, issue an invitation or two, and see what happens.'

I said: 'Aren't you afraid of getting old?'

'Don't be silly,' she said. 'You're really green, in some ways, aren't you? Men don't come to me for my looks. I'm not ugly, but I'm no oil-painting either. They come because I can cook, I can make a place comfortable, and I know what they like in bed. I'm not interested in sex. Any fool can learn to bite a man's ear and moan like a high wind.'

'Don't you ever like sex?' I enquired.

'If you're going to talk dirty, I'm not interested,' she said. 'I can't stand dirty talk. Never could. I like you,' she said, 'but there's things I can't stand, and one's sex-talk.'

Before she left, she made a formal visit, to say with the deliberate casualness that means someone has been planning a conversation: 'Do you imagine you're going to make a living out of writing?'

'It's a matter of luck.'

'You don't want to trust to luck. It's a dreary existence, banging away all day, having to think up thoughts all the time. I've been thinking about you. Now listen. You'll never have security. Now in my job you've got security if you've got a flat. It's the only job that has real security for a woman. You can always be thrown out of a job. And take you – a spot of bad luck with your writing and where will you be – in some double bed you don't like, I bet. Now you take my advice and get yourself a flat and set yourself up. Learn to cook. That's the thing.'

'I don't really think the life would suit me.'

'You're a romantic. That's your trouble. Well, I've no patience with those.'

Miss Privet borrowed ten pounds from me when she left, and about three months later I got this letter: 'I enclose your ten quid which saw me through, and thanks, my dear. No money troubles now as I've been doing overtime one way and another and my friends so pleased to see me, no talk of me being a common anything for the time being. Decided not to marry, no percentage in it. My flat very nice and I've paid for new furniture, and also all debts. Picked up a French chair, upholstered red stain. I have it in the bedroom where I can look at it. Well, that's all for now. If you change your mind just let me know. Or if in any trouble – I never forget a friend who has helped me in time of need. You've only got one life, that's the way I look at it. How goes the inspiration and if it fails, I've got a man might do. No good for me, doesn't care for a flutter, and doesn't like Art either. But he has *Proust* in his overcoat pocket. Come to think of it, I suppose he reads it for the dirt, so no good for you, cancel what I said. Give my love to that sex maniac downstairs, and to stick-in-the-mud Rose. (I don't think.) With best regards, Emily Privet.'

I tried to make it up with Rose in all kinds of ways. When I joked, saying: 'Look, Rose, I'll wash the cups in disinfectant in front of you,' she said: 'That doesn't make me laugh, dear.'

'But, Rose,' I said, 'have I changed in any way because I was friendly with Miss Privet?'

'Miss Preevay,' said Rose, with heavy sarcasm. 'French, I don't think.'

'But she didn't pretend to be.'

'It's no good trying to be friends. I can see you never did really like me.'

'Then tell me why.'

She hesitated and thought. 'You know how I felt about Dickie, didn't you? Well, then.'

'What's he got to do with it?'

'Yes? I made myself cheap with him. I felt bad, and you knew that.'

'You were very happy,' I said.

'Happy?' she said derisively. 'Love, you'll say next. Well, I know just one thing. You were my friend. Then you were a friend to that dirty beast, and that means I'm just as bad as she is, as far as you're concerned.'

'But, Rose, I don't feel like that.'

'Yes? Well, I feel like it, and that's what's important.'

Rose's face was now set into lines of melancholy; it was hard even to imagine her as she had been a few weeks before. Flo told me she was being courted by a middle-aged man who ran the pub up at the corner, and had a bedridden wife. Sometimes Rose dropped into the Private Bar to drink a port-and-lemon with him; and returned to watch television with Flo, sadder than before. For a while she had taken a chair upstairs to sit in the corner of the Skeffingtons' flat, watching Len and Mick paint, but her presence inhibited them and she gave it up.

'Auntie, they call me,' she told Flo. 'Auntie Rose. That Borstal, it hasn't taught Len any manners, whatever else it taught him.'

'Time marches on,' said Flo. 'Ah, my Lord, yes, and it's true for us all. Don't you turn up your nose at Charlie at the pub. His wife'll die, and you'll be set up nice for life. And there's nothing to scorn in a man what's broken in already – he won't play you up like Dickie.'

'You make me laugh,' said Rose, heavily.

On the last evening before I left, Flo invited me down to a farewell supper, telling me that I needn't worry about Dan, she had admonished him to be polite. Dan had not spoken to me for weeks. As far as he was concerned, I was cheating him out of two pounds a week. He was now asking five-ten for my big room and that little one downstairs, and knew he would get it. But not from me. And I had refused to pay the six pounds he demanded in compensation for an iron-mark on the table he had bought for fifteen shillings in a street market. He used to scowl and grind his teeth whenever he saw me.

'It's no sense quarrelling with her now,' I heard Flo tell him. 'Because if you put her in a bad mood, she won't tell all her friends what a nice place this is, and we might lose tenants that way.'

So I sat with them, and tried to remember the basement as it had been on that first evening.

The great table, which had been the centre of the room, had been pushed to one side, to make room for a half-circle of chairs used for the television. Aurora was asleep next door, with the cat. Flo no longer cooked two meals an evening, but food that could be eaten off people's knees as they watched. Len and Mick complained that her food was too rich; so she had banished herbs, garlic and oil from her cuisine. On that evening we ate undressed salad and cold meat.

The television was on, of course, but Len and Mick only half-watched it, and kept up their usual back-chat – what Rose referred to as 'talking silly'.

Len was a thin, spike-boned, white-faced youth, with great black watchful eyes. Mick was light, easy, good-natured; concerned with his clothes and his girls – he had several.

'Look,' said Mick. 'Look – what do I see?' He was chasing something around his plate with a fork. 'It's a snail, no it's a frog-leg. What my ma would say if she knew what I ate here, she'd have a fit.'

Flo sighed and shrugged. Rose said tartly: 'Don't parade your ignorance.'

'Ignorant,' said Len. 'Ignorance said Auntie.'

'And don't call me Auntie. I'm your sister.'

'I've got a worrrm,' said Len, holding up a piece of lettuce on a knife. 'Worms those foreigners eat.'

'Well, if you don't like what I cook,' said Flo.

'It's not bad now you've restrained yourself a little, ma,' said Mick.

'Cheek,' said Rose.

'Oh, let him talk,' said Flo.

'If he doesn't know any better,' said Dan.

Dan, Flo and Rose had the same attitude towards the two boys: puzzled, and rather sad. This was a new generation and they did not understand it. Flo said once: 'The way they talk – but they must get it from the telly, that's what I think.'

'Mind you, I've eaten stranger things in my time,' said Mick. 'Ever eaten a haggis, Len?'

'Not since I saw one alive,' said Len.

'Alive, did you? I've never seen that. What's it look like?'

'Don't be silly,' said Rose. 'Haggis is sheep's stomach.'

'No, Auntie, you've got it wrong. A haggis is a little animal, covered with fur.'

'Come to think of it I saw one, too, once,' said Mick. 'Where was it now? On the slopes of Ben Nevis, it was.'

'I like old Ben, don't you, Mick?'

'My best friend. Mind you, he's hard on those haggises.'

'You have to understand a haggis. They need kindness.'

'And sympathy.'

'That's what our old friend Ben Nevis hasn't got. Sympathy.'

'Those poor haggises'll die out soon, the way he treats them.'

Flo said, 'There's ever such a nice programme coming now.'

The screen was filled with spangled girls and the air was loud with South American type music.

Len raised his voice and said: 'That's why I hope I never see a mink. My favourite food, mink is.'

'Who ever ate mink?' enquired Rose.

'Me,' said Mick.

'Me,' said Len. 'Dressed with salad cream, there's nothing like mink.'

'It has to be a mutation mink,' said Mick. 'Well-dressed.'

'Better flavour,' said Len.

'You know what mutated mink is, Auntie – go on, you're just ignorant,' said Mick. 'It's mink that's changed from those atom-bombs. Twice the meat it had before.'

'That's right,' said Len. 'Like evolution.'

'The first time, it happened by accident,' said Mick, 'but now they mutate them on purpose for the meat. Now where is it they have that mutated mink farm, Len? It slips my mind for the moment.'

'Tibet,' said Len.

'That's right, of course. I read it in the *Reader's Digest* last week. Biggest mutated mink farm in the world, right up there in the Himalayas.'

'Since they mutated them, they look rather like llamas,' said Len.

Rose was staring hard at the television set. But her hands plucked at the arm-rests of the chair, and she looked as if she might cry.

'The Dalai Lama breeds them,' said Mick. 'He's not like old Ben Nevis, he has a real feeling for minks.'

'Sympathy,' said Len.

'Peculiar habits they have since they mutated,' said Mick. 'What is it now? I've forgotten.

'Monks' habits,' said Len.

'Naah. You've got it wrong. I remember: each mink has to live inside a magic circle all its life. Because it mustn't move too much or it'll get thin and tough, no good for mink pie when they get like that.'

'A magic circle drawn by spirits.'

'Spirit of turpentine,' said Mick.

'And, of course, turps is hard to come by up there in Tibet.'

'Poor Dalai Lama, I wouldn't be him, would you, Len?'

'Rather be old Ben Nevis. Haggises is easier.'

'And those minks, they're getting a real taste for turps. Drink it day and night. As soon as the Dalai Lama draws the magic circle, those minks lick it up again.'

'Not good for them at all.'

'Spoils the meat.'

'And they're getting scarce, they're dying out, mutated minks don't tolerate turps. Not that rotten stuff they've got in Tibet.'

'I'd put my money on haggises. For survival, that is. Wouldn't you, Len?'

'Too true. Give me a good haggis steak any day. You can keep your mutated minks.'

'You think you're funny,' said Rose.

'Ah, go on now – laugh, Auntie, laugh just once.'

Mick whirled Rose up out of her chair and danced her around the basement, to the music from the television, while Rose cried: 'Stop it, stop it.'

'You've got no sense of humour, that's your trouble, Auntie,' said Mick, dropping her back in her chair.

'No sense of humour at all,' said Len.

'Yes?' said Rose. 'I laugh, don't I? I laugh at plenty. How do you know what I laugh at isn't as funny as what you laugh at?'

'She's got a point, mind you,' said Mick to Len.

'A pointed sense of humour,' said Len to Mick.

'Did I tell you about that pointed sense of humour I saw last week on the building site?'

'Ah, shut up,' said Rose, and her lips were quivering.

Len shrugged. Mick shrugged.

'Don't you like watching our lovely telly?' asked Flo pathetically.

'Time for work,' said Dan, rising and reaching for his overalls.

'I'll tell you about the pointed sense of humour upstairs,' said Mick as the two boys got up and stretched, winking and laughing.

'I read about its habits last week in the *Mirror* strange to relate.'

'Related to the mink and the haggis?'

'No, it's a different kettle of fish.'

'Fish, is it? Didn't look like a fish to me when I saw it on the building site.'

'Ah, but that's because the one you saw's different from the old lot. It's got legs, since the atom bomb got at it.'

'Mutated, too, has it?'

'There are two *kinds* of pointed sense of humour now. The mutated kind and the old kind. Mind you, it's not a bad thing. I like to see a pointed sense of humour on land now and then.'

'Wasted down there in the sea, I grant you.'

'Even the sea kind have got different shaped waists since the atom bomb.'

'A sad thing, a pointed sense of humour without a waist.'

'They're sad, too. Need sympathy.'

'Plenty of sympathy.'

'Yes, Len, that's what we need, you and me and the waistless pointed sense of humour. Sympathy.'

'We're not going to get it here, are we, Mick?'

'No, Len. Not here.'

'Good-bye, Auntie.'

'Good-bye, Auntie Rose.'

'They went upstairs.

'Think they're funny,' said Rose. To me she said accusingly: 'And you were laughing. Yes, I saw you. Don't think I didn't. You don't want to encourage them.'

'Yes, she was laughing,' said Flo. 'Well, I don't blame you, dear.'

'Yes? I blame her. Them kids. Go on and on for hours. You'd think there was nothing in the world to worry about the way they go on.'

'That's right,' said Flo. 'Ah, my Lord, the way my life's going, and Dan's no time for some fun. I might as well go to my granny in Italy.'

'But she's dead,' said Rose.

'Yes, she died. And now I've nowhere to go if Dan doesn't treat me right. Perhaps I'll go to live with Jack in Australia.'

'But he hasn't sent you his address.'

'Ah, my Lord, nobody cares for me no more and Doris is not our friend because she's going.'

'She has to go some time, it stands to reason. The way I look at it, some people have an itch in their feet, that moves them on from place to place.'

'I don't blame you, dear,' said Flo to me. 'But we've been good to you, haven't we, darling?'

'You make me sick,' said Rose. 'Do you want her to say sweet things, and all this time Dan's as good as killing her because she has the sense to say no to your fancy rent?'

'But I don't understand these things, you know that, dear.'

'Yes?' said Rose.

'But we have been good to your little boy, haven't we, darling?'

'Very,' I said. 'I'll never forget it.'

'That's right. We should all be kind to each other. If we was all kind to each other all over the world it would be different, wouldn't it now?'

'That's right,' I said.

'Yes?' said Rose. 'A likely story.'

WORKS BY DORIS LESSING
Winner of the Nobel Prize

NONFICTION

AFRICAN LAUGHTER:
Four Visits to Zimbabwe
ISBN 978-0-06-092433-1 (paperback)

GOING HOME
ISBN 978-0-06-097630-9 (paperback)

**IN PURSUIT OF THE
ENGLISH:** A Documentary
ISBN 978-0-06-097629-3 (paperback)

**PRISONS WE CHOOSE TO
LIVE INSIDE**
ISBN 978-0-06-039077-8 (paperback)

TIME BITES: Views and Reviews
ISBN 978-0-06-083141-7 (paperback)

UNDER MY SKIN: Volume One
of My Autobiography, to 1949
ISBN 978-0-06-092664-9 (paperback)

WALKING IN THE SHADE:
Volume Two of My Autobiography,
1949–1962
ISBN 978-0-06-092956-5 (paperback)

FICTION

BEN, IN THE WORLD:
The Sequel to *The Fifth Child*
ISBN 978-0-06-093465-1 (paperback)

THE CLEFT: A Novel
ISBN 978-0-06-083486-9 (hardcover)

THE GOLDEN NOTEBOOK
ISBN 978-0-06-093140-7 (paperback)

THE GRANDMOTHERS:
Four Short Novels
ISBN 978-0-06-053011-2 (paperback)

THE GRASS IS SINGING:
A Novel
ISBN 978-0-06-095346-1 (paperback)

LOVE AGAIN: A Novel
ISBN 978-0-06-092796-7 (paperback)

MARA AND DANN: An Adventure
ISBN 978-0-06-093056-1 (paperback)

THE REAL THING: Stories and
Sketches
ISBN 978-0-06-092417-1 (paperback)

**THE STORY OF GENERAL
DANN AND MARA'S
DAUGHTER, GRIOT AND THE
SNOW DOG:** A Novel
ISBN 978-0-06-053013-6 (paperback)

THE SWEETEST DREAM:
A Novel
ISBN 978-0-06-093755-3 (paperback)

THE CHILDREN OF VIOLENCE SERIES

MARTHA QUEST
ISBN 978-0-06-095969-2 (paperback)

A PROPER MARRIAGE
ISBN 978-0-06-097663-7 (paperback)

A RIPPLE FROM THE STORM
ISBN 978-0-06-097664-4 (paperback)

LANDLOCKED
ISBN 978-0-06-097665-1 (paperback)

THE FOUR-GATED CITY
ISBN 978-0-06-097667-5 (paperback)

HARPER PERENNIAL

**For more information about upcoming titles, visit www.harperperennial.com.
Available wherever books are sold, or call 1-800-331-3761 to order.**